WESTMAR COLLEGE LIBRARY
W9-BTH-546

The Rise and Fall of a Proper Negro

The Rise and Fall of
a Proper Negro

AN AUTOBIOGRAPHY BY

Leslie Alexander Lacy

THE MACMILLAN COMPANY

E
185.97
.L23
A3

Grateful acknowledgment is made for permission to reprint the following: lines from "New York," "You Held the Black Face," and "Be Not Amazed," by Léopold Senghor, from *Modern Poetry from Africa*, edited by Gerald Moore and Ulli Beier, Penguin Books, Inc., Baltimore, copyright © 1963 by Gerald Moore and Ulli Beier; lines from "The Black Glassmaker," by Jean-Joseph Rabéarivelo, originally in *l'Anthologie de la nouvelle poésie nègre et malgache*, Presses Universitaires de France, Paris (translation from *Modern Poetry from Africa*); and lines from "Your Presence," by David Diop, originally in *Coups de pilon*, Présence Africaine, Paris (translation from *Modern Poetry from Africa*.)

COPYRIGHT © 1970 BY LESLIE ALEXANDER LACY

All rights reserved. No part of this book may
be reproduced or transmitted in any form
or by any means, electronic
or mechanical, including photocopying,
recording or by any information storage
and retrieval system,
without permission in writing
from the Publisher.

The Macmillan Company
866 Third Avenue, New York, N.Y. 10022
Collier-Macmillan Canada Ltd., Toronto, Ontario

Library of Congress Catalog Card Number:
71–95302

FIRST PRINTING

Printed in the United States of America

80063

For my father.
Now only a memory.
But what a man!
A special brand of humanity:
A good and honest soul
And such strong hands—
Yet gentle like the touch of children.
Nathaniel Lenard Lacy, Sr., M.D.
Loved his work,
Loved his family—and we shall miss him.
We loved him very much,
Very much . . .

CONTENTS

The black glassmaker
whose countless eyeballs none has ever seen
whose shoulders none has overlooked,
that slave all clothed in pearls of glass,
who is strong as Atlas . . .
A thousand particles of glass
fall from his hands
but rebound towards his brow
shattered by the mountains
where the winds are born.
And you are witness of his daily suffering . . .
but you pity him no more
and do not even remember that his sufferings begin again
each time the sun capsizes.

JEAN-JOSEPH RABÉARIVELO

The Rise and Fall of a Proper Negro

PROLOGUE

The End of Negro Existentialism

"LESLIE, Leslie! Wake up. Why are you still asleep?"

"Because it's six o'clock in the goddamn morning, and if you had any sense you'd be sleeping too." I turned over to go back to sleep.

"The government has been overthrown." His voice was serious. "It's no time to be in bed."

"Good. Now LBJ knows what it feels like."

"No such luck. Maybe he's next. It's the Ghanaian government. There's been a *coup d'état*."

"You're joking!"

"No, it's true."

"When? How could it happen? What's going on? When did it happen? Who's the new government? What are the people doing?"

"Just hold everything," Preston interrupted me. "Calm down."

"Oh, my God!" I was on my feet. "The Ghana government has been overthrown? Isn't that a bitch. Martin Kilson said that would happen."

"And nobody believed him." Preston's voice was calm.

"Damn, Preston, it seems like everything is going wrong. Malcolm, Rhodesia, Nigeria, now Nkrumah."

1

Preston just stood there. He seemed so sad. I could tell that he was worrying.

"Preston, we're going to be in a lot of trouble. The new government is going to blame us for a lot of the shit that went down. What are we going to do?"

Before Preston could reply, an American-built Ghanaian Air Force plane flew overhead. And then we heard the guns: pistols, rifles, machine guns, and a lot of other noises I could not identify. The noise stopped for about two minutes. Then there was a thunderous, sky-shaking explosion. Then dead silence.

As I looked out through the iron grating placed on most windows in Ghana to keep out thieves in the night, I could see Preston. What in the hell was he going to do? He didn't even have a passport. They'd probably arrest him and send him back to the Americans, who wanted him for draft evasion. What a waste! That was kind of funny: a black man from Georgia with an upper-class London accent trying to explain his problem to a bunch of Southern crackers who wouldn't know what the hell he was talking about. Fuck. And knowing Preston he would be logical to the end.

Preston answered, looking back from the direction of the shooting, "I don't know what we are going to do. Nkrumah's security police inside the government headquarters at Flagstaff House are still resisting. Many people have been killed. The National Liberation Council, which organized the coup, has taken over the radio station and other vital areas of communication. It's rumored that a few loyalists in Accra are calling for mass uprisings and a northern army regiment still loyal to President Nkrumah is believed to be nearing Accra. There's still some hope. I think the coup will be stopped. Get yourself squared away, old man! I'm going to the administration building to get more details. See you at the house later."

"Look man, the hell with the details! In a situation like this the police will shoot first and ask questions later. You shouldn't even be driving around—you might get killed. I know you want to help, but the best thing is to keep your ass at home and figure out what you're going to do!"

"I know you're probably right, but first things first." Preston smiled, got into his VW and drove away from South Legon, an old section of the university housing compound reserved for staff with little seniority. Preston was always logical and efficient. His mind worked like a computer. He would probably want to know the number of troops, types of weapons, tribal affiliations, ages, ranks, serial numbers, marital status, and wind velocity, so he could predict the outcome of the struggle. He had an answer for everything, plus enough integrity and seriousness to make you listen. When one of his university students was bitten by a snake, he became an instant authority on poisonous snakes. When he caught malaria (he'd refused to take the pills because, after two years of research, he'd discovered a way to avoid being bitten) his illness became something with at least ten syllables. Such a man in all this confusion. He had come out from England to help, but his badly needed talents had never been used.

As he sped off, I said, "Be careful," but he could not have heard me even if he'd been standing right next to me.

The silence of South Legon and the sounds of guns in town scared the shit out of me. I was not Preston King; I could not get myself "squared away." I could not move! I could not swallow; I became very conscious of my heartbeat. I believe I said a prayer. Many times. Me praying. The thoughts of new black men in power—violence, bloodshed, reprisals—of the unknown, of a new government with different conditions and requirements made me fear for my life.

Hurriedly I dressed and packed my old briefcase with my passport, a now-dated manuscript on political change in Ghana, my U.N. health card, two books, a toothbrush, a half-clean white shirt, and two sticks of pot.

Running out of my door, I saw two women hurrying toward me: a Brazilian and an East German who lived in the adjoining chalet. They had been awakened by the guns of change, and they, too, seemed terrified. I tried to hide my fear; I wanted them to see the cool Leslie they thought they knew.

"What's happening, Mr. Lacy?" demanded the German woman in near hysteria.

"Is it true that there has been a change of government?" asked the Brazilian, who had left Brazil with her husband because they feared reprisal for the role they reportedly had played in "subversive politics."

After I assured them that there was no cause for alarm, my two Marxist-Leninist neighbors seemed relieved. No doubt it confirmed their view that a revolutionary army would always crush the right-wing forces of reaction. As I left them, the German woman remarked to her friend, "My God, these governments in Africa are so unstable."

My destination was forty yards away: Christina Aidoo's bungalow. Christina was a Ghanaian playwright who had only recently published her first play, *Dilemma of a Ghost*. The work portrayed the problems that a Ghanaian faced with his family when he returned from an extended stay in America with an Afro-American wife. Because of Christina's socialist leanings and her belief in a black world revolution she was a special friend to the community of black Americans in Ghana. I wanted to hide in her house.

The only street in South Legon was humming with discussion. Most of the staff, both foreign and native, was trying to get the latest information on the coup. The expatriates wanted some word on their status (some had already unsuccessfully attempted to call their embassies); the Ghanaians were concerned about civilians and relatives either in the army or living in the Flagstaff area. I joined a small group of English and Ghanaian friends who had congregated in the yard to listen to Radio Ghana.

It was difficult to hear the broadcast because one of the English history lecturers, who had only yesterday hailed the political virtues of Nkrumah's policies, was today denouncing those same policies, politicians, and practices. This Englishman—the first white Uncle Tom I had ever met—was like a lot of Englishmen working in independent Ghana. To keep his job, status, private beach clubs, and remain in the land of the year-round summer, he was solicitous, opportunistic, and frequently dishonest. He and his kind would say or do anything to keep from going back to their cold-water London flats. Yesterday he was pro-government. Today—now that Nkrumah's political kingdom was being threatened—he was preparing himself for a possible new role. The Ghanaians seemed as

annoyed with these beliefs as they had been with his old
ones of the last five years. I felt certain that all of them wanted
to tell him to shut up and go back to England. But they
just listened, for they lacked the naked courage to do anything.
Academic freedom, or just plain honesty, was a painful luxury
in Nkrumah's Ghana. It usually brought official mistrust and
varying levels of political repression, ofttimes jail sentences.
This was because such utterances were invariably "anti-
Nkrumah," hence "anti-Ghana," and therefore "anti-people."
Thus the Ghanaians were cooling it as usual until the struggle
for Flagstaff House had been resolved.

While the Englishman was lighting his pipe, and therefore
silent for a moment, the following message came over the
radio.

"The National Liberation Council has taken over the country.
The few forces still loyal to the madman Nkrumah are still
resisting, but they will not succeed. We have broken the
myth which surrounded Nkrumah, and now we must dedicate
ourselves to bring true democracy to the country. Stay in your
homes and be patient. Long live Ghana!"

"We are back in power," shouted one Ghanaian lecturer,
who quickly went into his house. He came out soon afterwards,
got into his new Mercedes-Benz and drove toward the direction
of the fighting, some five miles south of the university. I was
not surprised at the lecturer's elation. The Ghanaian intellectuals—for the most part, English trained—had never been
committed to Nkrumah's one-party government. In fact, most
of them hated him, his abuses of power, his medieval political
norms. As one professor once said to me, "Unlike Gandhi . . .
Nkrumah with his bushlike tendencies really thinks that he is
an *Osagyefo*, a great ruler from Africa's past." These educators
of Ghana's youth wanted Nkrumah out of the way in the
very beginning so that they could have a Proper society:
British passports, British university standards, multiparties in
government. Most even felt that white legal wigs and gray
flannel suits were essential, and indeed comfortable, in constant ninety-degree tropical heat.

The voice on the radio sounded firm and passionate, and
the closing sentence, "Long live Ghana," was heartfelt and

dramatic. But then, the announcer was rather good with dramatics, for he had had a lot of practice broadcasting Nkrumah's propaganda.

Following the advice of this historic broadcast, the groups dispersed and the people went back to their houses. The Ghanaians were quiet but smiling. The expatriates were quiet, perplexed, and apprehensive. Only the Englishmen dared speak. While the message was being repeated for the third time, to the tune of the Ghanaian national anthem (which is musically European rather than African), I left the yard and walked slowly to my hideout.

Christina's house was typical for Ghanaians of her social and intellectual class. Superficially it had all the trappings and modern conveniences of any lower-middle-class American home, including a television set and an air conditioner Christina never used because she said it was too cold. But traditional pre-industrial Ghana gave the house its form, beauty, and character. There were chickens, some newly born, both inside and outside the house. Harmless foot-long lizards decorated the cement walls. Fresh fruits and vegetables—brought by a village cousin who usually stayed on to help Christina with her housework—were spread all over the kitchen and porch. The latter served jointly as a back entrance and a cooking area—one in which traditional pounders, sticks, rocks, and cook-out-type tools were more frequently used than modern kitchen appliances imported from the United Kingdom.

Christina was dressed and ready to leave. I said very little, for she seemed to know the reason for my early-morning visit. She told me to go into her bedroom and sleep. She would go to Accra to find out what was happening. She locked the door from the outside and went away. I opened my briefcase, lit up one of the joints, and stretched out on Christina's bed, safe and relaxed. . . .

Violence in the Third World, violence of the meek. . . . Black men fighting to rule. Stop the voting; guns can decide. Death and destruction—nation building must wait. Let's blame the English. Didn't they start all this? But then there was independence. Not a chance—neocolonialism. . . . The guns of

Flagstaff House; the coup—maybe somebody wants a change. What about the counteroffensive, a popular resistance? Maybe. Doubtful. The northern regiment? It would probably arrive late; even armies are inefficient in the tropics. *If* the army marched, against its nature, and arrived early, it was still an insufficient force to neutralize or destroy the military order which had emerged to challenge the legal government of the Convention People's party, in power for fourteen years. The scholars said the army held a privileged position. After three weeks in Ghana, scholars probably could not see for looking. And President Nkrumah—No. Sorry, his proper title was Osagyefo the President Dr. Kwame Nkrumah, His Lord High Priest, sometimes called the Redeemer—was in North Vietnam telling the Vietnamese people about the evils of imperialism. His U.S.S.R-officer-led security forces, all the members of Nkrumah's Nzima tribe, would not fight long for the bricks and stones of the government house at Flagstaff without the Redeemer. He was their national symbol, and he had only recently, and then very slowly, begun to institutionalize at the level of political action the charismatic splendor of his modernizing autocracy. They needed the Redeemer to lead the charge of the defensive.

If the attempted coup had taken place a year ago, I would have felt more comfortable with Preston's hope. And the year before that—my first in Mother Africa—I would have felt like charging the defensive myself. Coming from North America, I was prepared to believe everything, anything, anybody holding out even the slightest hope that black people would rise up kicking asses and taking power.

I had always been a believer. The first to see it had been the children we were not allowed to play with in the second town I lived in. They were too young to have called me a believer; what they did call me was probably more accurate: "One of those uppity niggers who don't play pussy because he's afraid of getting fucked." Thinking that they meant sex rather than stupidity, I lied to one of them and said that I had had sex. He quickly informed me, "So what? You still don't know cat shit from apple butter." Even when I gave myself the test, I failed. And later, after I grew up, got to college, and discovered America, I walked away from her ugly hate only to forget what the shit smelled like.

My awareness had been long coming and difficult to achieve. I was born in the corridors of the American outhouse. From birth to my sixteenth year I had been like most Negroes in the outhouse of America, walking the corridors, waiting for my chance to get into one of the rooms.

Thanks to my father's money, influence, motivation, and stupefying illusions of greatness for me, I had grown up behind a beautiful mask of Negro respectability which had no holes to see through or smell through. Thanks to my dear Negro preparatory school, which polished the mask, I could know without opening holes, the correct things to do, say, and wear. The real world of the corridor and the beautiful closed doors which lined it did not exist in my consciousness.

Leaving Louisiana to go to college in New England was surprisingly painful. The Room I entered was huge, filled with things I did not know existed. When I spoke to the person who greeted me, in an English that had been prepared exclusively for my role in the corridor, I heard my voice bounce on and off the many objects in the Room before I heard my echo. Since I did not know my way around, hands which I had never touched, because I was colored, reached out for mine and guided me to a small spot near the door. A fellow next to me laughed and said a few words. I recognized the sound of his voice. He was a corridor man, but only his parents had been born in the South. He was angry that I sat next to him. This was up North and I should not segregate myself he said. When I explained to him that I had no choice, because I had been brought there, he seemed to understand, but he still did not like it. Because of my training at Palmer Memorial Institute, I did not wish to annoy him. We were taught always to be gracious, thoughtful, and kind. But he was stuck with me because I could not see and therefore could not move. I politely called for my hands to guide me, but they were too busy.

Then I heard the cats and their kittens. Such beautiful voices. The fellow next to me began to talk with them. The resentment in his voice was gone. It made his voice difficult to recognize, until he laughed. I wanted to join in, but I had nothing to ask or add. I did not understand what the hell was being said. The McCarthy period; Red China; Nationalism, Communism; Jean-Paul Sartre; summer in Rome; "Did you read Tom Wolfe's *You Can't Go Home Again?*" These were things I had to learn about. But how did these people know about them? I had studied American and World History. And they were freshmen too.

I was frustrated. I wanted to see. I was in college and I wanted to learn. So I took off the mask. I screamed. I saw the shit. Voices and faces came together. There was so much to see, to know, but I could not stand the smell. The cats and their kittens, the light-skinned colored fellow next to me, the other freshmen, among them a young man with kinky hair from Africa, did not seem to mind the outhouse odor. How could they bear it? Some slept near it; others in it. A few stepped in it. One painted it; a young girl analyzed it; and another, a poet, wrote an ode to it. But nobody missed it, since it was a part of the air. And sometimes after class they sat and threw it around. "Nothing is so painful as watching someone trying to be something he is not" was a consoling thought. I was glad I had remembered that wise saying from my decorum classes at Palmer. Feeling more alienated as time went on, I thought maybe I had remembered the wrong quotation. Then I recalled the lesson on correct demeanor: "Don't argue with authority. . . . He is big enough to guide you in making a living, so give him the benefit of the doubt and forge ahead."

So I tried to adjust to my New England environment. It was easier than I imagined. Without my mustache, with a new three-piece suit, white bucks, speech habits like my ex-corridor friend, and shit-eating and -throwing lessons, I began to like and understand my place in the Room. And I got a new mask.

Getting a girl friend was still a problem. The corridor girls inside the Room were extremely selective. Maturity, prospects after graduation, fraternity affiliation, light brown skin, and the ability to stand on your spot as well as take the shit were the important qualifications. The more of each, the better your chances. I had dates, but never satisfying ones, because the pretty yellow girls I wanted were always too busy to go out with me. The corridor girls outside the room were unacceptable because they were beneath my station in life.

A few of the white girls were friendly, but I was afraid of them. After all, I was a black Southern gentleman who had never spoken to a white person my own age.

I decided to leave this Room. To broaden my education, I wanted to see the other Rooms in the outhouse. I walked up and down the corridor, seeing many of my kind waiting in line to enter one of the Rooms. I did not want any of them to speak to me. This was the North, and I had to avoid self-imposed segregation. I looked away from their eager eyes. I did not want to encourage them. And besides, many of the smiling ones would never get in anyway.

At the end of the corridor, I stopped to drink some of the outhouse water. I felt a hand on my shoulder. "Want this sign to carry?"

"Are you speaking to me?" I replied to the young white girl beside me.

She laughed. She thought my response was funny. I could tell she was a student even though it was obvious that she and the outhouse bathing water had had a falling out. She smiled, and I smiled while I listened to her speech. Judy was intelligent, a bit strange, and she called herself a nonobjective surrealist painter with Marxist leanings. She was cute, so I decided to listen in ignorance.

Her sign read "Down with Capital Punishment." How could an intelligent girl like this be interested in uncultured people who broke the law? I asked and she answered and my interest in her and her cause increased. Several corridor girls passed as we—no, she—talked. They were three I had tried to date. They were not pleased with what they saw, but to hell with them.

Judy never seemed to tire. A five-hour lecture was a record for me, and I was exhausted from just listening. "Change," "progressive," "fascist," "Germany," "Marxist," "social forces," "struggle," "working class," "revolution" were enthusiastically repeated throughout her discourse.

I thought all night about her revolution to rid the world of all evil. Time passed. Then we met again and later she suggested, as I'd hoped she would, going to her Room.

Like our Room, it was filled with people, individuals like Judy, a beat-looking generation of students with long hair, guitars, chess sets, magazines I had never seen, nude paintings on the walls, and books. So many books—about imperialism, capitalism, industry, war, poverty, Negroes, caste, class, ass, sex, love, poetry, revolution, Marxism, and Mexican muralist art. These strangers were white like the other cats and kittens, but they wanted to be birds. To fly out of the shit and its odor was the great dream. A few of the older birds wanted to stay and burn the house down. Too old to fly, they could get only as high as the encircling pot smoke would allow.

There was little furniture in the Room. No signs of wealth. Not even a bed. A few chairs lined the painting-covered walls. Everyone but me seemed quite comfortable on the floor. They talked—and how they could talk. "I'm leaving this sick room because I'm not getting anything out of it." "I feel alienated from all those rooms, and the corridor." "I'm against capital punishment." "We must have peace." "Society belongs to the workers." "Let's go smoke and be ourselves."

Surely they could not be serious about the "workers" running society. Without capital punishment, people would never stop killing each other. Why were they so interested in Negro rights? Where did these people come from? Georgia, California, New York, Ohio, Illinois—impossible. I didn't know people like this. They unceremoniously damned all the values I believed in. They talked of a better world, a revolution which would free the world of exploitation, color prejudice, hate, and hunger. They said they wanted to be free.

I did not understand, and I resisted, but I was excited by what I was hearing. It took quite a while, but finally, my anti-everything friends had introduced me to their way of life. I moved from my Room and got a bigger place in Judy's Room, next to her on the floor. Our love for each other made the change smooth and after a while I discovered sex. That day she took my face in her hands and told me that I was beautiful. I believed her, but I felt strange, because in the world of the corridor only the girls were beautiful, and the light-skinned ones at that.

I took off my second mask and put on another. I never knew that there was so much wrong with the world. It was like the falling of jail walls from my mind. Through a new process of discovering, accepting, rejecting, releasing, I was able to understand why my comrades wanted a revolution in American values and institutions. I was with them. I think I had started to discover my lack of manhood, for whatever I would have become, it surely would not have been a healthy man in the society these friends wanted to attack.

I was there for seven years. On that seventh anniversary of my coming, I again made a trip to the corridor. The people there were no longer corridor walkers, but Blacks and Afro-Americans. Followers of Marcus Garvey and the Nation of Islam, they advocated separation.

No, I said. That is not the way to do it. Blacks and birds together. But they rejected that solution as they had rejected the gradualism of the black bourgeoisie. For months I tried to get the Afro-American Association into the Room. I thought that they would be stimulating for the birds, because wings were always in the air. The Association had raised some important issues, but they were focused too narrowly, too conservative. The birds, for their part, were high in the sky and talking about ideal conditions of revolution, which did not exist.

The Blacks, especially the women, wanted me to leave my birds. I was afraid, because I wanted to be beautiful.

Then the groups started attacking each other. I tried to negotiate the disputes, but I was ineffective. The Blacks wanted to be beautiful, and by then the birds wanted to be cats.

I was not able to deal with the madness of these experiences. It was during those days and nights of failure and discovery that I decided to go to Africa. I needed a new dedication to life, more than I could find in an American city. I wanted to run away from this republic. I thought forever would not be long enough. And not just to Africa, but Ghana. Nkrumah had been our idol. He was aggressive, progressive, and militant. "Ghana shall not be free until all of Africa and all people of African descent are free" was his message. It became the special password, the secret exchange among Blacks, like me, who had come to believe with W. E. B. Du Bois—who had only recently joined the Communist party and left for Africa—that the American society could not reform itself unless there were radical changes in its basic institutions. Du Bois had said that a socialist Africa was the future.

So there was my answer. Unlike Richard Wright and his generation, who went to Paris, I could be both black and radical. I could finally have peace, be whole, be a man.

My first days in Africa were wild and beautiful. I wanted to belong, to get right in. I kissed the earth; I put my arms around strangers, who smiled at me in bewilderment. I ran and jumped on the beautiful untouched beaches near the Elmina coast and thought that from these very shores my ancestors had gone into slavery. Some of the things I did seemed unreal and affected, but I was trying to be happy. I wrote lots and lots of letters home, and finally one hot day I stood in front of the president's statue at the Parliament building in the center of this ex-British colony and waited for the conversion of my soul. I met others of my kind who claimed that they had it. But for me it did not come.

We were a strange and varied lot. Looking for a special kind of reality we could not find in our own countries, we had flocked to the Redeemer's throne. The modern world had come: ex-Garveyites from the West Indies and North America; black South Africans without a country; white communists and liberals from South Africa; African freedom fighters talking about revolution; Zionists who called themselves professional Marxists; black nationalists from America and white communists from America, bringing all their fights, factions, and fictions. The Chinese came, and the Russians were right behind them. Then the Japanese Marxists arrived, and of course the Cubans, who were being watched by the CIA living near the Peace Corps volunteers.

And to this already varied group were added other talents: black communists from Europe pretending to be radical black nationalists, with their white wives; pie-in-the-sky seekers; two hippies; one queer, who found little business; pimps, whores of all nations; a professional gangster and many minor thieves; a few serious scholars; two ex-Nazis; a few artists, many published and unpublished writers; broken personalities; rejects of the modern world; a professional hedonist; and me, an ex-upper-middle-class Negro from the state of Louisiana.

All had their reasons for coming. Some of them, like the two ex-Nazis, wanted the Redeemer's forgiveness. So Nkrumah forgave them; placed the doctor, who had sterilized Jewish women in Germany, in charge of a state hospital and gave the woman, who had been a special pilot in Nazi Germany and was now, along with the doctor, wanted by the West German government, a job as head of a useless gliding school. No one understood these curious arrangements; and I guess after their first year in the country, once we had been able to identify with the ruling class, no one really cared. A prominent Afro-American, a naturalized Ghanaian citizen and close associate of the President, once defended Hitler's helpers' presence in the country by saying with conviction, "Everyone is entitled to one mistake."

Some of them came to escape persecution, like the black South African freedom fighters and the white South Africans escaping prosecution for allegedly helping their black brothers. But there was no harmony between the groups. The Blacks were in one political club; the Whites another. They never understood each other. The Whites, most of whom were communists, did not trust the Blacks because they were nationalists, who in their turn could not understand why the white South Africans were there in the first place. That issue was somewhat settled when Nkrumah made H. M. Basner—the white South African who later used the government press to attack Malcolm X—one of his trusted advisors.

We were individuals who could not belong, a fatherless tribe of lonely, frustrated activists who wanted to achieve for the Ghanaian people a revolution which we were unable or unwilling to achieve in the countries of our birth.

But much of that had changed now. Many of the original tribe had left. Only the true believers had remained, including a few Afro-Americans who hated Uncle Sam more than they loved Mother Africa.

I, too, had changed. My energies, passions, false appetites, and ideas of greatness had not served me, because in my special state of exile I had discovered that the Africa I needed did not exist. But the Africa I found had been very good to me. I loved her. The very first year, I had gotten the white man off my back. The second year, I had not thought of him at all. And now, in the third, if I chose, I could talk to him from a point of health and civility. It seemed to me that I had gone through a kind of psychological metamorphosis, and although I had not discovered happiness, I had learned some important things about myself, my world, Africa, the twentieth century, and the country I had left.

The fathers of the coup, however, would not be concerned with the state of my psychic health. And they would probably not think that we had helped the country. After all, *we* had not brought about the revolution. The people in exile and political adversaries whom Nkrumah had gotten out of the way, but had not destroyed, would now vent their latent tensions and rise up together, crying out a single demand:

Revenge, revenge—death and deportation for those who dared follow Nkrumah.

While I was horrified by such a prospect, I was amused by the sights and sounds of Ghanaian history being acted out down in Accra. This was the first real shoot-out since the British turned back the spears of the Ashantis around the turn of the century. But whoever won the struggle for control of the black government, whoever killed the most soldiers and civilians, whoever controlled the mass media, whoever wore the black mask of power and privilege, would, with their party, tribe, army, or elite, still be irrelevant to seven and a half million people—to the Ghana that could be.

With their British training, right-wing leanings, and CIA backing, the National Liberation Council would not achieve the necessary level of political awareness to modernize the country. We had heard their plans before the Nkrumah period, and those who sat in one of Nkrumah's security prisons had not improved upon their ideas in the least. Direction for the plans would probably come out of the ruling elite at the university, and except that they were Africans, their thinking would be very similar to that of the group of New England Negro women who ran the prep school which took four years of my life.

Yet as I looked at the bedroom walls and saw the picture of Frantz Fanon which Christina had cut out from the back cover of his magnum opus *Les Damnés de la Terre*, I knew that Osagyefo Dr. Kwame Nkrumah should not remain either. His people did not need an *Osagyefo* any more. He had done his job. Much of it, in spite of his detractors, was done well. He and his party had broken free from those who could not deal with the implications of "freedom now." They had been brilliant, if not always effective, in the preindependence days. Nkrumah had raised the right issues, developed the proper strategies for revolutionizing the society, and told black people of the world that he was black first, African second, and socialist third.

Like Malcolm X, he had inspired the youth of the black world, who had looked for a leader consistent with their most visceral feelings. Unlike the Nigerian leaders, the first Ghanaian black man of power had unified the country and subordinated diverse racial, ethnic, and religious loyalists to a nation-state. And unlike other African presidents, President Kwame Nkrumah had vociferously championed the cause of freedom for all Africans and had made people of African descent elsewhere proud of their African ancestry.

The Redeemer had been a great man. But a new kind of leadership—perhaps more secular, more Ghanaian, more nationalistic, less ideological—was now needed. A form of government which would encompass more grass-roots populism and mass-party democracy was essential.

From that perspective, I thought what was happening down at Flagstaff House was a struggle exclusively about power, not about change.

And so, there I lay in Christina's house, waiting for the outcome. I could hide, but I could not run.

I tried to think of pleasant things. My beautiful home in Louisiana kept coming to my mind. I had loved that house. My rise began in that Southern mansion. It is a special kind of story that could only have happened in North America; perhaps it could not have occurred outside of the South. It is my short history of how it was that a middle-class Negro boy from a proper Southern family ended up in an African bed.

As Hermann Hesse said in *Demain*, "My story is not a pleasant one; it is neither sweet nor harmonious, as invented stories are; it has all the taste of nonsense and chaos, of madness and dreams—like the lives of all men who stop deceiving themselves."

I

To Make a Proper Negro

A CULTURE IS being destroyed. Toppins Avenue is in flames. Thick black smoke comes out of every building; falling flames ignite a mass of uncollected garbage, which, like the people, has been forgotten. People are everywhere. Panic is on every face, confusion everywhere—even the overfed rats cannot hide. A strange smell fills the air, for the night's summer wind does not move. The frightened firemen have begun to work, but they have to hide, duck the rocks and bottles which come from all around. Toppins Avenue citizens will not let them work, because they want their homes to burn. They do not know the firemen, but they hate them, blame them for bills which are too high, and will not let them extinguish fires in houses which offer nothing for the high rents.

Only the ashes are left. A noise which sounds like backfire has stopped, and then a scream which has seen death is heard. A mother, too grieved from the news of another war, cannot believe that she has now lost her youngest son. A tank in her community; she cannot understand.

Farther down, the street is quiet. There is not time to bury the dead. Men with guns, men who came from far away— some from other towns—stand and face the unarmed of Toppins

Avenue. The living are young. One cannot be more than ten; another is barely six. A small one, awake long past his bedtime, is hiding safely in his mother's arms. The boy called Perry is out front. He leads the living because the body in front of the tank belongs to his mother's family. His face is old, but he is thirteen. Like most of his kind, he is poor. He does not work, he cannot find the job he wants. School? Well, not for him; he quit last year. No one can see his fear. Perry looks into the faces of those with the guns; they are quiet and afraid too. But law and order must prevail; so they wait. The night is still. Perry suddenly moves another step. He is angry. He is talking, then he shouts, *"Shoot, motherfuckers! Shoot!"*

My first recollections of life are of a big comfortable house of white wood with front and back porches which in late spring and early summer were shaded with rosebushes. Spreading out eastward from the front was a beautiful street whose trees kept us dry during the spring rains. To the west was a spacious yard with a garden, two large doghouses for our German shepherds, and a garage which burned down three times because my brother and I enjoyed playing with matches.

My mother, Lillie, had little to do with decision making in our home. My father ruled absolutely. The house was run like an army barracks. Every morning, my father presented Mother with a work schedule, which was never to be questioned. All during my childhood Mother seemed confused, as though she never knew exactly what to do next.

Since she was my father's wife, she was not expected to do the housework herself. There were hired girls, sometimes as many as five, who came in the early morning to do the cooking, serving, cleaning, and whatever else had to be done. My father called these girls "Miss" and "Mrs." Much later he explained that this was the best way to "set off the hired colored help from the rest of the family." First names would have given them a lower social status, but from his perspective it would have made the situation far too intimate.

These house helpers were afraid of my father. Jobs they could perform well would always stay half done if my father came home before he was expected. And to guard themselves against him, the girls worked out a special warning system. When he left the office for an unexpected visit home, his secretary, a cousin of one of our housemaids, would ring the phone twice and then hang up. But even being prepared didn't relieve their anxiety, and as far as Dr. Lacy was concerned, a job half done was proof of inefficiency, an outward sign of inner laziness and inability to do hard work. Even when they did exactly what he told them to do, it was never satisfactory. And for all of this they received four dollars weekly, eighteen meals, and Saturday afternoon lectures on the "real art of saving your money."

In theory my mother was the overseer. But as soon as Dr. Lacy left she was immediately put in her place. "Child, now you just go sit down." She had known most of these women before she married; she had gone to school with all of their fatherless daughters and was caught up in the traditional hierarchy of age and respect. Even being married to a man they considered an outsider did not free her from their rules. So my mother, little more than a child herself, was told what to do. When the Colonel, a name they gave to Father behind his back, discovered this breach of discipline, he summarily fired the lot of them, reminded my mother of her origins and what he had done for her, and hired a new and younger group of housekeepers, whom Mother did not know.

There were other women in the house, who performed no domestic duties. Each of the three children had a nursemaid. I remember so well the girl who cared for me, Essie Mae. She did not want me to call her Miss Williams. Essie Mae seemed very strange to me; now I would call her defiant. She never accepted her place in the fixed Lacy household, even though she followed most of the Colonel's orders.

Always in my growing-up years I would think, Essie Mae never acts like the other help. As I remember I never had the feeling that she thought herself to be our social equal; she just seemed like a person who wouldn't be pushed around. She never appeared frightened when the Colonel shouted at her. And unlike the others, she always looked into my father's eyes whenever he spoke to her. I remember when I was four, or maybe five—my father always said that I was ahead of my years—I asked her why she was not afraid. I believe she said, "He just another nigger man." Once she had to confront Father as she was taking me downstairs.

"Where do you think you're going?"

"Following your orders," she replied without smiling, but looking directly into his face.

"What's wrong with you today, Miss Williams?" He sounded mad.

"Nothing, Dr. Lacy." She had the same look on her face. "I'se just fine!"

Father took his glasses off and rubbed his face in disgust. "Miss Williams, for the thousandth time, it is not 'I is,' but 'I am.' It is the first person singular of the verb 'to be.' You say, I am; you are; he, she, or it is; we are; you are; they are. Do you understand?"

"Yes, sir, Dr. Lacy."

He moved out of her way, and we went to play in the yard.

Essie Mae was not always mad; most of the time we had lots of fun. She answered all my questions, and unlike Mrs. Bottom and Miss Brown, the two ladies who watched my older brother and younger sister, she did not get angry or slap my hands when I tried to put the strange things I found on the ground in my mouth. Every so often she brought me delicious pieces of fried food, which we never had at home because the Colonel said that fried foods were not healthy. When my father wasn't looking or my sister didn't tell, I would sometimes give my Monday night baked chicken to my brother, because after eating Essie's fried chicken I had no room for it. The funny stories she told me about the "black ghosts" and the colored man looking for his mules could have cost her her job. The maids had strict orders not to fill our heads with nonsense or teach us bad English and superstitions. My father was very concerned about our speech, and as far back as I can remember, he conducted our daily speech drills.

My father seemed very proud of me. I always followed his instructions, and he never had reason to shout at me. I was proud of him also. He was very strict, but he was usually fair. I always defended him when people said he was mean. Hard work did not take his mind from his family. Even on busy days, he found time to give piggyback rides.

At one of our weekly family conferences, when we were much older, he told us that he had everything he wanted. "The good Lord has been very good to me," he said. He began to cry. He had met a beautiful girl of sixteen who had just finished high school and married her after two weeks. He said, "I loved her, but I did not really consider love a requirement for marriage. A wife must be from a reasonably good family, a lady with nice legs and free of venereal disease." Having these virtues, and a separate bedroom, she was in the position to give him the three children he wanted: two brilliant sons and a charming daughter. His Lord, whom he never went to church to pray to, was good to him. My brother, Nathaniel Lenard Lacy, Jr., was first. I followed the next year. And the charming daughter, Beatrice Elaine, with whom Lenard and I fought for most of our youth, was right on my heels.

Father said he got down on his knees when Beatrice was born and prayed that his children would "never have to endure a life of poverty and misery."

Our town was not very large, because like most Southern towns, Franklin, Louisiana, was two towns. We lived in neither town, though we were close enough to know what was happening in both of them. Our house and other houses like ours were located at the end of the first town and at the beginning of Essie Mae's town. We were a suburb to each. We had our own community. We even had our own little church. On Sunday we dressed up in our best and went along to a quiet service where people cried politely if they were moved by the Holy Ghost, but never screamed and never shouted. My family was very religious. I was given a white Bible for going to Sunday school for a hundred Sundays in a row. Father was religious at home, but he never went with us to church. That was because, as Mother always said, "The preacher does not allow him to run the church."

Willow Street separated our community from the first town. The people of Essie's town had to cross the railroad tracks to get to us. To pass from one town to the other meant passing my window. Town One was completely foreign, and two thousand foreigners lived there. Even when I was old enough to understand the ways of grownups, it was still incomprehensible. Yet, as I remember, everything happened in Town One; in fact, we called it Town. My father supplied his office with drugs from its stores. Our girls bought our baked and broiled food there. Except for our housemaids, all the people from Town Two worked in Town One. And, which seemed strange at the time, the people of One called the people of Two Ann, Sarah, Jim, or George and sometimes "boy," while the Twos always addressed the Ones as sir, Mr., or Mrs., usually while shuffling their legs or scratching their heads. When there were fires in Essie Mae's town, after the house had already burned down, new and bright shining fire engines would leisurely come out to make sure that the fires wouldn't spread. Power, lights, chocolate, the picture show, food, banks, stores, education, the law, candy, and ice cream were in the hands of the sirs and ladies of Town One.

People like Essie Mae lived in Town Two. I saw some of them early in the morning. The men usually wore blue jeans and brown shirts and in the winter they would wear old brown jackets with different colored patches sewn on the elbows. The women, like our girls, always had on clean white dresses. Most of the men worked in the sugar cane, rice, and fishing industries, and the women did the same chores for the Town One people as our maids did for us. Sometimes cars and trucks would wait for them on the other side of Willow Street. The women drivers always seemed in a hurry to drive away.

I remember that this morning sight always confused me. The morning people of Two seemed not to be like the people I heard at night. In their blue jeans and white dresses they were quiet; they seemed not to want to smile. After work I could hear them laugh and sometimes cry, and scream even louder than my baby sister. Their screams were always frightening. Their music, sometimes joyful but most times blue, could be heard for miles. I never did see their night faces, but I could hear their happy voices from the distance. Sometimes they woke up the people in Town, who would then send out the police, the overfed men with red necks and big guns, who would turn on the ugly sirens on the top of their cars to stop the night sounds.

I used to love the sounds of the night in Two. Essie Mae would occupy my thoughts, because I knew she would be having fun. In one of her other dresses she would be pretty like my mother. I used to dance with Essie in the backyard, and when I got older I used to lie on her stomach.

I was glad that I had my own room. I could open the window and see the distant lights. About midnight they would go off; I would feel so alone. On Saturday nights or the night before Christmas the lights would burn until it was time for the people to go to church.

The men from Town must have liked the night life of Town Two. The same cars which their women drove in the morning would come speeding by my window, heading for the lights and night sounds. Before the sun came up, they would speed back to their day life. Once or twice I saw one of the women from Town go into Two at night.

The men of One came into our community at night, but it was always to see my father. Our men had meetings with them in our basement. Sunday night was their night, and they were always quiet. I never saw any of them with our mothers and sisters, and they never spoke to my mother, since father would always make sure to send her upstairs before the men arrived for the meeting.

My father never had fun at night. He was always reading or counting his money. Sometimes he cleaned his gun, which he called "six brothers." The people of Two always disturbed his reading, even though I could never hear their music when I went to sleep in his room. He healed their wounds, stuck big needles in their arms, and pulled new children out of their stomachs. But their music was not his music. The music on his radio sounded like the movie music which we heard on Saturday afternoon in the reserved balcony seats of the picture-show house in Town. We had to listen to his picture-show music, and after a while we began to like it too. Only my mother continued listening to the music of the night.

There seemed to have been an imperfect balance between

Town One and Two. The noise of One produced the sound of the day, and the noise of the blue-jean and white-dress workers created the mood for the night. Town One never stopped the day noise, but could and did stop the night sounds. As I think back: if only the people of Town Two had not gone to work one day . . .

The thirteen children of our community were forbidden to enter the schools in One, and the schools in Two were below our standards—"immoral," as my father would say. We had to have an education in an environment which was consistent with our special status in life.

Saga Brown, a Methodist private school, was intended to prepare us for our life's roles. The "Forest," as we called it, was located in Baldwin, the next parish, about ten miles from Franklin. The only difference between the two towns was that Baldwin had fewer people.

Saga Brown was very beautiful. Tall pecan trees surrounded the four brick buildings, and the drive from the highway to the main building was lined with willow trees. One of the buildings served as a dormitory for students who could not commute. The girls lived on the first floor, and the boys slept upstairs. Two other buildings were used as classrooms, and Chester Hall was the building in which our teachers lived.

Most of our teachers looked like the people in Town One, but my father told us that they would be different because they came from the North. I thought that was all right at first, but then, I always had trouble pronouncing Massachusetts. Finally I settled for Mass.

Their speech was different; they smiled when they talked, and when they called my father Dr. Lacy they did not seem to be straining their voices. Away from the Forest their behavior was difficult to understand. Reverend Lowell, who taught me English, always looked nervous when I saw him shopping in Franklin. He spoke faster than he ordinarily did, and for a slow-moving man, he was always in a hurry to get away. The Colonel always told me that "real" teachers are busy people and have little time for childish games.

Reading, English, adding, substracting, and chapel were our main subjects. Eight of us had private piano lessons as well. I had already studied piano at home, but my father always said, "A real student must always listen." Father had a saying for every occasion. After he said one, I felt that there was nothing more to add. Often, however, I had the impression that the saying had nothing to do with the question I had asked. But if I had ever told him that, he would probably have said, "A real person always listens." I don't know why they ever called him the Colonel. A better name would have been the "Real One." The word "real" was included in most of his remarks. The real teacher, the real food, the real music, the real church, the real Bible, the real water, the real virtue, the real town, the real worker—even the real fool. One day he said that I was a "real son." Mother overheard and insisted that Nathaniel was also his real son. He just looked at her from over his glasses, and in his usual way, said "Sure, dear."

About this time the War was in progress. It had made Franklin a ghost town. For the first time, the factories did not run. The young men of One and Two had to go away to fight. A bus for One and a bus for Two always carried them away. The look on their faces was happy. My father did not have to go. Life was very different. We needed stamps and coupons to buy food. Sometimes my mother gave our coupons to the women in Two. Father always fussed when he found out, but sometimes he watched her do it and said nothing. There was never any butter, cheese, or chocolate, and the milkman only came four times a week. Mother had to clean the house herself, and Father was always angry. Essie Mae was gone too. Her little sister had come by to look for work and said that Essie Mae had taken her children and gone out West.

Two was now quiet at night. The men of Town One still came, but the lights had dimmed and the music stopped. Now my father could read.

Then Saga Brown was the center of my life. We began to sleep there all week and returned to Franklin on Saturdays. Saga was never still; there was always something to do. That year I was seven. At my party I met my first girl friend. Anna was tall and skinny and the first girl that I had ever met who was prettier than my mother. Since I was Saga's smartest student, and she the prettiest, we had a lot in common. I used to just sit and watch her, and when she would stand still for ten minutes, I would recite the three poems of Henry Wadsworth Longfellow I had memorized. And on Friday evening, after Social Dancing, I added Edgar Allan Poe's "Annabel Lee." I took my daily Longfellow recitations very seriously. When she would look away in one of my dramatic moments or suggest that we do something else the next day, I became very angry. Anna was always happy when I finished my speeches; I always got a big kiss on the cheek. I loved her very much. On her eighth birthday I wrote her my first poem:

> Your kiss is like sweet chocolate;
> "The day is cold and dark and dreary."
> Your face is very pretty;
> "The day is cold and dark and dreary."
> "Behind the clouds the sun still shines."
> We will be in love forever.

The fact that she didn't recognize Mr. Longfellow's lines made me even angrier than before.

I hesitated to talk about my new experiences with my father. His reply that it was not "real love" would have been unbearable. So Mother shared with me the thoughts from my first love; Father did not.

Coming home from the Forest one week, we noticed a strange sight. Right outside Franklin we saw many people, mostly people from Town One, looking at a small group of people enclosed behind a barbed-wire fence. The Town people were not being friendly to the people inside. The men and women shouted at them, and as usual their children were throwing rocks and shooting peas from slingshots to keep them ducking. After twenty minutes of pleading and promising to be quiet on the bus for two months, we persuaded our driver to stop and let us have a closer look.

The insiders had a look of questioning all over their faces, not knowing why they were there. They seemed afraid, the women crying and their babies screaming. Every time they cried and screamed, the younger Ones outside threw more rocks and shot more peas. I had never seen the people of One act so mean.

"Traitor, traitor," cried the outsiders.

What was a traitor? I had heard that word before—Benedict Arnold in our English book; yes, he had been a traitor. Surely these people had not done that. I moved closer to the fence. Mr. Kazuko and his family, who ran the restaurant in Town One—why were they there? He was no traitor; he had a flag in his store and gave candy on Halloween and firecrackers on the Fourth of July to the kids of One and Two. And Mr. Kato and his brother, who ran the picture show—how could they be traitors? And this was not an ordinary jail, for in our jail in Town One you never saw the prisoners. The only other jail like this that I remembered seeing was in a war movie. The American marines had put the enemy in prison camps, always behind barbed wire. But there was no war here; my father said that the fighting was far away in Europe and Asia.

Father knew about the camp before I told him; a "security camp," he called it. He was obviously annoyed by all our questions and just kept staring out of the window. Poor Mr. Kato. He was Father's friend. Several times they had had long talks; occasionally he had come to the basement meetings.

"Don't go there again," were my father's only words as he got up from his favorite living room chair to go to his room with the picture-show music.

A doctor came to town. Dr. Turner was a dentist, but the Real One was pleased because he could have conversations with another medical man. The dentist was good for Father because their talks took his mind off the camp and the war. In two weeks he was right back in step. Our Sunday evening car rides started again; he fussed about Mother's cleaning and cooking, and our weekly family conferences were even longer than before. But more important, *real* came back into his speech. We were all happy that the Colonel was back to normal.

Dr. Turner was younger and more talkative than Father. We liked him because he was so funny and because he had a pretty daughter.

Soon the arguments started. At first they were little ones, but after a long while they grew louder. The Colonel and Dr. Turner stopped speaking to each other for two months. Their wives finally brought them together again, but the peace was short lived. We never heard their serious talks; for, like the meetings Father had with the leading men of Town One, they were always in the basement. Hiding in the basement during one of their last meetings, I heard the Real One say angrily, "But this is not the State of Michigan. Don't you realize that you are in the stomach of the South?"

Dr. Turner just looked at him and stormed out of the house. Walking the basement floor in deep thought and talking to himself, the Colonel discovered my hideout. He was not angry; my presence in the still of the night was comforting to him. He hugged me so tight that I could not breathe. Imitating him, I said as he relaxed his grip, "Now I can take in some *real* air."

He laughed. He cleared his throat, and I waited for his reply: "And a real son never hides from his father." He picked me up with his strong arms and carried me to his room. While the picture-show music was playing and Father was reading, I fell asleep on his bed. That morning an emergency family conference was called at which we were told not to mention Dr. Turner's name in the house and to stay away from his family.

But Dr. Turner came to see us again. I remember because it was late, and I was up, as usual, watching the cars go by. The dentist knocked on the door and kept knocking, even though my father shouted several times, "Hold your horses, Turner; I'm coming."

Hiding at the top of the stairs, I saw little Dr. Turner stumble in. He was out of breath, and the more he talked, the more air he needed. He looked sick; perhaps he had been in a fight. His face and shirt were covered with blood. In my father's arms he said things I was too far away to understand. Father helped him walk down to the basement and looked over his shoulder, where he knew I would be hiding, and told me to fetch his bag. After giving Father his doctor's bag, I left the meeting room, but fixed the door so I could hear.

Dr. Turner had been trying to organize a group which would help the people in Town Two. The men of One did not want the group to function because they said it would cause trouble, and several of the troublemakers had been arrested because they had not listened. Dr. Turner had seriously disapproved of the arrest of these local NAACP officials, but the men in charge of the jail had refused to release them. That had been several weeks ago, and the officials were still in custody.

Father was opposed to the group because he had not organized it, did not approve of its members, and felt that they should "stay out of politics and concentrate on education and improved working conditions." Father had warned the dentist that he would start something he would be unable to finish.

Turner was still in a lot of pain, and Father was trying to stop the bleeding. The police had beat him. A young one on the force did not know that he was one of us and had spoken to him and his wife and family the way they talked to the people in Town Two. Dr. Turner had not stood for that and demanded an apology. Another policeman, who recognized the dentist, came over to settle the argument, but Dr. Turner was not satisfied and continued to talk. Like the NAACP officials, he was then taken to jail and beaten, but finally he was allowed to come home.

My father fixed the dentist's wounds and sent him home to rest. Turner's story disturbed him. He kicked the table and chairs in the basement room and just kept pacing the floor. Much later that night I heard him come up to his room.

Four nights later Father woke me and in a calm voice said, "Leslie, get up. We are leaving Franklin."

Out in the street there was much excitement—lots of police, the big fat sheriff, two of the leading citizens of One, men with torches, and men with guns screaming at us the same way they screamed at the people in the camp. I did not understand.

My little mother was ready to go. She was crying. Father tried to comfort her, but he could not help; her sadness was deep, and over his shoulders, her words came clear. "They shot him; they killed him; poor Dr. Turner is dead."

Outside, the screams continued; inside, we listened to Mother. Father was strong, but he could not help. Mrs. Turner was probably crying too. The walk to the garage was long and dark. Father had trouble finding the keys. The engine was cold, and it did not turn over very fast. We were being watched. The screams had stopped. We drove away. Father told us not to look back.

Now I know that we were run out of town. The agreement between Town One and our community had been breached. The basement talks had been no more than a holding operation, because no one expected a young, talkative tooth-puller to upset the balance. But that winter night in the middle of the War I was young and I did not know about rednecks. My father would take care of us. And I was happy and excited. I had never been out at night. If only the music had been playing.

II

Another Southern Town

NOW WE COULD not talk about Franklin. Nine years of your life ends in screams, violence, and the death of a man too young to be afraid; and your parents say, "We will not discuss it." Why, why, why, why? And a long list of other questions cannot be answered, because we can avoid the ugly reality of life by playing the piano, getting a "moral" education, and going to bed safely with warm milk and love supreme. Perhaps. You must therefore trust your protectors (who do not spell out why it is that you need protection). You accept the inevitable strong arm which is always around to lead you, and you go on laughing and enjoying. All you really care to do is to have fun and grow up. Children remember so little anyway. And if by chance your thoughts persist, a new environment will steal your mind before you have grown old enough to understand those experiences. Another big house—much bigger than our Franklin mansion, with a lot of rooms to play in—made me forget about the world I left; and when our furnishings and dogs came later, I had discovered the meaning of a new town. Mother would sometimes cry, but that would not be for long, since our silence was never an encouragement.

Shreveport, Louisiana, was a city, the second largest in the state and the largest in the valley of Red River. In the Civil War days it was recognized as the center at which men and arms could be assembled from Texas, Arkansas, and other parts of Louisiana. In those days of slavery, cotton was its chief resource, but after the fall of Dixie, crude oil, timber, and natural gas made Shreveport a major industrial center in the Southwest. In my youth it was a bustling, live, and modern city—businesses, skyscrapers, motor vehicles dashing and shrieking—with some 200,000 or more people.

All this tended to hide its most beautiful and enduring character: its two towns. Our middle community, however, did not function as it had in Franklin. It was larger and somewhat more diversified. Instead of eight families, we were fifty strong, whose occupations ranged from prosperous barber to physician. Our elite lived in the same general area, attended the same church, went to the same school, developed our own exclusive culture, and shared the same views of the surrounding world. Our reaction to the divided city was simple enough: beware of City One and avoid City Two. As children, youths, and grownups we saw faces in both worlds, but these faces had no characters, personalities, or identities. We were closer to City Two because we were all "colored people." Because of the segregated social order, certain contacts with it were unavoidable.

We had no special relationship with City One. Its leading citizens did not need us in their holding operation to contain the inhabitants of Two. Unlike their counterparts in southern Louisiana, they did not pretend to be gentlemen. Protocol which governed their relationships with "colored citizens" grew out of a historical tradition which went back to the founder of Shreveport, Henry Miller Shreve, trader, empire builder, slaver, Indian killer, and devoted Quaker who, like his father, Israel Shreve, disregarded his Quaker faith to fight in the American army. Mr. Henry was forever a source of inspiration to those white citizens who revered his qualities of violence, daring, hypocrisy, and courage.

The colored citizen who questioned this grand tradition was

tarred and feathered, or so I was told by one of the working-class children at my school. Second offenders, he said, always disappeared mysteriously.

School threw the children of the elite into direct contact with the children of City Two. For Father, that was a serious problem, given his negative feelings about public education. Little could he do, however, since there were no private institutions within three hundred miles. Nearby there was a Catholic school which was semiprivate, but my father disapproved of parochial instruction. "If you want to be a priest, go to Catholic school; if you want to live in the world, go to public school; but if you want to run the world, you need nothing less than a private school education," was his philosophy of education.

So West Shreveport Elementary was our school. Its motto, on the front door of the building, was, "Education makes better citizens." The one building on the grounds was falling down; the teachers were well dressed, but lousy; the students were uncultured; every day there were fist fights, which usually involved whole families. The English spoken by both teachers and students sounded to me like a foreign language.

Acclimatization psychologically and academically was difficult to achieve. There was no logic to the school's system; nothing worked. For what he was worth, we had a principal who represented the symbols of authority, order, and unity. But Mr. Tumbler, once a fine football player, had no special sensitivity for administrative work. He was remarkably stupid. If you journeyed to his office by following the signs he had posted to direct you, you ended up on the athletic field. I considered that a fantastic feat, as our school was housed in one building with two floors. And since he supervised the school's construction (from football, he had gone into carpentry), beware of the rain. The driest, softest place was under a tall tree. Thank God there was never a fire.

To cut down on the intake of foreign objects, you were wise to bring your own sandwiches for lunch; his wife was the school dietician. On the positive side, you always got enough exercise. If you couldn't run fast or didn't have at least two big strong brothers, you frequently got your ass kicked. The fellow doing the kicking, surprisingly efficient, was determined to win by any means necessary. Fighting was an art, but winning was essential. Status in the school and community was based upon physical strength, willingness to fight, and ability to beat all challengers. The more vicious the fighter, the higher his prestige. In West Shreveport, like most schools in this town, there was always a fighter supreme. He had all the pretty girls. Out of fear, everyone listened to him, and he was sure to get promoted in all of his classes.

Compared to Saga Brown the education was second class. Every classroom seemed like a school unto itself, with its own ethics, its standards of excellence, and its own power to determine whether recess would be two hours long or last all day. If you were fortunate, you got a teacher who could read and teach you new words in what was called vo-ka-bu-la-ree classes. The less fortunate got a good deal of exercise on the athletic field and a new desk to write and sleep on. To keep the students happy, the school provided an active athletic life, a small band, a better-than-average choir, which sometimes sang in the local Baptist churches, and a home economics class for those bent on a cooking career.

Even here, our exclusiveness as a class was preserved. The fifty big children—a dull and unimaginative lot—were in special classes. We had teachers who had finished high school and college, and we managed to control or influence the functioning of the insufficient cultural and nonathletic activities. I occupied a privileged position in the group because most of the teachers were my father's patients. It was assumed that I was intelligent, and the grades I received were usually A's, never less than B's. A poor kid who was smart received the grade he deserved, but he was never held up to be as good a pupil as the child whose parents had money or influence. These poor, without even a representative in our Parent-Teachers Association, naturally resented this discrimination and struck back at the only thing in the system they could hit: our heads. In the normal course of things, I was not a fighter; I even had trouble beating my sister. So I naturally tried to resolve my differences verbally. But that was not in the nature of the game. So, not wanting me to exhaust myself by running home, Mother was always happy to pick me up with the car after school. Because of this, I was called Punkin' Mary (actually Pumpkin Mary), a name given to a boy who refuses to fight and hides behind a woman for protection.

Fighting in the public streets would not have been consistent with my image. I was Dr. Nathaniel Lenard Lacy's son, and a certain intelligent, correct, and dignified behavior was expected. The only time we screamed and made unnatural natural sounds was at the barber's. Mr. Martin White—called Sammy by the rednecks who used to come by in the winter to drink his coffee and see some woman Barber White had waiting for them in the back room—used to shave our heads. He said that I had "bad hair," and I think he reasoned that the only way to make it good was to cut it off. I always felt sensitive with a bald head; the boys at school wore their hair longer and would shoot peas and throw water on my shiny head.

Sister was lucky; she got to keep all of her hair and was allowed to scream in moderation when Mother combed it every day. Great effort went into preserving its length, since long hair was our prize symbol of natural beauty. Every night, it was greased and plaited, and every morning, unplaited and combed out again—a process intended to make it grow. It seemed silly to me to tie the hair up with black cord at night, take it down in the morning, and tie it up again the next night. In order to keep it long and straight, or from looking like my hair before it was cut, Mother put hot combs in it every two weeks. This process, even more than the morning comb-out, caused my sister a great deal of pain because, more often than not, she got herself burned. The funny thing about this was Mother would burn out the hair she wanted to grow, or burn the curls she wanted to straighten, or curl the "bad hair" she hoped would drop out. But it had to be done. When the odor of smoke and grease had been cleared from the walls and Sister's face had been wiped with powder to clean away the tears, sweat, and whatever else would come off, she was always overcome with joy because Mother had made her beautiful. Why she kept her hair and why we cut ours was a question that I could not answer until I was almost a man. Homemade beauty still did not make her pretty, or so she was told by the light-skinned colored girls whose mothers were the guardians of our impressive culture (garden parties, Easter egg hunts, sorority affairs, cotillions, annual beauty contests, and the father and son banquet). To them she was naturally ugly because her curls were not a logical outcome of "good hair," which all of them had acquired from their Indian or European ancestors. Sister, like Lenard and I, was very black, with a wide nose and big lips. She was never told that she was ugly, but only who was pretty. With better shoes, socks, speech, mind, house, and more money, she was able to internalize such standards of beauty without severe psychological discomfort.

Skin-color differentiation among the Louisiana Negroes, especially the elite, was a curious phenomenon. New Orleans and Shreveport had the worst systems in the state, if not the country. In fact, New Orleans set the pattern for the whole country. The creation and preservation of an articulate and influential caste of colored people (the result of sexual experimentation between people of African descent and Europeans) was an integral and controversial part of New Orleans history. Although that city was one of the principal slave-trading centers in the South, free Blacks there managed to avoid being resold by selling slaves themselves and by moving relatively freely and openly in the city's white "society," while spending their summers in Paris and Algiers. That produced a light-skinned Creole caste, ranging from light-brown mulattoes to high-yellow octoroons which, until around 1966, formed an insulated society thought to be composed of the most beautiful creatures miscegenation had produced. Most significant Negro institutions were controlled or influenced by this caste, and it was impossible for the unassimilated to get any of its ass—unless, of course, he had enough money to buy a daughter from one of the established families:

> If you white, you right.
> If you yellow, how beautiful,
>   mellow, one of the fellows.
> If you are lucky, you're brown;
>   there's room for you in town.
> But if you black, God help you, stay back.

Male children, especially those from our class, tended to escape the harsher implications of this inflexible law, since their worth turned upon their productive potential as prospective husbands. I was partially fortified, first, because of my father's money and influence, and second, because of superior intellectual ability. Also, Shreveport was small. Later on, however, when these protections were neutralized by young men who had both looks and money, I was forced to seek out alternative devices to protect my self-image.

Somewhere around this time I discovered that all the "nice girls" did not live in our community. I was probably near twelve, because as I look back, discovery coincided with my father's decisions to have my birthday party on our new patio and to build a cement wall around the back and sides of our house. The "Lacy wall' was rather controversial. My father's detractors—and there were always many—said we were trying to close ourselves off from the rest of the community. Such talk was not without substance, given my father's isolationist tendencies. He joined a few select business-education ventures but stood back from most socially oriented groupings. The window-high wall was necessary to protect our hilltop home from falling dirt and movements of the earth which always occurred after a tropical storm. As in Franklin, our house was the last you passed on the way to Town Two. And between our house and that town was high grass and a cornfield. One day at the beginning of the wall's construction, disobeying orders, I stood on top of the huge tractor so I could see what was on the other side of the field. After nearly breaking my arms and a leg, I finally reached a place on the machine where I could see best.

The houses on the other side were very tiny in comparison to our fifteen rooms. History had played a large part in the continuation of the construction of crowded dwellings in colored areas in Southern cities such as Shreveport. From the books I had seen in my father's library, the houses looked like those dating back to the early plantations' slave quarters— compactly built in parallel rows of close-together rectangles, which the children called "shotgun."

In front of one of the two-room houses—which I later discovered was 10C—was a little girl playing in the dirt. Even from that distance and through all that dirt, I could see that she was pretty. When she finally looked up and saw me watching, she gave a sign for me to come over.

Through the high grass, we met in the middle of the cornfield. Running had made us both tired, so we breathed hard and just stood there and smiled at each other. She caught her breath first.

"You Dr. Lacy's son, ain't you?"

"Yes, I'm the younger one, Leslie."

She smiled with relief, as children do when they know they are right.

"How come you know who I am?"

"Everybody know who you is. But I know 'cause I seen your picture in the *Sweeport Sun.*"

The *Shreveport Sun* was the Negro newspaper. Our names and pictures were always on its pages, and for a local small-town paper, they took good pictures.

The dirty-faced girl was about thirteen; of course she could have been older or younger, since it was sometimes difficult to tell their right ages. She had long brown hair, but it was immediately obvious that her mother had not been taking care of it. Although her blue jeans made her look like a tomboy, her body, in spite of her skinny legs, was beginning to look like that of a young lady. In the world from which I had run to meet her, cleaned up she would have been considered a beautiful girl, but watching her walk around, looking me over, I had the feeling that she would have thought herself beautiful anywhere. How could a poor dirty little girl walk and look so proud? In her left hand she had a small stick like those some of the kids used to beat the bush with, and in her right hand —there was a toy ring on the third finger—she carried a piece of sugar cane.

After she had gotten a good look, she smiled again, got close to my face, and began to peel off the skin of the cane with her teeth. She offered me the cane, but I politely said no. Her beautiful brown eyes did not take my refusal well, but she was careful not to look hurt, jerking the offer away as if to say, "The hell with you. If you think you are too good to eat cane with me, I don't care. The more for me."

Most of the boys I had seen chew cane usually took off

the skin with their teeth, but her method of peeling and chewing was unique; hard for my stomach to take. If I had carried a knife, I would have offered to cut the skin and carve the cane into proper eating slices; but I was glad that I didn't, because her method seemed far more efficient. Besides, tomboys didn't take well to having real boys perform a job they thought they could do for themselves. Beyond that, I felt no real need to assist her, since she was not one of our girls, who, if they ate cane at all, would probably do it at home.

Her strong teeth produced a horrible sound, and with one ferocious bite, a side of the skin came off. The juices came directly at me and splattered all over my vest. She apologized, but made the spots worse when she tried to wipe them clean with her hands. With her mouth open and juice running out the sides, she had the appearance of a thirsty animal receiving his first drink. And unlike the other kids, she stored all the waste in her mouth until she had almost finished the whole of the cane, and she got all the strawlike substance out with one big spit. Again, I was the target. My pretty cane-eater apologized the second time, but before I could stop her from cleaning, rubbing, and brushing my clothes, I was as dirty as she was. I was a little annoyed as I continued to clean myself, but my efforts were even more frustrated.

I must have looked pretty funny, because she couldn't stop laughing. She was hysterical. She fell in the field and damaged some of the corn and just kept pointing at my once-blue vest and bald head. She tried to say things as she laughed and performed, but her words could not get through.

There I stood. I began to relax and started to laugh too, which, of course, made her laugh even louder. Now she began throwing more dirt on my clothes, and then a handful went right in my face; and the dirtier I got, the more fun she had. After a few minutes I joined the game, and we had a good dirt-throwing contest until we were too tired to stand.

As I was lying in the field and getting my breath, she handed me the rest of the cane. Refusing again would have spoiled the fun, so I took it after a slight hesitation—only to get my lips caught in the skin. She was too exhausted to laugh, but she managed a small one, took off the skin herself, and gave me the cane. Meanwhile she had got her wind back, and let out a good laugh when the juice came out of my mouth. And I could not have cared less about my new eating habits, because I was enjoying my first piece of sugar cane.

"Ain't you afraid out here?" Her voice was loud again.

"No! Are you?"

"There is snakes out here."

I jumped up to run. She laughed; she was trying to frighten me.

"I'se just funning. Ain't Doc Lacy going to be mad 'cause you talking to me?"

"No. Why should he?" As if I didn't know.

"Well you know how you people is. I ain't in your class. Look, you know what I mean. Well, anyway, I'se going home. Comin' tomorrow?"

"Yeah." I hesitated.

"See you." She ran back to her town.

The next day we met again. She brought the cane, and I brought some chocolate. We stuffed ourselves with all those sweets, and between mouthfuls, we laughed and took turns chasing each other through the cornfield.

After several of our secret meetings and cultural exchanges, I tried to treat her as I expected my sister to be treated. My niceties went unnoticed. She only responded to my laugh, Essie Mae's jokes, and the sweet chocolate which her folks could not afford to buy her. When I suggested that she wash her hair and perhaps occasionally wear a dress, she would laugh and dirty up my clothes. She was wild like the corn, hard like the cane skin, and ran twice as fast as I could. Only when we were resting were her words soft, her mind preoccupied, and her eyes sad. Then my poems would be welcomed, but never more than one at a time.

I knew something about sex in those summer days in the field, but she never stood still long enough for me to try it out. Once I almost kissed her, but her cough came up and got in the way. That kind of cough I had never heard. Up from the chest, and strong as she was, it made her whole body shake.

It was always there, waiting to come out and stop her chase, reduce her laugh, or cut off her speech. My cough medicine didn't help, and she was always saying she was all right.

As our summer passed, it got worse. One day she coughed the whole morning, and when I returned from lunch, "GONE HOME" was written in the dirt. The next day she was her normal, alive self again, but the day after that she did not come at all.

One night, after I had not seen her for three days, her brother, whom I had seen only from the edge of the cornfield, came over to see Father. He was weak from running and therefore found it difficult to explain. Finally it was out: his sister was sick, and Doc should come quick. Father tried to get more information about his sister's condition, but he was only a messenger. No doubt her cough was worse and probably in need of emergency service. I hoped she would be all right.

My father was not enthusiastic about going. Members of that family were not his patients. Like so many colored citizens, this family had a white physician who, even in emergencies, rarely, if at all, made night visits to Town Two. Father resented these night calls because the callers did not believe in the concept of a Negro doctor and would return to their usual doctor as soon as they could. Moreover, Father usually was not paid for his night visits, and the patients generally did not follow his advice. In a number of cases families stayed with doctors who had refused to come out to see dying relatives because it was after 6:00 P.M. Father had also found that several white physicians, in their haste to leave the world of poverty, had diagnosed illnesses incorrectly and recommended the wrong medicines. One woman died of pneumonia because her doctor treated her for a heart condition. Another doctor won a legal case against a family that had sued him for gross negligence in connection with the death of the twenty-four-year-old son. The facts of the case were indisputable: the man died from gangrene because the doctor had removed the wrong leg. The court held that the doctor was absolved from blame because he had exercised due care, since the unconscious man did not point out the sick leg.

Father had tried desperately, through his practice and in

his civic groups, to raise the level of awareness. But then, how could a Negro doctor in a fifteen-room house convince a colored citizen in a shotgun slave rectangle that white wasn't right?

Father and sun came over the hill together. One needing energy; the second bringing it. Tragedy and fatigue never mixed well in his face. I had seen that combination before, on another night, in another town, five hundred miles away.

And I never even knew her name; never asked her, was it Betty, Jean, Ruth, Dorothy, Jackie? She knew mine—everybody did, 'cause our picture was in the *Sweeport Sun*. Lacy, Lacy. Lacy—maybe it was Lacy. Couldn't even compare her to a summer's day, because I never knew her name. Her hair was dirty because her mother was dead. Her skin was yellow, but she was not one of the fellows—wrong world, wrong town; wrong name, Miss No Name . . .

> So take your rest, No Name.
> No home visits; remember, it's forbidden.
> No coughing, No Name.
> Sugar cane ripe, must be ate right,
> 'Cause you get your mess on my vest.
> I never knew your name;
> Just through the high grass
> And into the cornfield,
> A dirty face was all I saw;
> A laughing heart was all I heard.

III

Do Your Toilet Rapidly
and Early

Don't go where you are not wanted. . . . Don't lose your temper. . . . A gentleman is never rude. Don't be afraid of being courteous. Don't monopolize the washroom. Do your toilet rapidly and early with as little to say as possible unless the porter tells you that you are the only passenger. Do you swear, young man? I hope not, but the gods would forgive you once. . . . Don't drink from a cup containing a spoon. All food should be put into the mouth with the right hand.

THUS WROTE Dr. Charlotte Hawkins Brown—the New England normal-school trainee who founded, at the turn of the twentieth century, Palmer Memorial Institute—in the Introduction of her only book, *The Correct Thing to Do, to Say, to Wear: A Ready Reference for the School Administrator, the Busy Teacher, the Office Girl, the Society Matron and the Discriminating Person.* And in those days of becoming a gentleman, a bright and shiny ninth grader, this little red book was next to my white Bible in order of importance, and a perfect complement, once I had internalized all of its one hundred pages, to my own excess of inherited arrogance.

I arrived at Palmer three weeks after my little field friend was buried in her town's cemetery. Since I did not go to the funeral, I did not know the exact spot of her grave, but I hoped, because she liked to run, that she would be surrounded by graves whose spirits were also young. I had told my father after he had caught me crying that she was a "nice girl," and he promised before I boarded the train for Sedalia, North Carolina, that he would take a piece of sugar cane and place it near her grave. Naturally he was confused by such a strange request, so I backed up his promise with one from my sister, who was known to do anything once.

Palmer Memorial was reminiscent of Saga Brown in its beauty and general character, which of course immediately impressed me, since West Shreveport had never been to my liking. Not having learned anything there was not my prime objection. It had not been suitable because I found it difficult to relate to a structureless system, especially one which lacked even an iota of refinement.

After we passed through the usual unpacking, room assignments, physical examinations, and the official closet checking in order that the hall's matron could ascertain whether we had brought our five suits, white dinner jackets, tuxedos, and all the other clothing which was on the list, my four years at Palmer began with chapel exercises and a meeting with the president, Dr. Brown.

But before describing our chapel and further expounding upon the source of the *Correct Thing*, I want to say something about room assignments. I expected, like most of the young incoming gentlemen, my own room, complete with maid and laundry services. Sharing the bath was acceptable, since we had had only three baths in our houses in both Franklin and Shreveport. But I had peculiar sleeping hours and a long-time habit of having a separate room.

Looking at my three roommates on the day of arrival, I felt certain that they had the same sensitivities, for we had stood in our room staring at each other. To my surprise, none of them objected to sharing the room; they looked discomforted because they were nervously waiting the other's first selection of bottom or top bunks, and drawers, and closet spaces. It occurred to me that since they were that considerate and democratic, maybe I should not demand private facilities, as these timid fellows would probably not object to my peculiarities and to my being responsible for making ultimate decisions in the room. Besides, it was a new experience.

The building in which the chapel was located was named Alice Freeman Palmer Hall. Miss Palmer had been the school's major white philanthropist in the early days, and without "her, wild grapes, and Jesus Christ, Palmer would have never become." The Palmer woman gave the school her distinguished New England family name, her money, and guidance; Jesus, as usual, provided the holy blessings; and during hard times Dr. Brown ate wild grapes.

The chapel was like a religious museum because it had that sacred don't-touch quality. Like other chapels I had seen, it had the usual wall portrait with a small light over the head —a serious eighteenth-century figure looking into the sunlight. Seeing these pictures always gave me the feeling that the distinguished-looking wall face had done, said, or created something important; so I watched in silence and awe. To keep the place dark and add to the mystique, there were pictorial stained-glass windows that, of course, could never be opened. With a minister-type seat and two deacon-type chairs on each side of it in front of the podium, the room had an atmosphere of worship and consecration. Only the noisy seats kept me earth-bound.

The president sat in the minister seat, with her whispering assistants on each side. The other staff sat behind them in beautiful mahogany chairs. They watched us scrutinizingly as we marched in to the tune of some classical music I had never heard, the sub-freshmen (eighth-graders) first, until the tallest senior boy got to his seat. Then, all together, as we had done in practice session, we reached with our left hands back for our seats and quietly sat down. The girls on one side of the huge room; boys on the other.

The fourteen women on the rostrum were well attired, in black dresses, pearl beads around their necks, and just a little heel on their black shoes. A glow of confidence and competence bounced off their gloomy faces; if they could have spoken what they looked like, they would have probably said, "Look now, kids, we have ours, and you have yours to get." The three men included—who appeared to be hiding behind the wall of black dresses—did not seem to be the museum types. The football coach was mildly funny because he kept adjusting his long legs to the cross-ankled pattern which the women had set. Another male teacher, barely visible behind the amazon English teacher, was shining with joy as his bright eyes looked over her shoulders and fixed on the section where the younger boys were sitting. She must have known about his habit of looking, because she turned toward him politely and his eyes went down to the floor. Within two minutes he was looking and smiling again.

Everyone was waiting. Meditation quietness brought anxiety to the faces of the new; old students knew what to expect. One senior, in an ingenious camouflage, was already on his way to sleep; another student, probably a sophomore, was trying to hide a king-sized comic book behind a regular-sized hymnal.

While the heads were bowed, the fellow on my right handed me a sheet of paper. Printed at the top of the sheet were these instructions:

Guess the Number

At the close of the exercises the student body will stand and sing one hymn. For 10¢ you can guess what hymn it will be. If your number is correct you will win the jackpot. If one or more should win, the amount will be divided equally.

I could not believe my eyes. Gambling! And in chapel? I discreetly turned around to see who was responsible for this outrage, but all the heads were bowed in silent prayer.

"Well, make up your mind. This shit will be over soon," said the dignified-looking fellow to my left. Impatiently, he jerked the paper from my hand, wrote "42" next to the left-hand margin, and added his name to the list. When he finished, he quickly passed it to the next row, and within seconds, the paper moved with amazing speed to the row in which the junior-class boys were sitting. Later, when hymn 25 was selected by the chaplain, the winnings came from that row to the young fellow who had selected 25. Even though I was a little outdone, I found the whole experience amusing, simply because it was handled so efficiently.

Then Dr. Brown stood up to deliver her welcoming address. Perhaps because she was the president, or perhaps because of the way she looked, I looked directly and intently into her eyes. Even through her glasses, they possessed a magnetism and a gleam. Also, she was very distinguished. From head to shoes she was dressed in perfect taste; even the carnation on her well-tailored white suit was still slightly dripping with dew. She was short in stature, but from behind the podium she looked large and impressive.

My father had said, "Dr. Brown is a dedicated woman, so listen to her. That woman, along with Mary McLeod Bethune and Nattie Burrs, has done as much for the uplift of her race as did Booker T. Washington." My father did not have many heroes and surely no heroines. For him to admire a woman so much, after having known her for only a year, was a real tribute.

She began to speak. Slowly at first, so that her voice could speak to every face as her eyes took it in.

"I have chosen to speak to you this morning on a subject which is very near to my soul: the Negro and the social graces."

This brought enthusiastic applause. The sleeping boy applauded with his eyes closed. In fact, he started it. Dr. Brown accepted the applause like a modest and dedicated man of science who did not want to take an acknowledgement because he thought he did not deserve it.

"By social graces I do not mean an attitude of cheap servility assumed for the purpose of currying favor. I mean simply doing the courteous thing and making a pleasing appearance—the practice of everyday good manners so generally lacking nowadays in the conduct of the average young person, regardless of race. My message is to you, the young Negroes whose education and training is above the average; for unfortunately many of you are inclined to associate all forms of politeness, fine manners, and social graces with slavery-time performances of the maid and butler, and to discard anything which you might feel has come out of those days in which your ancestors were slaves. You forget that even in those days, many Negroes were schooled in the 'correct thing,' and what they were not taught they caught in the way of social demeanor."

She hesitated, but there was no applause. She adjusted her glasses, looked back at her attentive staff, and then forward again to the students. Dr. Brown spoke with a New England accent. Her voice was gentle and without flaws, for she took her time to stress each syllable and accent. Several years later, when I left Palmer and went to New England, I discovered to my amusement that her English was more New England than the New Englanders'. As I looked at Dr. Brown, I also noticed her shaking head, a nervous movement which brought to mind our deaf mute in Shreveport. Children used to run when they saw him, because the head movement always followed a terrifying laugh.

Soon more people were following the example of the sleeping boy. The bloodshot-eyed coach could hardly keep his balance in his chair. But Dr. Brown had my full attention, so much that I did not immediately notice the second sheet of paper on my right thigh. Another number game, I thought. When Dr. Brown's eyes turned to the other side of the auditorium, I read the paper.

Guess the Time
How long will Dr. talk today? Two hours? Three? Three and a half? You guess the time. Same rules as always.

These instructions were written, not printed. The game was probably just invented. As Dr. Brown continued, I quickly passed the paper.

"One needs only to read any book, fiction or fact, associated with the life of Negroes in the households previous to 1865 to see that it was the Negro butler and maid who actually taught the social graces to the children of the aristocracy of the Southern white group—everything from learning to curtsy to the art of walking with charm and grace across the ballroom floor. The canons of the social graces were learned by those slaves or servants as religiously as their masters learned the catechism."

Dr. Brown paused. Only the coach clapped, to keep from falling off his seat; the podium eyes of disapproval kept him from going back to a dream of a winning team.

"Fortunately"—her eyes turned from the coach—"there were

also those who, immediately after the Civil War, came under the wise and gentle tutelage of the flower of the white race that came from the North and Middle West, built private schools, became their instructors, and were their patterns for intellectual, moral, and social behavior. They taught our mothers and grandmothers the dignity of self-reverence and self-restraint. They taught our fathers—through example and precept—the proper attitude toward these women and what was expected of them in the new freedom which was theirs. These cultured Christian men and women gave to the students of the day open-sesame to the best culture that the world knew."

I discreetly looked around the room. Like myself, everyone awake was deeply engrossed. Dr. Brown believed in her wisdom, and because she was so dynamic, she had a way of making others believe in it. Our heritage had prepared us to receive this kind of wisdom. She seemed to sense our acquiescence, for as she moved ahead, the proselytizing mood of her beginning was replaced by a reverent compassion which was to characterize most of her speeches throughout my four-year term.

"It is perfectly natural that we want to forget much that was associated with slavery and its aftermath; at the same time, it is very necessary that we pay attention to some of the things that were gained by our foreparents through intimate association with an aristocracy schooled in the finer things of life. Well may we add to our modern culture and educational efficiency some of the fine manners of those bygone days."

Undoubtedly that last sentence was a familiar statement. Even the first-yearers, following the lead of those who had heard it before, clapped like we had heard God herself. Chapel clapping, as I sensed the first day, and was to confirm as the years passed, was contagious. It had a thunderous starting point, a subdued but continuous middle, and an intimidating ending, which usually caused the process to go over and over until hands refused to react to the brain. One clap session was sustained for thirty minutes. I watched the clock. I was tired and wanted to stop, but I did not want to feel disloyal. Included in the long approval sessions was usually a cheer, and in moments of emotional high gear, it was repeated over again, and again, and again.

"Dr. Brown," someone would shout.

"What Brown?" the audience would reply.

"Dr. Charlotte Hawkins Brown," says the first speaker.

"Dr. Charlotte Hawkins Brown," repeats the audience in a low voice.

"I can't hear you," says the first speaker in a louder voice.

The audience then repeats and repeats, because her name is never said loud enough. When each side's voices can go no louder, they spell out each letter in her name and end with shouts of, "Brown—Brown—Brown—*Brown!*"

No, the students were not crazy, nor were the sounds of approval artificial or contrived. It was intended to please; we actually, jointly and severally, believed in and welcomed her wisdom. Sometimes, like most youth who get tired from sitting, we were a little annoyed, especially when Dr. Brown spoke marathon style for four days. But we never objected to her speeches' content or missing classes, even though we heard the same thing over and over.

Dr. Brown ended her welcome speech: "We must take time to be gracious. After all, the success of the American Negro depends upon his contacts with other races who through the years have had greater advantages of learning the proper approach to life and its problems. The little courtesies, the gentle voice, correct grooming, a knowledge of when to sit, stand, open and close a door, the correct attitude toward persons in authority; good manners in public places, such as railroad stations, moving-picture houses, and other places where we are constantly under observation—the acquisition of these graces will go a long way in securing that recognition of ability needed to cope with human society, and will remove some of the commonest objections to our presence in large numbers. Alas, in order for the Negro to get even half the recognition which he deserves, he must be even more gracious, more thoughtful, more considerate, more cultured, more observant of little courtesies and social finesse if he would gain a decent place in the sun. . . ."

She had finished. Applause followed; the sleepers woke up; the staff went to their classes, to repeat for the first twenty minutes what had just been said. The numbers and songs had ceased, and we moved out, one step closer to the blessings of a civilized society.

Young and innocent, we returned each week, sometimes each day, to hear the doctrine of Brownism—even though it was easily accessible in our little red book. Even after we had taken our monthly red-book examination and all of us had gotten every answer right (sample question: "Should the lettuce on a salad plate be eaten?"; answer: "Yes. The idea of leaving the lettuce for 'manners' is outdated"), our expertise was reinforced with chapel services. As children of the elite (future members of the holding-operation communities of Houston, Texas; Apex, North Carolina; Tuskegee, Alabama; Washington, D.C.; Kimball, Virginia; Savannah, Georgia; Columbus, South Carolina; and other cities all over the Republic), we had to be ready. With students from Pembroke parish, Bermuda; Havana, Cuba; and Monrovia, Liberia, we also represented the international communities. In the course of it all, some became cynical, others slept, and games were played. We believed nonetheless.

All Alice Freeman Palmerites came from my type of family. They had to. Otherwise, after paying $1,500 for tuition and another $2,000 for clothes and transportation, their families would not have been able to maintain separation from Town Two. We were surrounded by each other's wealth. Graduation exercises of my first year looked like a General Motors reunion —there were mostly Cadillacs with black-suited chauffeurs. We had everything at Palmer except a landing field, so the private planes were left at the segregated airport. In fact, since we represented the collective efforts of the world's richest black bourgeoisie, when we wanted to go to the movie in Town One of the neighboring city, rather than sit in the segregated section, we would rent the movie theater for the day. Charge: $2,000. And we went to the movies at least three times a month.

We displayed the latest inventions from Town One. Bringing our own washing machines, driers, and portable refrigerators was not unusual. I had seven suits and other niceties, and of course my brother, who was a grade ahead, needed even more. One fellow, who had trouble passing, but who always scored

100 on his *Correct Thing* exams, had a shirt for each day of the school year. He was supposed to be one of the richer kids from Texas, and his bother had a fetish about clean shirts. Since they could not send Lucy, their housekeeper, to Palmer to do his laundry, his mother had done the next best thing. We all had checking accounts, but one girl, from Quitman, Georgia (voted most likely to succeed by her class), had blank checks sent from home, signed in advance.

We found none of this extravagant, since money was to be spent. The few Northern Negroes were not quite as rich, but they were to some extent psychologically compensated because, except in my classes, they got the better grades. Also—and at that point I did not understand why—we felt that they thought themselves superior. This attitude was too subtle for us to have confronted them with it. The Northern boys had a society called The Four Horsemen, but any Southerner who was interested in drilling and soccer could have joined it. Indeed, exclusiveness based on color, money, or region was hardly recognizable. Even the foreign students joined in the overall spirit of fellowship. The only exception was perhaps Saint Vincent. He was rich and colored like the rest of us, but he was strange, much older, very fat, with marks on his face, and he came from a place in Africa which none of us had heard about. To us Liberia was Africa, and being from Johannesburg, South Africa, was like coming from the other side of the moon. Also, we knew that the Liberian Palmerites were "civilized," because Americans had settled their country. Our geography teacher, a fine coach, had told us little else about the continent that was close to the sun. So when Saint Vincent proudly told us that he was the son of a "tribal chief," we were polite enough not to laugh in his presence, but confused enough to believe that his relatives came from that tribe of uncivilized natives who always got in the way of Mr. Tarzan's work. When we questioned him about his origins, he would only say, "When my people see blood, they kill." Because he was queer, the Northern boys called him a "queer." In turn, the Southern boys created a song in his honor, to the tune of the then hit song "Mint Julip."

Old Saint Vincent is the talk of the town.
He come in your room in the morning,
Ask you for some toothpaste,
If you don't have toothpaste, toothpaste,
He will play with your big penis
Old Saint Vincent, he is the talk of the town.

The most exciting day at Palmer, save graduation, was Roll Call Day. It was the day when each student made a personal contribution to the school. Each year after the Christmas vacation each class would compete with the others to see who could give the most money to the school. It was very fancy and elaborate. We wore special clothing; created special cheers, and brought special checks from home. During my four years, there were never more than two hundred students; once we raised $15,000, and never less than $5,000. It was only after the classes had handed their money in that the fun started.

The roll-call committee would read the amount it had received from each class: freshman class, $800; sophomore class, $850; junior class, $900; and senior class, $1,000. Then the auction would start. Freshmen would go into a huddle. Someone would hurriedly leave to make a telephone call. His or her return was cause for another class huddle and another telephone call, because Father had given his freshman child permission to give another $500. This would go on until we got tired or until Father said no. Once it lasted three days because one father was out of the city. Meanwhile we waited in joyous suspense and wrote letters home to have our allowances for January replaced. Naturally, the richest class won the day. The class of the blank-check girl usually won, a frustrating defeat for the runners-up because she never had to go and call her father.

I returned to Shreveport after two years. I had spent a summer with my friend in Bermuda, one Christmas in Virginia, and another in the beautiful city of Fort Pierce, Florida. I was nice and tall, my voice had changed, and I was charmingly arrogant. My father was proud; Mother was still quiet as ever; and Sister was busily readying herself for Palmer. Shreveport had not changed. But I was excited to get home, because my father had promised me driving lessons.

During the second week, the Fourth of July, the world of my youth was tested. I was driving in Town One. Father sat near me in the front seat. Suddenly a car passed close on my left side, and unable to judge the distance, I hit a parked pickup truck on my right. Father examined me quickly. I was shook up but otherwise all right. I was sorry, and my father smiled slightly and put his hand on my shoulder to relieve my thoughts of guilt.

As we got out to inspect the damage, a little white boy about eight ran inside his house, shouting in his horrible Southern accent, "Daddy, Daddy. Come quick. These two niggers done hit our truck."

Within no time, his father, the father next door, then all the fathers, mothers, and children of the street came to confront my father and me. The anger in their faces was out of proportion to the damage to the truck. Five dollars would have more than covered the bill. I knew about rednecks then, but I was only half afraid, because Father was close. They were poor and dirty, but their eyes held us in contempt. Their added indifference was humiliating because it was quite obvious that they were not listening, nor were they interested in the truth. My father's yes-sirs and flawless English provoked no response. Their collective thoughts were voiced by the owner of the truck:

"Yeah, yeah. We wait for the deputy."

"Put your guns away," said the deputy to the mob as he drove up.

"If you say so, Carl," replied the truck's owner. "We jus' didn't want dese niggers to get loose."

The handguns went back into the pockets, a woman put a butcher knife under her apron, and the riflemen rested the butts of their guns on the ground.

I hardly heard the deputy. I was thinking of Franklin. Poor Dr. Turner. Were the Japanese still in those security camps? Then I remembered that Mother had told me that they were out and back running their restaurants and picture shows.

Looking back at the mob, I almost laughed out, because the redneck woman standing almost too close to me looked like the picture of Alice Freeman Palmer hanging in our living room. It was probably in thousands of homes throughout the South. A good joke to tell the kids in September would be that Freeman Palmer wasn't dead, but bankrupt, no longer a lady, and now living in Shreveport. The resemblance was remarkable. Same eyes, nose, hair style. Only the look of destiny and clothes were different.

Father seemed a little relieved to see the deputy. A little explanation would get things back to normal. But to his surprise, the old deputy ignored him, and unlike the others, inspected the small scratch on the bumper.

"Doctor, what you doing over here?"

"I'm teaching my son how to drive, officer."

"Yeah? Why was he driving so fast?"

"He wasn't driving fast. He was in the proper speed limit—twenty miles per hour."

The mob did not agree. First they said fifty miles, but they finally agreed that I had been going seventy miles per hour.

"Are you calling these white citizens liars?"

Father hesitated. The crowd waited for his answer. I wanted to tell the rednecks, "Yes, you are lying," but I got the shut-up sign from Father.

"Well, not exactly. . . ."

"And what does that mean?" The deputy put his hand on his gun but did not draw it.

"I didn't say they were lying, but mistaken."

"Yeah?" the deputy said indifferently as he looked through our car. He opened Father's medical bag and threw the contents on the ground. As Father moved to pick up his tools, the owner of the truck pointed his gun at us and told him not to move.

"Don't you think a new Oldsmobile is too expensive for you to be driving?" asked the deputy.

"What does that, sir, have to do with the case?"

"Shut up." The deputy was angry. He pulled his gun but did not point it.

I looked at Father's face. He was afraid. His body shook

slightly. He was also angry, because of the way he held his arms, but he had a way of not letting people know it. I was afraid too. So many guns. I wanted my daddy to speak up. He had always told us to be honest and stand up for our convictions in spite of the consequences. He was like a different man, a man I would not have recognized if I had not been looking into his face. The real Father, nothing but talk. Pretty speeches for the people of Town Two; silence and fear for the people of One.

Free at last. Dr. Lacy was driving; I sat in the back seat and turned from his eyes in the rearview mirror. My spirit was like the falling sun. "Shut up!"

"Shut up yourself," he should have said to the deputy. How proud Dr. Brown would have been. Chapter X, "How To Behave," page 37, number 4:

. . . a gentleman is never rude. Don't go where you are not wanted. He rises above street speech by his language. No one encourages the cowardly in any man . . . his culture asserts itself in the discretion with which he makes his choice when to speak and when to be silent.

Home at last. Father's face was normal again. I don't believe that he realized what had happened to him. His manhood was not city wide. It counted only among his kind. Everything else was temporary, and you adjusted to it without making it a part of your conscious existence. If you were intelligent, like my father, you could play tricks with your mind. If you were poor, you beat your wife. In either case, it was all in a day's work.

The table, better than that of those who had shouted at us, was set for four. Nathaniel was abroad, studying French. I did not like the thought I had in my mind, but when I finally allowed myself to accept it, I had to laugh. It was funny: how do you say "No, sir" and "Yes, sir" in French? My brother would go directly back to Palmer. I would have to give my sister to Dr. Brown alone. Everyone ate, except me. I was hungry, but my thoughts confused me, and Mother added to it. After dinner I told her. She was impatient; she wanted each detail. Her reply shocked me.

"What did you expect your father to do? If he had stood up like you wanted him to, like a man, and talked back to those crazy people, they would have killed him. And who do you think would have taken care of us?"

The train ride back to Palmer helped me forget. Mother knew best and had repeated her words before she gave me my little sister's hand. I was now to be responsible for another human being.

Train travel also reflected the Town-One–Two pattern. This train was especially representative. Three cars for the "colored" passengers, six cars for the whites, several service cars, including diner and club cars. In theory, the Pullman car was integrated, but very few Negroes had the money, and courage, to use its facilities. Ordinarily we traveled by Pullman as an alternative to flying, but Father had decided that on this trip we should have the experience of "being with the people."

The entire institution was in the hands of the white conductor, supported by three other white men: assistant conductor, a passenger representative, and trainman. Negroes entered the structure in their usual service roles, as dining-car cooks and waiters, Pullman porters, chair-car porters, and special assistants to the assistant conductor. Unofficially, the special assistant was the "head nigger in charge" (H.N.I.C.) of the other Negroes. His job—placing the identification checks on the seat after the conductor had punched them—put him into special relationship with both towns. Ironically, he performed the same function on the train which our community had performed in Franklin. He religiously followed the rules handed down from above and reported back to his superiors the attitudes and functionings of those below.

Wishing to serve his master at the highest possible level, the H.N.I.C. was usually authoritative and abusive in his dealings with his fellows. In his zest to maintain his privileged position, he made his superiors aware of employees' mistakes they could not have detected otherwise. He was indignant for days if a fellow employee forgot to call him Mr. Roberts, but he would laugh for hours and come a-running when his boss called him Tom.

The behavior of the Negroes in the car was a study in inferiority, although at that time, I did not understand its nature or its consequences. Whenever the conductor entered the car, whatever was happening stopped happening and something else happened. An angry wife became civil to her still-angry husband after the conductor spoke to her. The conductor's entrance brought complete silence; so intense was it that if he had stayed in my car for the three-day ride, I could have prepared all my homework for September. Children, too young to know, cried from Mama's beating, because they had seen no reason to stop playing. It was difficult to stop laughing in the middle of a laugh and difficult not to breathe loud after a fast run in the aisle. But the children soon got the message; one even posted himself to watch for the silver-buttoned blue-shirted conductor. There were no rules to follow, and the conductor never gave us any orders. We just knew how to act.

Nevertheless, the conductor knew of his special power. And like a king walking into his court, he would grant us the right to relax. It never occurred to the relaxing subjects that their king had been paid to give the service. It was both interesting and ugly: they laughed to relax, and on one occasion one of the relaxed offered the eighth-grade-educated conductor a leg of fried chicken. And of course his smiling assistant got a wing.

With the conductor or any of his white overseers, the passengers were like children who seemed not to want to understand why their own children wanted to play in the aisles. "Now, Mary, don't run in the aisles; you know better than that. Johnny, you sit down and go to sleep." But Johnny and Mary (both three years old) did not "know better than that." From their dress and speech, it was quite obvious that they lived in the rural South. Everything was quite new to them, and it was their first train ride. Every time bald-headed Johnny and straight-haired Mary were told to stop doing what came naturally, something tragic must have happened to their youth. Or at least I thought so, because one of the few fathers in the car reminded me of my own.

The white kids could play baseball in their car, and by opening the doors between the cars, they were able to use our car as their outfield. And when their balls bounced off our heads and got lost under our seats, the little rednecks would order one of the bald-headers to find it. Running and looking was then tolerable and could be done without fear of punishment, because we were only doing at play what our folks did naturally.

In the dining car there was always a table reserved "for colored." My family and people like us always ate at that table. The waiters were nice to us, even though we were the last to be served. The other people of color brought their food with them. Eating in the diner was too expensive, both financially and psychologically. Every family had a box or bag of food which had been carefully prepared the night before. Even though you never saw the food containers when they boarded the train, you knew that they were there, hidden behind some clothes in one of the small suitcases. It was quite a ritual: no one opened those hiding places until the right moment. Seven, twelve, and six were acceptable eating hours. One family would lead off; the others would quickly follow. They would set up their tables on their laps and gather around for fried chicken, ham sandwiches, hog head cheese, cold hoecake, fried pork chops, fried chitlins, apples, oranges, and other food which would "keep" for a four-day trip. The homemade food always looked delicious and was always nicely wrapped and generously shared with each member of the family as well as with other passengers who sat nearby. Mealtime made all of them look like one family.

They ate very quietly. Conversation would have seemed like a breach of table manners. In fact, even though they ignored all the rules of *The Correct Thing*, their style and form was quite sophisticated and impressive. They had no knives and forks; their clean hands seemed good enough. If a mother was enjoying a piece of food, she shared the unfinished part with her children, who did likewise among themselves. They smiled and laughed with love as they put the cold food in their systems. I did not share in their meal, but I was not blind to its beauty. I was glad that they did not eat in the dining car.

My last years at Palmer passed very quickly, yet not fast

enough. I loved the school and had internalized most of its values, but I wanted to get away—to "escape," as one fellow put it. This was the first (perhaps the second) time that I had thought of Palmer as a prison. The thought did not remain long, because I knew what a real prison was like. What I felt, no doubt, were the pressures and strains of my inability to resolve all of the contradictions of Palmer. We were supposed to be in training to take our fathers' places, but we spent more time in chapel than in classes. And every day, every month, for long memorable years, we heard the same sermons. We were treated at every chapel session like we had not heard the one before. The majority of the students did not find this situation objectionable. I therefore assumed that something was wrong with me.

I do not mean to give the impression that I was a young rebel. I was not. Probably the best way to describe my differences with the system of Palmerhood was that I approved of its overall objectives, but I thought the procedure was inefficient.

One of my teachers, whom I respected, put my young mind at ease by assuring me that everything was for the best and that she held for me "the highest hopes of success in all future educational adventures toward a full, fruitful, and happy life." On graduation day, she reminded me with a little pull to her heart that she expected me to achieve worthwhile goals. She spoke about George Washington Carver and Booker T. Washington. I could be one of them if only I worked hard and kept "the banner of Palmer always aloft." She said goodbye. I cried. I was sorry to leave. I had loved everything very much. The training and virtue which I had been given would help me face the world. Now I would go on to higher education, to be a doctor like my father, or perhaps, because of my verbal skills, a lawyer.

IV

The Cats and Kittens

"My name is Leslie Alexander Lacy. I have just arrived. I would like to be assigned to my room." I liked my name. It was long and melodious and I always enjoyed saying it. My name, unlike that of my brother, who was stuck with my father's name, being the first son, had special significance. Leslie was the name of my father's best friend; Alexander the Great and Winston Churchill were his special heroes. And my father always said that men of destiny and empire builders needed impressive names. I believed him when he said it.

My name with all of its history did not seem to impress the white middle-aged woman sitting behind the desk. She did not look up. As I stood there waiting for a response, it occurred to me that the noise of the typewriter had come between my words and her ears. I had spoken in my best English, practiced the phrase for nearly a week, and she had not heard. I knew I had to repeat it, which I felt I could not do, since I had given everything I had the first round. What a fine statement—lost to the noise of a machine. We had been taught at Palmer that "a gentle voice is the best way to reach an open ear." I seldom shouted, not even when angry. And the few times when I did shout, I could not recognize my own voice.

With soft and gentle speech, I could manipulate with fine precision the cross between my picture-show and Palmer diction. And of course, having to repeat—especially to someone you were trying to impress—threw the whole contrivance into disarray. Finally, my initial courage returned, and in my best English and somewhat louder than before, I said my name again.

"Yes, Mr. Lacy. I believe everything is in order," said the middle-ager with great enthusiasm as she stood up and shook my hand. I momentarily lost my equanimity (my cool). Not only had I never spoken in that manner to a white person, but I had also never had the pleasure of shaking one of their hands. But I smiled as she smiled (just a little one), and felt uncomfortably comfortable.

"Mr. Appleseed has been expecting you," she interrupted my thoughts. "Go right in and he will give you all the necessary details." The smile left her face, and she returned to the noise.

Mr. Appleseed looked like his name; in fact, I almost laughed when I saw him, because he resembled the comedian Jerry Lewis fifty pounds lighter. Also, he was extremely nervous. My presence in the office seemed to make him anxious—a kind of subdued anxiety which well-educated and refined Whites experience when they unexpectedly encounter a face that is colored. Like most, the funny dean of men tried to conceal his psychological changes behind a pleasant castle of fine rhetoric, but I was not fooled: I looked right in.

Something was wrong. Surely I was not the first Negro to live in the residence; and if in fact I was, he had had five months to prepare for my coming. Soon the anxiety left his face; only nervousness remained as he shook my hand, welcomed me to the college, and invited me to take a seat.

My responses were perfect. I was Palmer all the way. The only disturbing feature so far had been the handshakes. Handshaking was an important ritual in our community back home. Since the hands you held were invariably prominent, your grip was gentle but firm, with a vigorous shake. "Their" handshakes lacked the character to which I had been accustomed; they were too fast—rapid fire—a touching action rather than a cordial shake.

Mr. Appleseed began talking on the telephone. He swiveled his back to me and whispered into the receiver, turning now and then to comfort me with his funny smile. The conversation was difficult to decipher, but the phrase "I think it will be okay" gave me the feeling that they were talking about me. Also, it was clear that he was talking to a superior and that the problem had to be resolved immediately. For him and for myself, I was a little embarrassed, but remained calm and collected.

"Well, Mr. Lacy"—he had finished talking—"your accommodations are in order." Now very relaxed and without the funny faces, Mr. Appleseed painfully and in great detail spelled out the rules. Half of me listened; the other half wallowed in a state of euphoria. I was finally here. Indeed from the age of ten—probably even earlier—I had known that I would receive a university education. Half of my classmates were going to Howard University, and the other half, the richer sector of the deep Southern middle class, would be heading for Nashville, Tennessee, to attend Dr. W. E. B. Du Bois' alma mater, Fisk University. Their futures, like their counterparts' in the nation's capital, would be set: the boys would be near professional schools, and the girls—no, ladies— would be near professional husbands-to-be. I was not interested in the Negro colleges. I thought them to be inferior, and most of their graduates whom I had met over the years would have had difficulty maintaining a passing grade at Palmer. Dr. Brown had assured me that a college in the Boston area would have just what I needed. And my father had had the same impression: "Go North and finish the attainment of your culture. . . . We need some new ideas for our Southern empire."

For the half of me which listened, Mr. Appleseed made the dull history of the college, as well as the history of the residence, seem somewhat interesting. In fact, he became intensely excited by his own account, especially when he introduced me to the distinguished gentleman hanging on the wall, who, strangely enough, looked very much like Mr. Appleseed. At one point, putting his hand on my shoulder, he assured me, in a very reverent tone, "This can be your tradition as well." Adding in a lighter tone, "If you have any problems, please feel free to come and let us know. Our sole concern is the comfort and convenience of our students." I got another hand touch, another smile or two, and was escorted up on the elevator to room 421.

A voice inside, with an accent I did not recognize, said, "Enter." I entered first and received the shock of my life: all four of my roommates were Whites. Consciously—since the schools in the East accepted Negroes—I had not expected to be segregated; but my deeper thoughts had not entertained this kind of situation. I had known that I would finally meet, talk, and perhaps study with young Town Oners, but the fact of living with them had never occurred to me. It is a very interesting Negro middle-class psychological state. You know that you will be reasonably safe and secure in your integrated environment, even though—given a new set of demands, coming out of a wide range of possible situations of which you are unaware—you know that you may feel apprehensive and unable to deal adequately with every situation that arises. Hence the better your training, the better you are able to function. In the Deep South no Negro from my class would have assumed that he could have been safe (emotionally, psychologically, or physically) around Whites from the South or working-class Whites in the North. But in the North, especially in the universities and related cultures, the white people are gentlemen and scholars. Everyone back home that you respect has told you so. Thus far the two greatest influences in my life, Father and Palmer, had told me that. Therefore, without any considerable thoughts on the matter, you trust the white folks' judgment and allow them to make decisions for you. You do not expect to be severely embarrassed, because you feel that "they" will be embarrassed too, so you expect them to deal with you in a context which is comfortable for all concerned. It's a kind of built-in balancing point around which Whites and Negroes like me "in the good old days" moved.

In a firm and somewhat authoritative voice, Mr. Appleseed said, "This is Mr. Leslie Lacy." The "Mr." sounded good without the Alexander. "He is the roommate you have been expecting. All of you are fine boys, from some of the best families in America, and I am sure you will get on. I am sure that there will be no problems. But if there are, please do not hesitate to come down to see me." He gave me the touch and quietly left the room.

Their smiling white faces did not arrest my anxiety. Before today, I had never seen white faces smile. They were hard to understand. I got some relief when they darted over to welcome me, because it was then that I realized that they were nervous and scared like me.

"I'm David Wienstein," said the smallest one. "I'm from Scarsdale, New York, and I'm going to study medicine."

"I'm David Miller. I come from Springfield, Massachusetts."

"I'm William Lord Tyler. I come from Richmond, Virginia. I'm interested in music." He did not have a Southern accent. He sounded more English than New England. Later I discovered that he grew up in Richmond, and except for short summer stopovers, had lived there for sixteen years.

"I'm Ed Frost. I'm from Houston, Texas." Strong Southern accent and big smile. "We are from neighboring states."

They knew about me before. They had gone to the office and inquired. They had become curious when I had not arrived on schedule.

"You are a long way from home," said the first David, smiling and breaking into the uncomfortable silence.

I smiled back in approval, but said nothing, because my speech was not yet prepared. In the next second I said, smiling and very forceful, "I sure am, I think I'm going to like it." I wanted to keep talking, but the words would not come.

Both Davids were sixteen like me; the two Southerners were eighteen and nineteen respectively. We were *very* polite. Each time they addressed me they called me Mister, and I followed suit when addressing them. They watched me, and I watched them—and we smiled at each other from time to time—as I worked to get unpacked and squared away.

We had two bedrooms, a spacious living room, a beautiful study area, and a private bath. It was a suite. The residence had once been an upper-middle-class hotel, which the university had purchased. The Southern gentlemen slept in the first bedroom, and I slept in a bed between the two Northerners in the second.

As the days passed I gradually settled in, and the "Mister"

relationships continued. "You may use the bathroom first."
"I'm sorry, am I playing my music too loud?" "Your clothes
are very nice." "Mr. Lacy, your voice does not have the
usual Southern accent." "I am sorry I used your Vaseline for
my cut. I had no idea you used it for your hair." "Go, man,
go; your records are really hot." And we were together all
the time. They and their male friends were the only people I
knew. We went to school together; except for the two
Northerners, we went to the college church together; we ate in
the dining room together and shared, with exaggerated
laughter, the impersonal anecdotes of our histories. Every time
I spoke, everyone was sure to listen. One day during the
third week, in a real moment of laughter, we agreed that
"Mister" would not be necessary, even though the Southerners
had related to each other on that basis all along.

At the end of that week, the old students of the college
sponsored an "Orientation Hop" for the freshmen. All of my
roommates except Wienstein had dates. I went alone. The
hop was a curious mixture of those social affairs I usually
avoided: funerals, receptions, and father-and-son banquets. The
band played strange music, but no one danced. The young
men stood together, lingering around and stuffing themselves
with goods from the refreshment table. The young ladies, all
white, attired mostly in black dresses, sat dutifully around the
auditorium wall, amusing themselves with quiet talk. Even
the fellows with dates had abandoned them for the rah-rah
fraternity spirit around the fruit punch. This was not my
idea of a party, but everyone seemed to be having fun. Not
wanting to feel conspicuous and displeased, I moved quickly
and graciously toward the refreshments.

The faces were pleasant. Some said hello. Some smiled.
Others introduced themselves, but no one lingered to talk. I
was terribly conscious of the staring eyes. I had to remember
everything: the hand for the punch; not too many sandwiches—
you can always come back for more; chew your food slowly;
be pleasant. It took me thirty minutes to eat my first sandwich.
I reached for another. I finished it; took another, even though
the first one had been more than enough. Finally my Southern
roommates came over. We passed a few friendly words, but they

hurriedly left to talk to a man—surrounded by other men—
who I later discovered was the president of the Southern
Gentlemen's Society.

While I stood with a full stomach and without anything
else to do, my anxiety increased. I assumed one position, then
another. And without looking at anyone, my eyes from time to
time moved around the room.

Dancing and very little conversation was my definition of a
party. Two problems, however. The music and all the girls
were white. But I could not leave, so I abruptly rushed across
the floor and asked the first girl in front of me to dance.

"Yes, thank you very much."

A white girl! My age. She came from Vermont and was
surprised and curious when I told her that I came from
Louisiana. I could not do the Lindy, so I held her two feet
away and created a new dance between my slow drag and her
jumping up and down. Her piercing questions disrupted my
Palmer conversation while dancing. Mary Bothwell wanted
to know things which the Palmer young ladies had never
asked. "Why did you come so far to go to college?" "Is the
South as bad as people say?" "Do you plan to rush one of the
fraternities?" "Are you planning to stay here the whole four
years?" "Do you like the offbeat poets?" "Do you ski?" "How
do you feel about Senator Joseph McCarthy?"

My answers were mixed: "Yes." "No." "Very much." "It's
very interesting." When she did not consider no or yes an
adequate response, I added clauses which were equally inadequate.

We danced five numbers. I wished to walk her back to her
seat after the first, but she held my hand until the next number.
Nothing personal, but just a part of her dancing ritual.

All the Whites watched, but a few stopped looking after
the second number to do a little jumping up and down themselves. As the others jumped, some of my tension subsided.
We ended our dancing with the usual formalities; I graciously
walked her back to her wall seat, and then with shoulders
erect, made the long walk back to the fruit punch. After a good
and pleasant face for those who were still smiling at me, I
left for the residence.

My roommates were very concerned about my dance partner. "How did you know her?" "What's her name?" "Where is she from?" "You sure know how to pick the pretty ones, Leslie." I answered all their questions like a frightened defendant. As I look back through my history, I realize that I must have been trying to assure them that she was just a dance. And if she was pretty, I hadn't seen it. I had danced with her, held her body, remembered her face, hair, eyes, the quality of her mouth. But I could not know about her beauty because I had not *looked* at her.

I felt like I was on trial. They were as concerned for that stranger as I might have been for my sister. An unseen Vermont girl suddenly took on importance, *probably* out of proportion to her actual worth, because she had jumped up and down with an anxiety-ridden Negro from Shreveport. I was beginning to understand.

Wienstein hadn't gone. He went to church on Fridays. A Jew. I had never heard of a Jew. One day I put his Friday-night cap on. David was angry. It was not a cap but a yarmulke. After that he explained that Jews were different. They shared a common history. They were chosen; they had suffered, and six million had just been murdered in Nazi Germany.

I listened as he told me his sad stories. I could not feel sympathy for him immediately because I had never thought of white people from his vantage point. I knew that some were rich like us, richer even. Some were poor and uneducated, like Essie Mae's people. Some were Catholics, others Protestants. I felt stupid because after he talked I had the feeling that I should have known about his special history. Poor David! Why had people been so mean to him?

The other David—Miller—recounted his history of suffering more with sophistication than with compassion. He was not a serious Jew, David One always said. He did not want to be reminded of his orthodox upbringing and would rather converse in English when David One tried to reach him in Yiddish. "We are not in Europe, David. Please speak English to me."

Wienstein and I became special friends. I was not his first.

One of his best friends in high school had been a "colored boy." He had liked him very much because he was a "great guy" and had won a lot of new trophies for the school. One day he told me a delightful story. "We thought you were white." White? That was funny. The school charter prohibited it from asking a prospective applicant what race he was. When there was doubt, because you were too far away to be interviewed or it was not clear from the other facts what you were, an alumnus who lived in the area would come to visit you and with all deliberate speed make his report to the administration. This was thought to be essential, so that the incoming student would not be uncomfortable. Why, then, was I in room 421? When the alumnus had come to visit me I was in New Orleans visiting some high yellow friends of the family. If he had seen my father, he would have known, but only their voices met over the telephone. He did not know about our voice training. As fate would have it, I missed seeing the alumnus, who spent two hours talking with Dr. and Mrs. Clark about my character. He assumed that I was white, because he assumed that the doctor and his wife were white. When I explained the mystery to David, he examined his own skin . . .

Living with and being surrounded by whites was not easy. Always I found myself vacillating around a circle of emotional and psychological reactions—awkwardness, tension, anxiety, fear—and usually accompanying a particular reaction was a great deal of pretension. Gradually and with a careful control, I worked out behavior patterns which corresponded to my state of being. David Wienstein, without even knowing it, became a great help. I was not relaxed around him either. This suffering Jew simply made the adjustment easier. I practiced on him. Talking with David gave me an index of what I could expect from other Whites. When I was at school, walking with other classmates, he was someone I could say hello to, wave to, which I felt made the Whites in my presence stand easier, since another white person knew me.

To a lesser degree I tried to have the same type of relationship with my other roommates and their male friends. We played games together, hit each other on the arms and back and made statements which made us sound like friends. We read the same books, believed in the same God, had the same ambitions, shared the same family structure and values; and after months of consistent practice at night in the bathroom, I finally sounded like them. We got on just fine. And other Whites I met were helpful, considerate, and never abusive.

Nevertheless, I could not relax. I saw their eyes watching and their ears listening. When I greased and combed my hair in the morning, my roomates watched in disbelief, amusement, and amazement. Also, they could not understand why I greased my legs or why I got angry when one of the fellows in the gym classes said that I had put powder on my legs. (They did not know about Negro ash.)

And I did not understand. Sixteen! What an innocent age for proper Negroes. What am I saying? Simply this: I wanted desperately to belong to this new and exciting environment—or rather, I wanted to enjoy and take part in the benefits, but I had no conscious desire to be absorbed by them. I had come North to study. Eventually I would take my skill home. My father was a big man there, and I could be bigger. Beyond that I loved—worshiped—my middle-class culture and its life style. It was the only universe I knew. The only one I wanted. I therefore expected to meet my New England counterpart. Naturally enough, I knew my social and financial equals in Houston, Dallas, New Orleans, Atlanta, Richmond, Washington, D.C., Nashville—all over the South. But we had no relationships, except for the few Northerners at Palmer, with the centers of the Northern elite. In fact, I intended to establish the links by, among other things, marrying into one of the prominent families. Indeed, my father had been overjoyed when I suggested the possibility. "You are right," he had said. "We need some Yankee blood in the family." I was, however, waiting to get established before I made my move.

"Excuse me. My name is Leslie Alexander Lacy. I'm from Shreveport, Louisiana. I'm a freshman hoping to major in political science. What is your name?"

The Negro boy sitting down at the table in the lunchroom

looked up slowly from the daily school newspaper. He looked annoyed and bewildered and turned the page before he spoke. "Roy Farmer." His face was frowning. His voice was tough, and his manner was not friendly. He continued to read his paper.

"Are you a Bostonian?"

Without looking up, he replied, "Yes."

"I don't wish to disturb you; I just want to be friendly. This is my first semester, and I haven't met many people. I saw you sitting here, so I thought I would come over and say hello."

"Hello."

"Are there any parties or anything like that this weekend?"

"Look, man, I am not a social calendar. If you want to find out what's happening, go look on the bulletin board. And another thing: out of all these students sitting in this lunchroom, why did you ask me?"

His question surprised me. Surely he knew why: he was the only Negro eating in the lunchroom. "Well . . . because— because you're colored, and I figured you would know."

"Look, Lacy, this is Boston, not Louisiana. You don't have to worry about segregation up here. You can do anything you want and anything you please. Didn't anybody tell you that before you left home?"

"Yeah, I know all about that. I've gone to a lot of things, but you know how those affairs are. What I want to do is to meet some of the chicks. Know what I mean?" I laughed. Too loud, judging by the look on his face. He began getting his books together to leave.

"Lacy, this is not Mississippi. I told you that you can do anything you wish. That's what's wrong with us; we always segregate ourselves."

"Hi, Roy. Still knocking them down?" said a white boy walking with another white boy past our table.

"Say, Mike. What's happening, Tony? You guys sure are drags. What happened to you last weekend?"

Before they could answer, he turned to me and gave me some more advice about how to survive up North. Then he went to sit with them at another table.

It took that experience, and others, to make me realize that the Northern Negroes of education were a different breed. *They did not wish to segregate themselves.* At first that was difficult to understand. Segregation was a part of my self-definition. We were segregated from Town One, and except for business reasons, we segregated ourselves from Town Two. But we have to go further. This student not only did not recognize me as his equal, but given whatever other assumptions he had made, he was not the least bit friendly; in fact, he was hostile, very hostile. And he was not alone. Most of the Negro students, especially the upperclassmen, got upset and annoyed when any of the freshmen (usually Southerners) approached them. Couldn't they understand that these new-comers had come to them on Negro business, a kind of business that white students didn't know: Where is the local Methodist church? Where's the best place to meet some dignified people? Where do we get our every-two-weeks hair-cut? Where do we go so we can relax? How do I join a Negro fraternity? You see, I must ask you these questions because you ought to know. It is our culture about which I ask.

My father and mother were very consoling. They told me not to worry, because everything would "turn out for the best." I listened. My family knew best.

But soon I found myself acting like the other Negroes. At first I attempted to stop myself from acting that way. But after a while it got mixed up with my facility to be charming and I could no longer recognize it. In psychology parlance, I developed a special reaction toward middle-class Negroes. In Shreveport I never had too much contact with lower-class Negroes, so reactions to those I met in Boston remained the same. I looked and acted like I possessed the universe, but the content of my life was very simple: school five days a week; breakfast, lunch, and dinner with David Wienstein; an occasional movie or hop; nights of loneliness; datelessness; increased anxiety and lots of telephone calls home for shots of moral support. Father and Mother convinced me that my difficulties were temporary. I had to be properly socialized. "You must adjust and become part of the wider world of sophistication and charm," I was told.

I worked hard to adjust. Working to develop my Boston accent was first. I loved the way the Bostonians spoke, and practicing in the bathroom mirror after my roommates were asleep was a nightly ritual: *park* (like in *bark*) the *car* in the *garage* because there is no room on the street.

School was interesting. I was learning logic, rationalism, and sociology. And Appleseed was always around if I needed anything.

Then I met James Derward McDaniel. To say that he was different than the other Negroes I met would be to understate his dynamic character and the ultimate effect he was to have on my evolution. It all started one evening in the dining hall as I was having a quiet meal with David. Our eyes met as he walked in; he said hello by bowing his head slightly, and looked around for a seat. I did not acknowledge his greeting; turned quickly to David, hoping that he would not sit with us. Through the corner of my eye I could still see him standing in the door, moving from time to time to let others pass in. The look on his face was one of anger and disgust. One boy said to him, "Excuse me," in order to pass, and violence came to James's face. He was not properly dressed for dinner, but like a few of the boys who wore ties with the sport shirts they had worn all day, he could have passed inspection, even though, unlike that minority, he wore a sweater, not a coat. "Please don't sit with us," I wanted to say. "There are other seats."

"May I sit here?" He was standing in front of our table. He had asked to sit, but everything about him was a demand. I was frightened. I don't know why. David was still talking. He was out of it. He did not understand. And before David could say, "Why, certainly," the angry colored stranger sat down.

He did not introduce himself, and when we told him our names, he bowed his head again to me, but not to David.

"Pass me the salt."

Without looking at him, David responded immediately, and continued his conversation with me. I listened to David's words but watched the stranger eat. He had not gone to

Palmer. In fact, I had a feeling that he was doing all the wrong things just to annoy me.

At last he was finished. He looked up at both of us with contempt, lit a cigarette, and turned his eyes from us to view the entire room. He then stood, stretched his long arms, and strutted out of the hall.

"Who was that?" I asked David in disgust.

"Who?"

"That fellow who was just sitting here."

"I don't know. Why? I didn't really have a good look at him. Don't you know him?"

"No! All I know is that he is very rude."

"What did he do?"

"Well . . . nothing, I guess. Let's just forget it."

"Whatever you say. Say, let's go see a movie. They say Jack Palance is very good in *Sign of the Pagan.*"

The tall stranger had done nothing. His manner, however—his whole being—had infuriated me, and I was unable to feel superior. Indeed, I felt intimidated. He had style; that I had to admit.

I was alone in the suite during the semester break. My roommates had gone to visit friends and relatives. It was Sunday, and I had just returned from the university chapel. I loved the chapel exercises. They were quiet and sedate, and Dr. Howard Thurman, the first Negro dean and minister of the school, was eloquent, incisive, and inspirational. I was reading my Bible when suddenly there was a knock on my door.

It was James Derward McDaniel (he introduced himself arrogantly) with three other Negro fellows I had never seen. They almost pushed me aside before I invited them to enter. McDaniel walked and looked through all the rooms while his questionable-looking friends stared at me. Momentarily he joined us.

"These are some of my boys. Meet Lip, Bob, and Bill," he said, not quite so unfriendly.

I shook their hands but was somewhat puzzled by their visit.

"We came up to find out whether you had any sounds," said Mac, as he insisted on being called.

"Sure, I've got some sounds." I went over to the box and started some records.

Mac took a pack of cards from his pocket. "Want to play a little poker?"

"No," I said directly. "I only play bridge, and occasionally I might play bid whist." They all laughed. I did not have the heart to tell them that the men of our community back home played poker every weekend.

"I don't mind if you play. Make yourselves comfortable. My roommates are gone for the break."

They sat down to play, and Bob took out a bottle of whisky from the bag he had been carrying. I gave them each a glass and took one myself. I sipped the whisky and water slowly as I watched them play.

"How do you like living with these white motherfuckers?" said Bob in a very pleasant New England accent as he fingered his cards.

"Why do you call them that? Actually, they are pretty nice fellows."

"That's right, Bob, they are very nice fellows. Now you should apologize to Mr. Lacy for calling his *white friends* motherfuckers." Mac's statement brought laughter from his friends.

"You're right," Bob said cynically. " 'Motherfucker' is probably too flattering. A better description is probably ass-holes." They all laughed again.

"But you fellows don't even know them. Why are you so hard on them? Besides, if you got to know them, you'd probably like them."

"Look, stupid"—Mac's voice was angry, his words cut into me like a sharp knife—"don't defend those silly punks in my presence. They got the whole world at their disposal, and they don't need your defense. As far as I am concerned, they can all kiss my ass. Now let's finish the game."

Whenever Mac spoke, the whole room stopped to listen. His words went by you unchallenged. He was crude and profane, but you let that pass without offense to you because what he said was always said so well. At first I thought he sounded like an intellectual playing gangster Humphrey Bogart style. After watching and listening to him for six hours, I was not sure. I felt (bits came out from time to time) that there was a logical system behind his words. His accent, without the nights of practice, was Harvard, but I had the feeling that his statements, usually preceded or followed by "motherfucker," were more important to him. Everything about my background had prepared me to dislike him. He was cold, crude, detached, and insulting even to his friends. But strangely enough, that made him attractive.

That Sunday afternoon of gambling began our friendship. Mac came by often to listen to my Nat Cole records, usually when my roommates were out. It was a little strained at first, but as the weeks passed, we became inseparable. The students called us the Gold Dust Twins; never in our presence, because most people were afraid of Mac's wit and sharp tongue. Mac made and enforced all the decisions in our relationship: the parties we went to, the girls we met, the Scotch we drank, and the books I read. He used to say, "I'm the teacher; you are the student. I'm a one hundred, and the best you can ever be is ninety-nine point nine." When I reminded Mac that an infinite number of nines after 99.9 was 100, he sharply replied, "Only symbolically."

McDaniel was argumentative and aggressive. Every afternoon, he waited at our table in the lunchroom to disagree. He challenged everyone. Arguing for its own sake was not his thing, but invariably if an individual spoke more than two minutes, he broke some of Mac's rules. As a debater he was effective and ruthless. He destroyed you intellectually, and if his opponents were white, they were destroyed in total. He never shouted and had a fetish about interrupting your statements. He let you finish and then finished you, leaving the room dull and quiet because there was nothing left to say. Where and whenever he argued he brought his world to the table—a Northern Town Two world—a world of violence, mistrust, alienation, despair. Yet he did not claim to speak for the other town dwellers. Unlike the white radicals who were to capture the remaining innocence of my life, Mac was a dissenter without an ideology. If anything, cynicism ruled his complicated being. He understood social and political movements, but did not distinguish between them. And he hated reformers; had no use for the "cause" people. He would "make it alone."

"Individuals make history"—but only those who have risen from "obscurity to power." Like Hitler and Napoleon, whom he quoted from so often, he would rise to power. "When the door of opportunity is almost closed, I shall ease in" was his celebrated phrase.

It was, eventually, McDaniel who first called to task my system of values. Reading Ellison's *Invisible Man* seemed to have started the cycle. I liked it because Mac had given it to me, and also because it was a good book written by a Negro. Then, I did not appreciate or understand the significance it had for my angry friend.

Mac's favorite target—and at first for me a great source of discomfort—was the Negro middle class. He attacked them personally, collectively, and institutionally. Anticipating what E. Franklin Frazier was to say more coherently and systematically a few years later in his magnum opus, *Black Bourgeoisie*, Mac castigated the black B (as he called it) for its isolationist proclivities and constantly predicted its fall. Like a bounty hunter, he sought its members out, crashed their parties, engaged them in debates at school. On several occasions he visited Negro middle-class church services, stood up during the middle of the quiet sermon, and preached his own brand of secular ethics. He shocked his opponents. And before they could recover, we were on our way. His only reward was seeing them squirm. If he had been superficial, his behavior would have seemed childlike. But his words were profound and violent. He made you think. You were forced to re-examine; at the very least, to listen.

Ironically, it was through Mac that I was introduced to my Northern counterparts. They were much more complex, more diverse than I had imagined. Indeed, in the sense that I understood it, "community" could not accurately describe the Boston Negro elite (probably typical of the North, with the possible exception of New York City). Although most of its families lived in the "better" area of the Negro section of Roxbury, they had no stable concept of themselves as a class and no social ideology on which to base their exclusiveness and separation. Money and membership in various social organizations, including fraternities and sororities, seemed to be the major condition precedent to group acceptance and solidarity. Social relationships were highly diffuse and organizational expression highly decentralized. Probably the best description is a loose conglomeration of professionals and semiprofessionals living in the same area without the benefit of a centralized authority and interconnecting institutions. And they were perhaps not as rich, educated, discriminating, and cultured as was the elite I had been accustomed to. Given my values at that level of consciousness, the Northern black bourgeoisie was crude and underdeveloped. There were two distinct types in the group: those who wanted to integrate, and the few who didn't waste time trying. The former were hard to figure. I had always lived in a segregated community; that there was value in selected forms of integration was not debatable, but the notion of moving from my peers to live in a white community indefinitely was *then* incomprehensible.

Because I liked Mac, had a profound respect and admiration for his brilliant mind and the manner in which he expressed it, I did not accept his criticism of the black bourgeoisie (bougies) as an indictment of me or even the class that I was supposed to represent. His approach to them was, in fact, rather contradictory. He put them down as stupid individuals. "They're phony." Their behavior was false, and he criticized their wasted energies and superficial social relationships without seeing them as an expression of a philosophy of life created by a class that felt itself superior. He shared most of their regard for wealth, prestige, and power, but felt that they could be used more effectively.

Nevertheless, I was beginning to understand some of the contradictions in my own life style. Once I told Mac about Dr. Turner. He became furious and accused my father and the other leading Negroes of Franklin of being Uncle Toms. Intellectually his position seemed sound, although emotionally I could not accept it. Correct or not, I had been put on notice, and for the first time in my life, I was examining myself.

And for the first time, I had to confront the *intra*racial-dating color problem. In Shreveport and at Palmer I had been immunized. I could join any group I pleased, take out any girl I wanted. Not so in Boston, mid-nineteen-fifties. What I possessed was not sufficient: I needed a *fairer* skin. My dark face was not comely to the pretty young colored girls I wanted. They were never available. Their rejections were discreet and carefully worked out, for the girls were too polite and intelligent to speak out their real reason. If I could have sued a girl for alienating my affections, objective evidence would have been hard to produce. It was more of a sub-terranean feeling, an inner consciousness which existed only between me and my alienated object of desire. Unless you can share the strain and stress of inner insecurities with an intimate friend, they become your private neuroses. You want to tell someone, but ego won't allow. For telling an insensitive friend—insensitive because he has not been one of the rejects—is likely to produce the following kind of response. "Come on, Lacy. You're being too sensitive. The women are not that way." Then he goes on to prove it: "Look, Shirley is going out with Frank. Mary is seeing John. And Richard can't possibly feel that way; he's living with two African guys." He's right. But your case is different. You explain further, until finally you feel absolutely ridiculous, either because your friend has given you a sudden burst of courage or because it's too painfully exposing to continue. So you end by reciting some few statements giving him the impression that you have made a mistake. What really happens is that your ego is exposed without relief and you hurry to hide. Or at least that's what I did. I couldn't even tell Mac, my best friend. I was already 99; how could I become 98?

If you are unlucky, hiding becomes your private life style; and just to be sure that no one invades your sanctuary, you erect all kinds of clever defenses. I had two: hostility and James D. McDaniel.

Whenever I thought I would be rejected, I struck out first. "You girls are really silly. Why don't you read more? If you spent less time at the mirror, you'd probably see more of life.

I don't want to go to those frat parties because the people never talk about anything." Etc., etc. Most of the time, I'd feel guilty even here, because although I was not *wanted*, the person was at least civil to me. Sometimes your hostility is directly proportioned to your imputed ugliness, and you strike out harder at those you think find you ugly.

The men and women share the same standard of beauty. The girls are harder hit. Their beauty is more important. They cannot be aggressive; they must be ladies, so they must wait and wait. The great problem comes when someone sees your face, is pleased by it, and tells you so. Too late. You do not believe her, or try to pretend that you have no time for her. And if you come to your senses and see her, watch out— she's in for abuse. Note: the rejects avoid each other; if I had been able to accept my own "ugliness," I would have had a girl of my own.

Mac was my main stick. With his intellect I could vicariously whip. In fact, the first time I ever used his word ("mother-fucker") was an occasion when he had intimidated one of my rejectors.

"I'm glad you straightened that stupid motherfucker out," I said with a sigh of relief.

"Yeah, she is stupid. But a pretty motherfucker, you must admit."

The next year was quiet. McDaniel had graduated and was now serving and freezing in an army unit stationed in Alaska. I had transfered to a smaller college near Boston, and without the excitement of the Mac era, I had settled down to some serious studying. From time to time I endeavored to carry on in Mac's tradition, but I was never quite as effective, never grand.

For a Negro, one New England college is like another: same patronization, same paternalism, same burdens, and same benefits. My advice to those of my kind still coming is: stay away from the small colleges. The towns near those ivory towers will kill you. Nothing you want is in those towns, and every anxiety you would feel at a city college or university will be doubled. The only thing you will find to do besides

masturbate to break the insane routine is to steal books you
do not need or want.

Near the end of the second semester, I could tell from my
mother's letters that something was wrong on the home front.

That summer the family met for its last conference: Father
and Mother were getting a divorce. My family? Impossible.
They were happy. They had everything. Father's practice was
better than ever, and Mother could still spend to her heart's
content. I had just finished a paper on my family for social
science class.

I did not want to hear the talk. My quiet mother had learned
to shout. They both shouted. Words I did not want to hear
came from their shouting mouths: "sexual incompatibility,"
"infidelity," "mental cruelty." They hated each other.

"We knew the first year of our marriage that we could
not make it," Father told us.

The first year of the marriage? That was two years before
I was born! Nineteen years ago. How can you live with some-
one for nineteen years and not share love? Don't be stupid,
I told myself. The children—remember?

"I want a hundred thousand dollars."

"And I want the moon."

"Cash."

"What?"

"You can afford it. After all, I've given you the best years
of my life. . . . What can I do now?"

Like a tennis spectator's, my head moved.

"I can't afford it."

"You can."

"How do you know?"

I thought about reconciliation. But no one was interested.
"No." "Never." "Emphatically not." For us they had stayed
together. How much did they blame us? We had watched their
models as our personalities grew. Separate bedrooms. They
lived in sin.

My sister was not prepared for this. She was too old not to
understand, too young, like all of us, not to be affected. She
had just graduated from Palmer and was to compound her

illusions by going to Fisk. "Fair Palmer, thy sons and thy daughters give cheer." Beatrice cried. Nathaniel, Jr., too logical to be helpful, cried too. I could not. I wish I had. I would cry later.

After the divorce Mother moved to the West Coast. I did not return to New England. I went to Los Angeles—to help my mother, I told myself. Perhaps I did not have enough "culture" left to be noble. I thought the West might be good for me as well. I was still charming, but I could not hide the truth from myself: my culture had been shaken. My land down South, my huge home and spacious yard, my colored servants, my wealth, fine speech, a special kind of security and faith in the future had not served me, not prepared me for the white world I was expected to deal with. I had discovered that my world of Palmer and company was exceedingly small, barely visible from the outside. No one had told me about white people or minimally what one was supposed to do in order to avoid the anxiety.

"The world is out there. It's waiting for you, but you've got to be ready." Thus my father had spoken, and his words were repeated more than five thousand times at Palmer. Bullshit. What world were they talking about? And be ready for it how? Well, all I remembered was how to sit, stand, walk, and of course, talk; a few courses in English, biology, and the other usual. Far from enough. What I needed was a course on white people.

That should have happened. Sure, I passed my exams. Got on. I am talking about my psychology. When I left the South I left my security, my individualism. You realize it one day. For me it came early one morning as I was looking at myself in the mirror. What a difference. The secure, arrogant Leslie was no more. I felt inferior.

No, I did not do a dance when Whites came into the room. In fact, I looked and functioned rather normally. I simply felt inferior. (Is the word bothersome? Well, then use "anxious.") Nothing at the Boston colleges gave substance to my being. Palmer, by contrast, had much more going for it. At least some of the buildings had names of Negroes, and the Negro faces which passed through them spoke and gave you a friendly hello. I will be told, "Not so." For I have heard many Negroes say just the opposite. But Negro middle-class inferiority is difficult to detect if you are not a middle-class Negro; if you are, and are not careful, you might even miss it in yourself, probably by calling it something else: education, exposure, adaptation, socialization—just to mention a few possibilities. It starts when you come in contact with your white counterparts. While train conductors, policemen, clerks, postmen, and other Whites below you professionally may annoy and at times make you feel uncomfortable, in your Negro mind you see them as "ignorant" or "uncultured," but never superior. You only feel inferior in that white world you hold in esteem. On an individual level you do not know that you are going to feel inferior, so it is nothing that you can prepare for. You can, however, be prepared by others. But those of your kind who have gone before cannot honestly share that experience. For a Negro in the middle class can never admit that he feels inferior—even if he's aware. It would destroy him psychically and vitiate the whole system of values on which his precarious position in society is based. And even those who have the psychological breakdown still function. You begin to build your whole life style around this anxiety-awareness. For now you know you are going to feel it and you structure accordingly.

Mac had made the transition easier for me. Now that he was gone, California would be better.

V

The Birds

"WANT this sign to carry?"

The sign the young student was holding read "Down with Capital Punishment"; subtitled, "*Only a new social and political system can eliminate the causes of killing.*"

"Are you speaking to me?" I replied very formally.

She laughed like I had laughed at a disheveled Negro who (when I spoke to him in front of a restaurant in a small Mississippi town of three hundred people) replied in an English accent.

"Yes, I'm talking to you. Why don't you join our demonstration? It's for a good cause."

"What cause are you demonstrating for?"

She stepped from the group which had assembled in front of the school of art and told her "comrades" that she would meet them in front of the jail. She stretched her short legs like she was going to touch her toes, and put the sign on the ground between her feet. She smiled, then threw her long hair back over her shoulders and took a cigarette from her pants pocket. After fumbling through what looked like a green laundry bag, she finally produced an old book of matches. After which she returned four novels, several pamphlets, and about three hundred mimeographed notices announcing the demonstration to her bag. Then she took two quick draws on a cigarette too old to respond and in disgust stomped it out on the ground. She nervously searched her pocket for another year-old cigarette, and although the second smoke brought forth the same result, she struggled through it as she talked. She was now seated on the ground. I did not want to stain my suit on the grass, but after a few hours of talking with her I was as relaxed as she was.

"I am with a group called The Society for Human Freedom. We are against capital punishment and other related dialectical evils. We aim to raise the level of social consciousness so that the people of this country will see and understand some of its unjust social practices. The first thing, however, is to get the students and instructors involved. Only then can we, with other groups, form a common front against these unjust conditions."

"You can't be serious. Capital punishment is given to only those people who commit capital crimes—murderers, rapists, and other criminals who express extreme antisocial behavior. If you didn't take care of these criminals, the whole society would suffer."

"That's just it," she said excitedly as she looked for another smoke. Again she searched her pockets; again she emptied the contents of her bag on the grass, talking and cursing, looking in vain. "Do you smoke?"

"No, I'm afraid I don't." I was sorry I didn't, for she seemed helpless without her cigarettes. She thought for a second, looked around and saw another student smoking, and ran over to ask him for a cigarette. I hoped he had her brand.

"As I was saying," she continued talking, smoking, smiling, putting her things back into her bag. "Society causes people to commit crime. Individuals are not born antisocial. They take on explicit aggressive behavior because forces in the society shape them. They have some choices, but they are highly conditioned. If a man is hungry and he steals, can you call that stealing?"

"Of course it's stealing. Besides, there are social agencies to take care of the poor."

"Social agencies make things worse. They are a part of the system." She seemed indignant.

"Look, I know things are not peaches and cream. In the last few years I have discovered a lot that is wrong in this country. But I still think stealing is stealing, and people who kill other people should pay for their acts. . . . Other people might get the point and think twice before taking somebody's life."

"Everybody says that, yet it has been proven that capital punishment is not a deterrent to murder. In fact, in many of those states that have abolished capital punishment there has not been an increase in homicides recorded; and in some states it has actually decreased. . . . If you look very closely, you will discover that it is the system which causes people to act as they do."

Sociology 1 had made me aware that individuals go through a socialization process, and from Emile Durkheim I had remembered that the "individual is but a microscopic reflection of the social world." She was, however, saying something more. I wanted to make her aware of this, but she spoke approximately two hundred words a minute, taking a breath after the first hundred. Finally I was forced to interrupt. "You seem to place so little emphasis on individualism. Ultimately, it seems to me, each person is responsible for his social behavior—"

"That's bourgeois," she interrupted.

"Wait, Miss . . . uh. . . . What's your name?"

"Judy."

"Judy, you didn't let me finish."

"Sorry. Go on." She seemed slightly annoyed and somewhat impatient.

"What I am trying to get across is that individual behavior is very important. History—"

"But I—"

"Please just give me a chance. History is full of examples showing great men who have risen from obscurity to power. I believe that individuals make history through hard work. I think also that the real problem in this world is that we don't have enough *real* individuals. Ayn Rand was correct in *The Fountainhead* when she said, 'The world is perishing from an orgy of self-righteousness.' " I was very firm. I thought that argument would convince her.

"Ayn Rand is a fascist. She and other writers like her perpetuate the capitalist myth in fine rhetoric, deceiving people in order to hide the real problems of this corrupt society. Her central protagonist, Howard Roark, was simply a sadistic intellectual who placed his rights above the people's rights. Imagine blowing up a building which was to be used for the poor because someone changed his silly design! Sure I believe in individualism, but a kind which is defined in terms of other individuals, people committed to the general good, not destruction. I guess you think Hitler was a great man?"

"Well, not exactly."

"Not exactly!" She stood up furiously. "Don't you know that he murdered six million human beings?"

"Sure I do. Why don't you sit down?"

"Then why do you say 'not exactly'?" She sat down on the grass again.

I was trying to answer, but it was difficult because I had never thought through these opinions. Hitler was Mac's hero, who he used as an example to support his definition of individualism and strength. But he had never talked about or ever been required by those he argued with to explain this side of Hitler's nature. Ayn Rand was my author; Mac had introduced me to her writings. I quoted freely from *The Fountainhead*, memorized very painfully Howard Roark's summation to the jury, his only statement throughout his trial defending why he had destroyed a building which he had designed without payment, asking only that the construction of it strictly conform to his design. Perhaps his behavior was an overreaction, but theoretically I had approved the principles involved. And how could an American author writing on individual freedom— even an extreme manifestation—be compared to fascists in Nazi Germany?

"Well?" Judy wanted her answer.

"I guess—"

"You guess!" she shouted, interrupting me.

"Wait now. Why are you getting so excited? You never let me finish."

Her cry of disapproval brought increased concern from the white faces sitting, standing, and passing around us. I felt the usual anxiety but carried on quite normally. Judy apologized and I continued.

"I guess in a way—in a very limited way, mind you—Hitler was great because he was able to move people. But he was also very evil."

"You see, I would never make such a distinction. In my mind the issue of his greatness never arises, because of his madness and inhumanity. As a Negro living in this society, you should be the first to understand that."

"And what is that supposed to mean?"

"Now, don't get emotional. I'll explain what I mean. Look, what are you doing right now?"

"Well . . . " I hesitated slightly. "I had a class, but it's over by now. So I guess I'm free."

"Good. Let's go over to the Student Union. We can get cigarettes and coffee."

Her walk was fast and confident. I had to almost run to keep in step. She was quite independent. She paid for her own coffee and cigarettes and had opened the door and seated herself without my assistance. The Student Union was nearly empty because most of the students had gone. It was nearly 6:00 P.M. We had talked for quite some time.

"Now," she continued as she lit up a fresh cigarette, "Negroes are discriminated against in this society, right?"

"Sure." I was slow to reply because I didn't know where she was taking me. I had seen Mac use a similar technique on white people.

"Why do you think that happens?" Her confidence made me a little uneasy.

"Well, because people are ignorant. Once you educate the whites and they see that Negroes are as good as they are, the problem will be solved."

"But can't you see that it is not in the interest of the system to carry forth that kind of education? And even if it had the will, the content of it would probably not be creative. Discrimination and prejudice are very profitable, and no one is going to cut off the white hands which feed them. Don't you know that most of the people who die in the electric chair and gas chamber are colored. Why? Because the whole legal system is set up for the rich and powerful, and unless a Negro is rich, he is not going to be able to prepare a proper defense. This system is very contradictory, indifferent, crude, and inhuman. Beauty and justice are mere words here. Have you ever been to an Indian reservation?"

"No, I haven't," I said slowly.

"Well, I have. It was horrible. Once a beautiful people; now they die defenseless, intimidated, and without honor. . . . An inhuman system destroyed them because it was not interested in the Indian's dignity nor his culture. Travel Route 66 to Oklahoma City. Red mud and long, silent highway will tell you a horrible story of a land which was good, where people lived and worked. Then the settlers came. . . . Today the Indians are gone. . . . Dead. American Indian, a thousand years dead. He served his country, his fellow man, his God. That's Route 66—Arizona, New Mexico, Texas—quiet, silent, indifferent . . . dead. The settlers, backed up by the government, called it progress, manifest destiny, railways, telegraphs, and more land for more settlers. Why couldn't the two cultures live in peace? Because the civilization of the settlers was aggressive and inhuman. Indian art could not be understood because Indians were considered less than people, pagans without souls, without love. . . . That's why we act. We must reverse this trend and revolutionize the system."

I was speechless. And I did not understand everything. I thought Judy very unusual and very interesting. A question came to mind. "Constantly, Judy—in fact, throughout—you have talked about the system, how corrupt it is. This may sound stupid to you, but *what system are you talking about?*"

She smiled slightly, lit her seventeenth cigarette, and began to talk. Her words came out slowly; at first they were autobiographical. Her father had been defeated by a Senator McCarthy and had subsequently died of a "broken heart." She had been "born a rebel" and had been on picket lines since she was two months old. Can you imagine protesting injustice from a baby carriage? Out of her mouth came a world unknown: Rosenbergs, Japan, Spain, civil wars, China, demonstrations, sick society, freedom, France, a different conception of love, Hermann Hesse, moral crisis, a world without war, imperialism, and hate; and a dream of a better world which had changed the whole course of her life. It was a growth in reality and not a mere reflection of things as they were. America was responsible. American democracy? Impossible. Her voice was sometimes firm, and a few times I saw tears which did not come down. She spoke freely and passionately. Some of her words: "I became, as a result of these experiences a confirmed and committed person. I became a new woman working for a new existence, a state of being that *shall* give a continuous increase in the capacity for humans in the world to provide for their needs. It is man's actual success in providing food, clothing, shelter, more and more abundantly for a greater and greater sector of the human community, that is progress. Real progress. It is the gradual abolition of the crudity of primitive conditions, the elimination of hurt, hunger, disease, the provision of a more adequate supply, for more and more people, of the necessities of life, and a life itself which is psychologically free, sexually sane, and morally sufficient. . . . This leads me to believe that it is possible to change the corrupt nature of our society and other societies which it supports and which resemble it, and build a new and better land. A universal society of men and women who shall all be equal, sane, and free without distinctions such as race or nationality. Does that make sense to you?"

"Yes, in a way it does. Go on."

Judy reached for another cigarette. "I believe that, given proper conditions of life, people everywhere can live in peace, justice, and mutual sympathy throughout the world; that it is possible to bring to a final end the exploitation of men by men, of class by class, of nation by nation, of black, brown, and yellow men by white men, of male chauvinism. This is the love that inspires me to a heroism of self-deprivation and struggle for the benefit of those not yet born, to an arrogant indifference to persecution and death. For, ultimately, it's from us that the change will come. Individuals who are imaginative enough to push in the new order with as little pain and blame as possible."

Finally she finished. I was excitedly relaxed. Her concern for people, people she did not know, fascinated me. But I thought less about her words. In a way it was like a new emotion, because I was suspended between liking her and not daring to. For a long time, I was looking at her, deep in her eyes, and she was looking back. No faces to watch us, nothing but wanting came between our eyes. . . .

"Well, I have to leave now." Her voice was quiet, filled slightly with emotion. "Maybe I'll see you some other time. Be good." She got up quickly, before I could stand, and hurried out of the door.

Before I had reached my Lincoln, I heard Judy's voice shouting, "Wait," from the other side of the parking lot. She rushed toward me. When she stopped and got her breath, she asked, "I don't even know your name. What is it?"

"It's Leslie."

"Leslie what?"

"Lacy."

"Leslie Lacy. Sounds Irish." We both laughed. She took my hand, looked at and squeezed it, and smiled, and ran away.

A conversation with Judy Goodman: white, rebel, sixteen, a nervous surrealist Jew, learning how to paint at the University of Southern California in Los Angeles. My first day of school and I had met my first representative of the American left. For one day, for two, for a whole week in my mother's new $40,000 home, I thought about this girl and her cause, to rid the world of evil. Mother constantly asked me why I was so quiet, but every time I tried to explain, I knew that I had not heard enough to make my replies comprehensible. But how would she have understood in any case? I had been exposed to much more, and I couldn't even explain.

What a miserable feeling: the world of reality or unreality about which Judy spoke should have been introduced to me at Palmer. You can forgive—once you understand—your rich, educated parents and your $3,500-a-year education for not telling you about white people. You might even conclude that on that issue they did their very best. But how can you forgive your American and world history teacher, who taught you about the Second World War and failed to mention the U.S.S.R.; neglected to define communism or fascism; forgot about the "cold war"? And he was a smart one, at that: New York University M.A., Phi Beta Kappa (he showed us his key every day), a captain in the army, service in North Africa, and then two years in Paris after his discharge. My brother said his French was beautiful but he had difficulty finding Africa on the map. He didn't have to be Du Bois or believe in Marcus Garvey. (Who was Du Bois? Who was Marcus Garvey?) It was 1953. We didn't want to be radical, Mr. Teacher. We were rich. We paid $3,500 a year. We wanted to know about the African students in our classroom. Sierra Leone, Nigeria? What were they? We didn't want to identify with them; we just wanted to know who they were. The world was changing, Mr. Teacher. Independence movements? What were they? No details, Teacher. Okay. Fine. Why didn't you give me a word, define a phrase—give me something, M.A.—so I wouldn't sound stupid when I faced the world.

Dear Mr. Teacher,
   I am now in Boston. My white counterpart is stupid too. But he knows the words, a phrase or two. He still believes. You see, Mr. Teacher, it is not just middle-class isolation. Thanks for everything.
                              Sincerely yours,
                              Leslie Alexander Lacy
P.S. Mr. Teacher, we were in North Carolina—the heart and mainstay of Ku Klux Klan. They rode at night. They were happy. Didn't you see them in Greensboro? For them, something important, eternal, and sacred was about to happen: *Senator Joseph McCarthy for President.* Teacher, M.A., you didn't tell us about *this Senator* and the implications of his reign of rightness for us. We saw, we listened, but we were children entrusted to you.

> And like children, we were
> Playing like giants in a land
> Of midgets.
> In the red mud we played,
> Acting out the dreams of our fathers.
> Kissing and being kissed.

Loving and being loved too.
We played with commitment or
Comfort.
When the midgets scratched our beauty
We cried in our innocence
And hid our beauty.
We laughed when things were funny
And prayed the prayer our fathers prayed,
Because we believed what they believed.
We had ice cream sodas on Sundays,
School on Monday,
And without scholarship or citizenship,
We returned on Tuesday.
Like our fathers would do,
So we did,
Asking nothing,
Knowing nothing,
Being something.
Demanding nothing,
We were happy.
We were young.
And in the midgets' world of Separation
And Segregation
We grew up:
Proper,
Intelligent,
Correct.
Like our fathers did, so we did.
We knew joy,
Never discovered sex.
Caught in a whole reality,
We were not then alienated;
We were back in our youth.

Carrying a picket sign was not initially an outward manifestation of what I felt inwardly. I did not see my personal crisis as having anything to do with capital punishment, farm workers, Woolworth department stores, or anything or anybody else who had a grievance. Marching around and around, singing folk songs I did not like or understand and occasionally stopping to pass out leaflets to people who did not read them did not seem as much of a necessity to me as it did to my fellow walkers. And since I was not a rebel in the sense in which I then understood the term—struggling against social and political attitudes generally or specifically—I feared that someone who knew me would ask me to explain. A friend of the family who was a psychologist did his medical best to convince me that in my innocence I had allowed myself to become involved with "those people" because I was unconsciously acting out hostilities directed at my social class. On reflection (fully aware that my skills in such matters were then and now acquired without supervision), I cannot agree. Unquestionably we all are haunted by the vestiges of our origins, and I, no less than anyone becoming aware, sensitive, tried to create a balance between what I had internalized and what was being discovered, which, given my earlier influences, was likely to be contradictory. What my learned friend failed to see was that although I was disappointed with those who had trained me, I was still very involved with being a middle-class Negro.

Sure, there had been middle-class white Americans in New England; then Mac; and now Judy. All from different vantage points, picking away at my inners. My life had been affected. I questioned. Indeed I had even done some value house-cleaning. But, correct as ever, I was still basically Leslie Alexander Lacy. And picketing was not fun; no 1956 Los Angelean could have called it anything but the contrary. We took every conceivable abuse, including the lack of police protection. Judy and I always walked together. But that proved to be dangerous, so I changed positions. Imagine yourself Negro, young, scared, uninvolved politically, singing foreign folk songs, tired, embarrassed, walking happily hand in hand with a blond Jewish white girl of German descent—who got you hit in the head at least once a week because she stuck out her tongue and called a Southern-born white policeman (trained in the art of "dealing effectively with niggers and wetbacks") a "fascist cop."

Even without the protection and comfort of a white skin and inner involvement, I carried a sign, because fundamentally I was attracted to these people. It will be said, "But they were white, like the cats and kittens who had caused you anxiety in New England, and before that—before consciousness —in Franklin and Shreveport you had on occasion been made to feel miserable by them." Determined to cure me of this "adolescent capitulation," my Negro psychologist friend extended his earlier analysis—first, proclaiming me a sadist, and later, after the fifteenth demonstration, promoting me to a masochist.

Now it seems to me, though I may well be mistaken, that Judy and her morally indignant young friends sold me not to a cause, but exposed me to the ethics of their character. Their vitality filled me with astonishment, and I respected their courage. What they said and did politically was less important than the day-to-day, week-to-month-to-year content of their lives. They shared very easily, and always with a smile, the voices and thoughts of their insides. They were never afraid of intimacy. They were always trying to be honest. Terribly honest—too much for me at first. I began to understand the meaning of a relationship and painfully came to see that some of my best friends had isolated themselves (I too) in order to avert the insight that intimate association facilitates. Without malice, usually from a point of commitment, they argued and fought about the direction of world politics and were usually most critical of the people they respected. At Palmer we prayed for peace; they walked for it. Normal men could use the words "love" and "beauty" in describing their feeling for each other. To me it was a strange and exciting world. Nothing which was to be shared was considered taboo, repugnant. A depressed one, sometimes near the death wish, got love first, therapy second. One ear would listen first, quietly, sympathetically, but before the day passed, before the anxiety extended, everyone knew and everybody cared. Judging by my standard of human existence, they were all destitute (in fact, I wrote a poem about them: "My Destitutes—poor, plosive, proud,/Dreamers who speak of politics and peoples,/Individuals who live with peace"). But a more-destitute-than-thou could always know of a hand to hold and a meal to eat. After which he could rest, that day, tomorrow, as long as he had to. And in between, he could talk—man, how they could talk! About

love, class, caste, justice, race, war, and the thing they wanted
most: peace—a world without war and hunger.

I can recall one of their conversations:

Judy: "Did you hear what Professor Taylor said about
Brotherhood Week?"

Ruth (seventeen, sophomore, history, Jewish): "What?"

Judy: "That it was a purifying ritual during which each
year people relax their hostilities for seven days. He said he
would not participate."

Joseph (nineteen, junior, philosophy, Jewish): "Good. It's
about time the progressive staff learned its real relationship
with the liberal organization in this school."

Esther (eighteen, junior, Phi Beta Kappa, English literature,
Jewish): "That's shit. You don't understand the function of a
progressive instructor at a liberal university. His or her pri-
mary function is to get involved with the liberal establishment,
and through this, working with others, he can help reshape the
direction of the group."

Samuel (eighteen, sophomore, French, Jewish): "I agree
with Joseph. I have talked with Dr. Taylor, and he's beginning
to radicalize. He's going to be very beautiful."

Esther: "Samuel, you are very beautiful and I love you,
but you are a male chauvinist. . . ."

Laughter from the group. Samuel is a little angry, stands
up and gets himself a piece of cheese, and brings the quart of
cheap Gallo Vin Rosa out of the refrigerator. It looks like a
long night.

Samuel: "If I am a male chauvinist, you are indeed a
feminist."

Judy: "Esther, you're being personal because Samuel refuses
to sleep with you."

Esther: "Don't you think that's rather presumptuous? How
do you know I want to have sex with Samuel?"

Judy: "Because you told me."

Esther (slightly embarrassed): "Well, I think I remember
that talk, but it was rather theoretical. In fact, we were discussing the possibility of having a healthy sex life in the
absence of personal commitment to love."

Samuel: "That's all right, Esther; we understand. If you weren't going to a female Jewish psychiatrist you probably would have discussed that about yourself years ago. Maybe you ought to try mine."

Joseph: "I'm sure the inner dynamics of your sexual lives are interesting . . . but tomorrow. Today I want to hear your comments on Taylor so I can make a statement at the forum."

Esther: "Well, it seems to me that self-imposed isolation from the liberal or semiliberal group is defeatism. The progressive should be aware that his views are not popular. It is therefore not his function to go to a liberal forum and hold forth. He or she must be able to work with liberals and progressive conservatives, constantly trying to expose them to the error of their position. Taylor is a good person, but he's a bourgeois progressive. By that I mean he doesn't understand how to work at the committee and caucus levels. He wants to persuade his detractors to his position, a position which is itself highly vulnerable, by the use of powerful and effective rhetoric."

Samuel: "I disagree. Taylor may be a bourgeois progressive, but I think his reasoning is perfectly sound. It is foolish, even reactionary, to waste time trying to reform people who don't share any of your assumptions about the true worth of man. He distinguishes what he calls 'the entrenched liberal' from the defensive liberal. The former, people who run most of the organizations, like the Brotherhood Week nonsense, cannot be reformed. You can criticize and expose their positions, but you will become ineffective if you join them. The defensive liberal, a very good person, but generally misguided, is reformable and can be made into an effective person."

Esther: "That's partially true. And because it is, it tends to conceal the true function of the progressive. His role is not to reform, but to expose. His role is not an ideological one, but an educational one. The so-called entrenched liberal may not support a move for the overhauling of the penal system, but if his bourgeois Judeo-Christian secular ethics are exposed, he might get on a picket line. His real job, it seems to me, is to educate by sharpening the contradictions. If we get them involved in activities, eventually they will themselves want to change the penal system. Before long, we'll have the revolution."

Samuel: "That's like telling Trotsky to stay in Russia after Stalin has come to power."

Judy: "Sam, that's a bad example."

Esther spoke again, and predictably, Samuel disagreed. As the night slowly passed, other friends joined us, and with the help of a third bottle of wine, a quiet early morning, Hiferts, a girl and her guitar and Dylan Thomas, we never reached a consensus.

But we never did. We had talked; that was the important thing. We had raised new issues as well as discussed some of the old ones. I met two more friends. Joseph got his information. And Esther and Samuel resolved their other problem before the rise of the morning.

Although they thought intensely and talked incessantly, they were also spontaneous. They could always explode, give out, do whatever they wanted to without fear of ridicule. My middle class had a kind of spontaneity too, and in a sense (purely physical), we were indeed more active. Our music and culture had provided us with a life force which could easily allow us to *break up*, or as Cesiare said, "give up ourselves to the essence of things." But when to break up, when to give up, was highly circumscribed and particularized. We could do *our thing*, release our souls, only when it was proper, acceptable, and of course, intelligent and correct. Around my Negro peers I was thought of as cool, articulate, and highly sophisticated. Editors in the Palmer yearbook had described me: "Head One [actually, but it could not be printed, it was Head Nigger], prexy, attempted dignification, tries to be a cool breeze, real businesslike—most likely to succeed." If I had been that way at Palmer, I was now discovering a new psychological mechanism, which allowed me to *give up* when the spirit hit me. It took me a long time to achieve such emotional freedom. Freedom to dance without music; freedom to use my hands without fear that I would be thought a homosexual; freedom to curse; freedom to talk without being labeled; freedom to read; freedom to tell the truth; freedom to have sex before marriage.

Sexual freedom came last. I was afraid, like most little Negro gentlemen, of getting the girl pregnant, and of catching syphilis. Beyond that, I believed in the overall values inherent in and connected to middle-class morality. I was therefore from time to time intimidated in conversation about sex, but this passed very quickly, because Judy was my girl and she was chaste too. She abstained for a different reason: she would have sex before marriage only if it was an act of love. We discussed it but never worried about it. Like many who wait, we slept in the same bed when I was at her apartment or when Mother was out, and went through the usual kissing, holding, touching, pushing—wanting.

When friendship extended into love, the nonsexual rituals were no longer bilateral. Judy was ready; I was not. I tried to ignore it. Judy understood. We stopped sleeping together. I told myself all kinds of things: we are too young; she will get pregnant; love is not enough; she's white—never. But her open and my repressed desires did not pass.

One afternoon two years from our meeting, I said, "Yes." I had become saturated by her tenderness, and nothing else seemed more important. The rain had finally conquered the smog, and we inhaled the summer air together. Judy's face was happy. She knew. But I told her anyway: "I love you." And again, and again for the rest of the day.

Later, much later, she took my head in her hands and told me something I had never heard: "Your face is beautiful." I believed her. But it was a little strange because in the colored world I was not even handsome. Only the girls were beautiful, and the light-skinned ones at that.

My values were far from balanced, but there was so much we shared. The signs I carried now had meaning. The protest, painting, wit, bridges over the rivers, books, and long hours of trying to be honest were no longer adventures or a serenade to a group of young people I loved. They knew that death in an execution chamber was not such a universal experience, but each time a life was choked out in San Quentin the gas seeped out into our society. They took a stand against this death. I was with them. They wanted "people to be people." They were also like birds. To fly away from the shit and odor of America was their great dream. But they were always people, because they could not fly—they could only get as high as their pot and encircling ideas would allow. That vitality and love of life had become a part of my self-definition. I could not resist, nor did I want to, for I, too, had come to believe that there was something immoral and corrupt about life in America. I had traveled abroad. I had questioned, taken in, thrown out. I had also been questioned—once by an FBI worker who shared the views of my medical friend and assured me that I had been duped. In those days I was foolish enough to talk with him because I thought that his Harvard Ph.D. meant something. I had gone to the Soviet Union, and he was very concerned. I shocked his Harvard mind when I recalled to him a conversation with a Soviet worker who had asked me, "Why is there unemployment in America? Do you have everything you want? Aren't there any more roads to build? Aren't there any more houses to build?" That my purpose in going to Russia was not to join their revolution, but to cuddle near other young people of the globe escaped him.

Also I had seen America—their America. I had seen things happen in coffeehouses America needed but rejected. I had listened to poets—too high to go to school—create, not caring that it was profound. I had seen long hair, short hair, conformity, and motorcycle travelers who could not go on. I had seen the beat generation of Western America paddling along, some like hooting owls damning the idiotic and maniacal, some betrayed, some laughing and not caring, having looked in vain for something to believe in. Others had the advantage of being wild.

I had known intimately the ones who cared a lot, my birds, the students of that generation who came from all over America. Jews mostly; some trying not to be. Each had problems and a psychiatrist who never understood. Some did not want to return to perfume and dashing cavaliers. The ones like Judy did not want to return to "Jewish Mother" who had served in the communist effort. They spent lots of hours at my house. They always rearranged the house when they came—like moving the television into the kitchen to see such things as the Bolshoi Ballet. They grew on Mother like they grew on me. Mother saw me changing, but did not worry, because I got A's in school. She also figured, as I had at first, that I had the best of two worlds. I could fight the war on imperialism and also return to my life of splendor. Lillie (they called Mother by her first name, like they did their own parents) was sometimes great. Once while we were at my house the telephone rang. It was for Judy. She returned crying—as I remember, everybody cried—because some colored man on the land down South in Louisiana had been electrocuted. His living had become our cause. We were not lawyers, but we knew about the natural laws of Mississippi. We had circulated petitions at school (Mother had done some of the typing), and had sent five thousand telegrams to the governor of the state. And quiet, studious Sidney—who spoke in verse and read fifteenth-century philosophy—had suddenly come down to earth and hitched to a place near my home to console the condemned man's family. What he told them we will never know. The State killed him too.

VI

Black

GRADUALLY I DISSOLVED all of my relationships with middle-class Negroes. Reading E. Franklin Frazier's *Black Bourgeoisie* helped. As a black sociologist at Howard University, he could view the social organism at close range. He threw a hard left at the salient values of our group and exposed its illusory and pretentious autonomy in the overall body of American institutions. The shallowness of the bourgeoisie, which he deplored, coupled with my reading Marx, Simone de Beauvoir, Jean-Paul Sartre, Albert Camus, just to mention a few, gave added intellectual and political strength to my growing sense of radicalism.

I finally left the University of Southern California with a M.A. in political science. I saw little value either politically or intellectually in the degree, and potential employers tended to agree. Partially from pressure at home and partially from my indifference to pursuing my studies of American political parties, I went to northern California and enrolled in law school. I was still very much involved with Judy, but her disapproval of my law studies, greater involvement with her art, frequent visits to New York, and the distance from Los Angeles to

San Francisco placed the relationship on a telephone-and-letter basis.

Some unfortunate person, probably a Supreme Court jurist, said that the law is a jealous mistress. It took five months for me to discover that the law did very little to protect her lover; that the study of contracts, torts, crimes, real property, was concerned not with justice, but with clever rules set out to protect vested interests. And Perry Mason's finding-the-crook ethic was an anomaly in the real legal bureaucracy. Special concentration, however, is necessary to see the layer of contradictions. Most believers get lost, hopelessly inundated by the rhetoric. How beautiful it sounds: law is the harmony of the universe; it is the perpetual rose in the garden of man's universe; its special fragrance is justice for all. Once or twice I reminded a law instructor that the rule of the rose was suffering from a lack of fertilization. He quickly—and once defensively—in his acute Texas accent, reminded me that the law had been followed in the state. If I had an ethics objection, I could raise it in the third-year equity course, or—as a stopgap measure—I could see the chaplain who was located in the school of divinity across the Bay.

On a full-time basis I continued my radical politics. No longer was I merely interested in protesting specific grievances; I was now quite actively working with political groups which espoused explicit socialist alternatives to capitalism. Indeed this new activity was an extension of my political commitment in southern California. The young birds of California's south were (probably) both in moral temperament and political orientation very similar to the early Marxists of Europe: idealistic, humanistic, secular moralists. As intellectuals—or not far from it—they were concerned with man's alienation, spiritual fulfillment, and abstract rights and correlative duties which they thought each individual should possess. They held up socialism as a general answer to the exploitation under capitalism, but were highly critical of its institutionalization in eastern Europe. Not wanting to be confused with the liberal, they disliked the proclamation of the grand ideal, but tied their ideals very closely with a rational analysis of world societies. Some of their families had been in the Communist party or one of its many front-runners; although the birds would work with them, especially on issues of loyalty oaths and discrimination, they were generally indifferent but not hostile to them.

The San Francisco flock came from another nest. They were not alienated students fighting specific evils. They had organized themselves (or joined other groups, parties, or fronts) on a working-class basis with some degree of consciousness and were attempting "to make articulate the miseries of a larger proletariat," one far beneath them in income and education. During my three years in San Francisco I met radical organization men from the far communist left to Christian Socialists on the right. I was, however, closer to, but did not join, the Socialist Workers party (SWP), a group which had broken away from the Communist International in support of Leon Trotsky after he had been expelled. They ranged in age from one day (born recruits) to (a few) in the seventies; most were over thirty-five. They came from a cross section of American social and economic classes, but most tended to be from the working proletariat, usually skilled artisans. All the ethnic groups were represented, with the Jews forming the largest minority bloc. Broken down on ethnic lines there were approximately 50 per cent WASP, 40 per cent Jewish, 2 per cent Catholic, 7 per cent Negro and Mexican, 1 per cent foreign-born—and one Apache.

A university professor would not have called them intellectuals in the conventional sense of the term, even though, sometimes extremely elegantly, they could quote and interpret much of the Marxian and related socialist-communist literature, which they had painstakingly absorbed over a period of many years. From their perspective, they had an image of themselves as "professional revolutionaries" and had party affiliations, foreign travel, FBI dossiers, proletarian involvements, and libraries full of the "people's literature" to prove it. They could explain *everything* in history, especially modern phenomena, in terms of Marxist ideology. In fact, as I heard so often, "The history of all human society, past and present, has been the history of class struggle." Their confidence in the coming revolution was their main appeal. It was coming in five years. "The class struggle between the owners of production and the

workers will have sharpened the inherent contradictions in
the capitalist system, and the workers shall rise up to usher
in the new order." One guy who had been in the movement
for twenty years had inside information; he assured me that the
five-year prediction had been based on "revisionist dialectics";
the Real revolution would arrive in three years and four months.

Even more than their southern California allies, they de-
emphasized personal grooming. Suits, haircuts, ties, hairdres-
sers, perfumes, and deodorants were a part of the bourgeois
ethic and should therefore be avoided at all costs. As in all
movements which breed conformity and eccentricity, there were
a precious few who refused to adopt the revolutionary dress,
figuring—unlike their teammates—that they would have time to
get changed into uniform before the revolution came over the
Bay Bridge.

Beyond these general sociological characteristics, the San
Francisco–Berkeley "professional revolutionaries" could be specifically divided into three units. There were the "out of it"
people—withdrawn, otherworldiness orientated, usually young,
timid, passive, subdued—who appeared to be hiding; who, like
the Boston Strangler, had gone insane because they could not
confront the evil which they had been a part of; who, like the
present-day hippies, had been beaten down by their inability
to stop feeling *guilty* and had nothing left but a guitar and a
few memories and sustained themselves on a little food and the
occasional pot and wine. Then there were the strong ones, the
organizers, the picket-sign carriers, the ones who kept the
party together. Last came the intellectuals—political intellectuals
—the ones who talked most about the revolution they all
wanted. They would have all been offended if you had told
them that they had divided themselves into *classes* and sooner
or later would have their own *struggle*.

Every year the Revolution got farther and farther away.
Each year, another year was added, even though the five-year
figure was constantly repeated. The contradictions had not
sharpened; the working class was still divided; and most dis-
tressing of all, the police were getting stronger. Strangely
enough, most of my comrades were unmoved by these objective

conditions. How they believed in the coming order! Not for a second did they relax their orthodoxy. If an objective condition called a socialistic postulate or prediction into question, it passed as though it never happened. If someone had the courage or insight to argue the point, he would commit political heresy and would be certain to be labeled a "revisionist" or a "bourgeois intellectual." When I pointed out to one of the party's leading theoreticians that Lenin was the first revisionist, he accused me of being an FBI agent. They were very critical, but always within the context of "accepted truths." Sometimes it was absurd—like the time I listened for three hours to four otherwise intelligent people who were convinced that the struggle of the Mexican farm workers against the large Californian farmers was a logical extension of the Stalin-Trotsky debate. A lone dissenter, who sat quietly with me during the whole affair, whispered in my ear after the talk, "They are all wrong. It's the Spanish Civil War."

Fighting on another front, and inspired by a non-materialistic conception of history, were the black graduate students at the University of California at Berkeley. I knew most of them individually but had little to do with them politically. They wanted to change their relationship to the university. Individually they had encountered at a very high level of subtlety every conceivable form of white intellectual racism. Highly sensitive and very perceptive, these students saw then what others were to know later: that American education was a European mixture of *poppycock* and *what works*, neatly arranged and called intellect. They saw—under the leadership of Donald Warden and Henry Ramsey (two men I respected)— that this mixture was not enough: first, because it made them strangers to each other, and second, because besides their professional skills, which were dubious, they had been furnished with little in the way of social information which they could use in those communities to which they were destined to return. Donald Warden (who resembled a picture of Marcus Garvey) one day suggested to a group what he called "a retreat to the bush," and I listened.

"Black students must come together in an attempt to work out this academic death." Donald and Ramsey had already formed the Afro-American Association, and he now reminded the five hundred people listening that it was *only* through groups like this that black dignity could be achieved. His knowledge of American history and his ability to marshal the facts were incredible. "We are Blacks," he shouted with passion. "We are not Negroes. Where is Negro land? There is none. We are from Africa, brought here as slaves. They—the Whites —called us Negroes, nigger, boy, colored. But we are Blacks, people of African descent, Afro-Americans. In Africa we had our own language, culture, God; and that's where we were free. Imagine getting your degree from a racist.

"We must return to that freedom—physically or spiritually or both. We must leave these corrupt white people. We must leave them alone! The Honorable Elijah Muhammad tells us that this so-called civilization will be destroyed. We must separate. Build our own land."

Thus spoke Donald Warden, early 1961. The nation of liberals, progressives, and radicals was leading us to integration, and Donald was talking about separation.

Over the months, the Afro-American Association gained chapters and supporters at every college and university in the Bay area. And by the end of the fifth month it extended its appeal into southern California. And again and again Donald Warden, the Phi Beta Kappa from Howard University, bombarded his integrated audiences with his notion of separation. When accused of preaching hate and separation, he quoted from the world's reservoir of black thinkers, but ended in the tone of the Negro Baptist preacher:

"Let me bring you home. You call me a hater. Negative. Do you hear me? [The Blacks in the audience would reply, "Yes, we hear you, brother—preach on."] I am an anti-hater hater. They say I preach separation. Well, I say, go to Harlem, go anywhere where there are black people, and you'll see that we're already separated."

In spite of the trend toward integration, Donald and his Afro-American Association had a tremendous influence on the black students. (In fact, after listening to Donald, and especially Ramsey on this issue, I stopped using the words "Negro" and "colored.") They were brilliant, articulate, and some of them had gone to black colleges, which gave them another experience to share. But more important, Donald was respected by the sometimes embarrassed Blacks he lectured to, because he had the courage to say publicly things they felt privately.

Mr. Warden also shook up white academia. The segregationists agreed with his call for separation, but without the added dignity, pride, and sense of history which Donald thought Blacks should have. The liberals were outraged: "We have been working with you people, fighting the bigots, and now you tell us we can't even join your Association. Why . . . that's racism in reverse." The progressives (including my comrades) were really up tight. Profoundly they shared the liberal's rage; agreed with Donald's overall thesis, but thought he was wrong because he preached nationalism, "a regressive step in the building of socialism." This is a very interesting point. Following the Soviet line on "national liberation movements in Africa," the radical left in America and Europe regarded Blacks like Donald as "bourgeois nationalists," historically necessary but dangerous because they might come to power before the trade unions were ready to lead them. Much later that year the Soviets changed their position toward "bourgeois nationalists," and naturally the American comrades followed.

But Donald was not impressed: "Surely we are against the system, a white system. Colonialism is white. Imperialism is white. We in the Afro-American Association do not make intellectual and political distinctions which have no meaning. We know that all white people are not 'the oppressors.' But all white people benefit from it either politically, financially, emotionally, or psychologically. The others are indifferent. All Blacks suffer a correlative burden. . . . Now, let me be understood. By white people I mean everyday white people, going-to-church white people (the most segregated hour in America is from eleven to twelve on Sunday), foolish white people, smart white people; liberals, conservatives, racists, Trotskyites, Stalinists, any ists; progressives; good, bad, indifferent—all the whites, 'cause they're all devils."

Right around this time I had an additional concern: the draft. Given my political convictions, I was unalterably opposed to service in an imperialist army. My Louisiana local draft board had refused to give me the usual student deferment and had not accepted my alternative conscientious objector appeal. The unemployed white sharecroppers who controlled the board were unable or unwilling to make a distinction between a man of peace and an "unpatriotic coward." To add to my confusion, my comrades accused me of lacking political integrity. "Tell them that you are a socialist and that you refuse to support a capitalist war machine whose job it is to put down people's wars of liberation. . . . You will go to prison for five years, but it's the price you must pay for freedom." Beautiful. I believe you; but not for me. Some fine young men had paid this price; I respected their courage, but I was not psychologically prepared to spend that length of time inside. I saw the contradiction, but I did not have the necessary inner strength to sentence myself to confinement. If this says something about the kind of radical I was, perhaps future events will absolve me.

Desperate and guilt ridden, I searched for advice from among the Afro-Americans. Donald and one or two others had successfully avoided Uncle Sam, and I needed some new directions. I could not find Donald or Ramsey, and there was a cloud of secrecy surrounding their whereabouts. The young long-haired students at the headquarters could not be convinced to be cooperative; I was "with the Devils" and could not "be trusted."

"Why have you come way over here to get help from the brothers? Have your devil revolutionaries run out of predictions?" He was cynical and cold.

"No, they haven't, but I want to find a way to beat the army and jail."

"Just tell those devils to kiss your ass and don't go."

"But it's not that easy. I want to know what you guys are doing."

"We're not 'guys'; we're *brothers*, *black brothers*, soldiers only for Africans and people of African descent. If you left those *devils* alone and got your mind together, you would know what to do."

"And how does one do that?"

He laughed, and I laughed too. "For me it was easy. I just had to be myself. For you, since you have a white mind, it will be more difficult. First of all, you have to love black people."

"But I do."

"Nigger, stop lying! Your mind is white. When was the last time you had some good soul work?"

"Well . . ."

"Just as I thought. You've been fucking those blue-eyed beasts so long you've probably forgotten how to fuck. . . . And that's the second thing you have to do—get you a sister. But before you do that—"

"What about the draft?" I interrupted. I was a little uneasy.

"You want to change the subject? That's what white people do," he said indignantly.

"I don't mind talking about being black, but you're so self-righteous that you wouldn't believe anything that I said anyway."

" 'Self-righteous' is a white term. What you hear is pride, baby; pride."

"Did you ever have white friends?"

"A white friend in a contradiction in terms! I knew some white people. They called themselves progressive, but no matter what they call themselves they're all the same *mother-fuckers*. In fact, I got an idea." He started to laugh. "Go to prison, and when you get out you will be an important man; might even get a position in the government."

"Why do you say that?" I was puzzled by his remarks.

"Now, I'm surprised at you! Don't you know the revolution is coming in five years? By being in prison you will avoid the bloodshed and be a hero in the socialist order when you get out. Dig it! Can you see it—white Marxist soldiers storming the prison to let you niggers out. I hope that the SWP wins, 'cause if the Socialist Labor Party comes to power, you might go to Mississippi and work on a state farm."

The next week I got my notice to report for April induction. I had still not worked out a strategy, so I wrote my draft board—my files had been transferred to San Francisco—that my aunt was ill, and since there was no one to care for her, I would report the next month. When I received the second notice, I wrote another letter:

Dear Sirs:
    I am ill. My schedule has been heavy, and I have come down with a serious case of the flu. I hope you have not been inconvenienced and look forward to seeing you soon.
                                        Sincerely yours,
                                        Leslie A. Lacy

In two weeks I received my monthly attempt-to-reconvert visit from the FBI. Although the agent knew about my draft status and assured me that they would come to get me next month if I did not show, now he was concerned with my participation in the Fair Play for Cuba Committee. The committee had been organized in New York by friends of the Cuban revolution, and a chapter had been established in San Francisco by representatives from all of the leftist groups.

FBI agents are very friendly at *your* house (but never go to theirs to be questioned). My comrades always ordered them to leave ("Subpoena me if you want to talk to me!"), but I couldn't; my early conditioning, both culturally and socially, always got in the way. With great passion he assured me that he knew I was busy and didn't want to disturb me, but he was only doing his duty.

"You are a nice fellow, Mr. Lacy. You come from a fine family. You are going to be a fine lawyer. You must separate yourself from these communists. They are ruthless people who are bent on using you. The Fair Play for Cuba Committee is subversive. We all respected Fidel Castro in the early period. Cuban society was in need of a change. Subsequent events, however, have made us reverse our stand. Castro has been duped. He is a communist being controlled by the Russians."

This time, like always, I said very little to the man in the brown flannel suit. And when he finished, he left with a smile.

Without a supporting demonstration, I reported for induction on receipt of notice three. I dressed Brooks Brothers head to toe—sharp, as clean as an Easter coat. I hadn't looked that way for nearly five years, hardly recognizable. My style was offset by two books: under my left arm I had a copy of Karl Marx, *The Communist Manifesto*, and I was reading Eric Lincoln, *The Black Muslims in America.*

I was two hours late. Most of the young inductees-to-be, among them an American Indian with cold black eyes, had already moved through the first phase of the physical examination.

"You're late," shouted the white Southern sergeant.

I looked slowly up, and contemptuously, at the cracker, and said softly but firmly, "My ear passages are extremely delicate. If you must speak to me at all, modulate your sound. Otherwise I might suffer permanent injury." I placed my induction notice on his desk, continued reading, and waited for my instructions.

The sergeant's face read: "That's all right, boy; we'll get you straightened out later." His voice said cynically, "Yes, sir, Mr. Leslie Alexander Lacy. Follow me this way."

We marched to the first examination room; he gave my records to the white Southern doctor and made a few remarks I could not hear. The room had the usual medical equipment and three men, who apparently had to be re-examined.

"Take your clothes off," the doctor ordered indifferently.

I ignored him and continued reading.

"Did you hear me, Lacy? This is the army. Put that book down and follow my instructions," the cracker said angrily.

"Please don't shout—"

"Yes, I know," he interrupted. "You have delicate ear passages. Okay, Prince Charming. Please, pretty please, take off your clothes."

"May I be taken to a private room?"

"A private room?" he shouted.

I closed my book, put it with the other between my legs, and put my hands over my ears. When he calmed down, I continued reading.

"Why do you need a private room?" His voice was calm.

I looked at him for a while and then said, "There might be homosexuals here. They are strange people; you never know what they will do."

This continued until his disgust led him to go to the resident colonel for assistance. The colonel arrived quickly. My God!

Another cracker. Weren't there any Northerners in the army? We were indifferent to each other, and after his short discussion with the doctor, I was taken to a private room.

I took off my clothes. It took me fifteen minutes. I walked to the center of the room, knelt down as though I was going to pray, and urinated. I stood up, shook my penis three times; stopped; then three again. Then I told the doctor that he could begin. When he got within arm's reach, I began screaming and grabbed his red neck. Within no time the room was filled with police. I stood against the wall with the stethoscope around my neck and a long scalpel in my hand. The colonel broke through the wall of police, demanding an explanation while rushing to comfort the urine-soaked doctor gasping on the floor.

Saluting the colonel, I spoke right up. "This inductee fails to conform to army regulations. I tried to examine him, but he refused. Then he seemed to go mad, coughing and urinating on the floor."

So accustomed was the colonel to military procedure that it took him a minute or two to realize that the real doctor was in his arms.

"Why, you. . . . Arrest that maniac," the colonel shouted to the police.

After I fought the four policemen, I was taken to see a psychologist or a psychiatrist. We had a lovely conversation— after I disarmed him by telling him that a white "healer" who had been in the army for twenty years probably did not believe that Blacks had sophisticated psychological problems—about my fish eggs. I choked him too, and we went through the same process again. Later that day I was released and ordered to report the next morning.

I was tested for six months. I was really sick. Finally I got the word: "Dear recruit: We are sorry to inform you that you are not qualified for acceptance under the present standards."

Meanwhile Donald and his zealots stepped up their campaign to recruit more Blacks into their Association. Like a prophet calling for the millennium, he walked and preached through the streets of Oakland, Berkeley, and San Francisco, in and out of schools and colleges, office buildings and coffeehouses, telling black people wherever they were: "The time has come to break with white America."

I joined the Afro-American Association after much inner probing. I thought that they had a positive program, although I still had reservations about their long-term objectives. The white left in the meantime had not achieved its predicted victory over capitalism, and besides, I thought I had had enough of its pussy, poetry, and politics. I still believed in socialism, but I also felt a need to assert my blackness. Later that year, partially because I wanted to convince my new comrades that I was trying and partially because I supported the idea, I had a debate with Wesley Johnson (Black) at San Francisco State. Resolved: Black Nationalism Is a Solution to the Negro Problem in America. I supported the resolution. Here is how George Irizary of *The Golden Gater*, State's daily college paper, described the proceedings:

A mixed audience, including interracial couples, black nationalists, Muslims, and an outspoken white Baptist evangelist with a bagful of religious literature, left a campus debate Saturday night after a lively and sometimes emotional question period. . . .

Medical biology major Wesley Johnson argued black nationalism was a deterrent to the Negro problem in America, that it is unrealistic to the situation. The "whys" are the challenge, not "withdrawal" said Johnson.

Black nationalist Leslie Lacy, the other debater, said the Negroes should look for a place in history. "Personally, I'm going to Africa," he said.

"America is a sick society," argued Lacy. When Johnson replied that Negroes as a part of American society are probably sick too, Lacy rebutted with, "There would be enough medicine in Africa to cure it." (American sickness). "Integration would be a combination of Negro inferiority, white liberal guilt, patronization, and paternalism, despite the morality of civil rights. This is the freedom of self-negation," said Lacy.

"Amens" were intermittently voiced by the Caucasian Baptist evangelist in the audience, who has recently located on campus. The evangelist's "amens" followed most statements in favor of black nationalism. At one time he yelled out to a black nationalist across the lounge, "We'll give you George Washington if you give us George Washington Carver." "I'd like for you to take him," said the black nationalist.

Both the comrades and the Afros criticized my presentation. The former said I had been duped; the latter's criticisms were expressed by Gerald X in the same paper, in a letter to the editor a few days later:

> Both participants did a thorough job of representing the "Negro," or the product of the white man.
> Les Lacy represented the bitter "Negro," an individual who appeared to be angry at the white man, but perhaps more angry at himself and his black brothers. Angry at his black brothers because they don't act right and achieve their dignity, and angry at himself because *he is caught in the web of whiteness.* That is, he would like to see dignity restored in the black man, not so that he can associate with and appreciate his *own kind,* but so that he can associate with his white comrades and hold his chest out and say, "Man, now I have dignity too."

This criticism was mild in comparison to later ones. I constantly lived under a sense of pressure. Although I spoke for the cause of black nationalism, I continued *openly* my association with whites, and Judy was still my girl.

I was also under fire from the air; less formally, but with equal power, the birds told me that I had gone over to the enemy—the "reactionary racist provocateurs."

Nevertheless, I continued working on both fronts. I was the sinking universal man foolishly trying to bring the diversity to harmony. "No, Leslie, no," each side shouted (listened to itself). "State your preference. Are you for or against?" And now that Judy was in town, I was even more confused.

How could I know? People can tell you that you are "duped" or "white loving," "fucked up" or "brain washed," as Gerald X summed up, "a duped Negro, fucked up by white-loving comrades and brainwashed against your own people." But I couldn't help believing that if you are honest, an honesty which develops out of your zigzag history, it is hard to be *one thing* (even if that thing is what you should be) if in fact you are possessed with many things, as I was. Political movements demand conformity, and those who serve them are never willing, if able, to understand the complex patterns of a personal evolution. And why should they? It's not a problem if you know where you belong. I guess people who are sensitive and ask much from life will inevitably suffer from a lack of consistency. And the frightening thing, the thing that could have driven me mad, is that I thought I was consistent.

I needed both worlds. Politically the Afros offered Blacks like me a revolutionary alternative to an inflexible and doctrinaire white left. For a long while I had been dissatisfied with the politics of comrade revolution, and with the comrades' inability to be creative and do some serious thinking about the profoundly changing nature of contemporary politics in general but particularly America.

Also, my racial consciousness and emotional anxieties were far from settled. Ironically in a sense, my identity crisis had been augmented. The radicals, true to their humanity, creed, and ideals, wanted to eliminate such distinctions. I was reminded often, until I started to believe it, that I was not a Negro, but an individual: "Please stop saying he's white, black, Jewish, or Mexican—people are just people, only individuals." The imperialists had created those distinctions, and we had to eliminate them. It was easy for me to accept, since it was my color which had made people hate me.

But their "democratic crucible" had a witch standing over it. The problem of America went deeper than a class analysis. And what was a Negro or a Mexican supposed to be in the period between now and assimilation? Their idealizations were far too neat. Sartre (in *Anti-Semite and Jew*) had already told the Jews to beware of the "democrat," for unlike the anti-Semite, who wants him eliminated as a man, the democrat "wishes to destroy him as a Jew and leave nothing in him but the man, the abstract and universal subject of the rights of man and the rights of the citizen . . . separate from his . . . ethnic community in order to plunge him into the democratic crucible, whence he will emerge naked and alone, an individual and solitary particle like all the other particles." By implication I was also much more than an individual. All my mental and psychic projections were an expression of everything that I had been, and for a long time I had been an American Negro. I had changed, rejected, grown up, discovered America and part of the world. I was becoming a man. But, however tenuous, I still had roots, memories, and a history I was just beginning to understand.

The political culture of the left I knew was unequivocally Jewish, or very much influenced by Jews. There was nothing evil about this. They were the major intellectuals, the major participants, and it was natural that their movement reflected and glorified their history. I had intimately embraced this history and discovered its meaning and beauty. I had learned very much. I had felt a profound sense of freedom and commitment and discovered a great deal about the human heart. I believed in socialism and its capacity to help man. My leftist comrades were some sort of the finest people I knew, and I know that some of me will always be there.

But what they could not know was that a world revolution *must* be based on a world culture. Until then, each culture for itself. Hence what I needed was a political culture which not only would extend and express my radical convictions but which also addressed itself completely, but not necessarily exclusively, to my brand of human alienation. Marcus Garvey, Donald Warden, and Kwame Nkrumah may have been "bourgeois nationalists," but they had a special historical meaning for me because they were black. I had to be free to know what that meaning was.

But I soon discovered that the Afro-American Association was not as viable an alternative as I had anticipated. Indeed, they were black: ate it, slept it, bought it, read it, lived it, and said they loved it. But like so many radicals fresh out of the womb of enlightenment, they unfortunately thought that history began when they became aware. You were either "together" or "shaky," and there was no real place for stumblers like me.

Politically and economically they were capitalists. And a capitalist without money was a strange breed. Marx was white, and Adam Smith . . . well, strangely enough, he was not. Du Pont *et al.* would have white America, and Donald Warden —who later came to Ghana and established an Afro-American chapter—would rule black America. And of course, the question of where we would get the resources was one that only a "Negro so-called ex-Marxist" would ask.

But the Association's weaknesses should not obscure its many virtues. The group was very relevant. They raised many important issues about the future of Blacks in America. They explored the racism in white America and made the white left more aware of itself. They did things which the comrades never thought of, like going into the black community each week and effectively explaining to the people what was happening in the world. And to extend their community efforts, they set up night schools which taught African history, English, and current thoughts on black affairs. But more important, the Association helped the alienated black students feel a part of the stagnant intellectual community and provided them with a weekly forum in which they could express themselves, and to my knowledge, were the first Blacks in recent history to demand a reshaping of a university curriculum with an addition of a Black Studies program. When the history of black protest is accurately written, the members of the Association will have an important place in it. They had the best qualities of their generation: intelligence, radicalism, courage, and indifference.

But I had decided to go to Africa. Flying from the birds to my new black nest had not been easy. I had had my wings clipped, learned new political songs. I learned all the rhetoric, said things which were black, attended all the Association's meetings; and once or twice, when other speakers could not be found, I had been allowed the privilege of speaking to my people at street rallies. Yet I did not quite feel at one with this Leslie. The brothers and sisters knew I still saw my leftist friends, and constantly reminded me that only a clean break with the "devils" would free my soul. The meetings were off limits to Judy, yet I always had the fear that she might defiantly stop by the office or wait for me outside. The earnest questions I raised during the meetings were branded as "white"—therefore not worthy of reply. I believed in what I was doing, yet from their frame of reference, they were right in finding fault with me. When I look back upon those moments, I am almost tempted to make some sort of apology to the black people to whom I spoke, because my whole heart was not there. Such was the existence I led by way of seconding my commitment to the movement.

I could not reconcile the contradictions of my life. And instant conversion was impossible. I had made the intellectual decision and I had applauded a speech in which President Nkrumah said he was black first, African second, and socialist third. My emotions, however, did not follow intellect. I needed too many days, perhaps years, to work out my inner confusion. I needed a community of people that could afford to be patient, and I did not believe that I could escape the taunts and attacks of America's racial madness in another American city. And Dr. W. E. B. Du Bois had made my decision clear. He was black and radical, and in his life was the back-and-forth political pattern which was beginning to characterize mine. I had recently heard him at a peace rally. He was going to Ghana. "A socialist Africa is the future," he said.

The Blacks respected Nkrumah, but I should fight *here* not *there*. Why take my white hangups to Africa? I couldn't solve *my* problem by running.

The birds, on their side, were dismayed. Why Africa? Strange. They hadn't questioned me last year, when I went to Spain, or the year before, when I went to England. And had I questioned them when they returned to the lands of their forefathers? No. I was beginning to see the subtle racism in these comments. But to me it was obvious: where else could a black man go to discover his dignity? Drinking beer in English pubs or discussing existentialism by the banks of the Seine had little to do with my present evolution.

Before I left for New York I wrote the Association the following letter.

Dear Brothers and Sisters:

I am going to Ghana to live. Some of you—and you may be right—will say that I ran away. If that is true, please forgive me. But I cannot continue. I love you all. I will never be that far. We will always together be a part of the same revolution. Goodbye, Donald, Ken, Ramsey, Belvie, Jim. Again, I love you.

> Ghana, Ghana here I come,
> Right back where I started from;
> Open up your heart to me,
> Ghana—here I come.
>
> Leslie

VII

Exile to Search

Senegal

DAKAR, Senegal, was my first stop. It was 7:00 A.M., and hot, very hot, like New York in the middle of August. The Atlantic Ocean had been my universe for ten sleepless days and nights and the fish had eaten well the food my unsettled stomach had thrown out to them. The ocean had never been my cup of milk, but I had the foolish and romantic unconfessed notion that I had in some distant gene been brought from Africa by ship, and that on my return, I should travel likewise. A word of caution to those who come to Africa: fly if possible, and if you have to travel by sea, leave your ulcer at home.

I had all kinds of fantasies during my seasickness, which I am told is psychological. I remember only one of them. I imagined myself in the "middle passage," being beaten by President John F. Kennedy. That was relatively easy because on the ship was Rev. John Kennedy, fresh out of missionary training and using my lost soul for his apprenticeship. Because he had never really listened to black voices in America, he assumed (and I did not correct him) that I was African. If you like missionaries, his credentials were impressive: white, young, Mississippi—cracker-born, -reared, and -trained—and the Lord had sent him to Africa to contribute to its development by translating the Holy Book into "native dialects." I was surprised that he was going to Nkrumah's Ghana. Kennedy's wife (and let us not forget about his screaming children, the only other passengers on this American freighter, which was called *The African Princess*) cannot be described. She had given up her humanity to her Baptist church, but she looked forward to new vitality teaching English in the Ghana school system.

Playing pagan was fun. It took my mind away from my stomach. I created horrible stories about missionaries missing in action de-ee-*ee*-ep in dark Africa. The children, of course, were happy, because they thought that hunting "lions and natives" would be fun. But the Holy One was quick to remind his offspring, "You should never make fun of uncivilized people. That's why we are here." Naturally, my stories did bother him. He was afraid for his little Southern woman. He had heard about those uncivilized Mau Mau in Kenya. Finally he had to confess that if the Lord was busy watching out for fools and babies in Latin America, the American Embassy in Ghana would stand *in loco parentis*. His racism was balanced off by his dramatics. Rev. Kennedy threw his Bible overboard to prove to me that he had free will, only for me to discover that his other Bibles were packed away below. A very nice captain suggested that maybe the fish could now pray for him. Damn, that's no fantasy: he was a real phantom. A white missionary in 1963 Africa.

Dakar at last, and a cure for all of my illnesses: America, ocean, and Rev. Kennedy. I walked down the gangplank looking for my Senegalese friend Jean Paul, who was supposed to meet me. My feet felt good on the African soil. I wanted to kiss it, but I was saving that act for Ghana. But even if I had tried, it would have been virtually impossible, because I was surrounded—completely mobbed—by the smiling faces of Senegalese stevedores. They grabbed my arms, took my bags, and seemed excited to see me. What a welcome! Africans coming to meet a returning son. I was stricken by elation. I held each one's hands and put my arms around the shoulders of each—all fifty of them. But how did they know I was coming? Then I thought, Jean Paul had told them. He thought of everything.

Finally I greeted them. "Brothers, I'm so glad to be home. This is the greatest moment of my life. It was worth spending every hour in America just to be able to live this moment. You have made me very happy. They tell black people in America that the Africans don't want them. I know now that they were lying to keep us apart. Black people in America belong on this continent, and I bring you greetings from all those who cannot be here. I am truly happy."

"Give us dollar," the man in front said enthusiastically.

"Dollars? But I don't understand." I was confused.

"Yeah. You from America. You got plenty dollar. You be Big Man. American. Rich country. This be poor country. We need dollar. You give dollar."

Suddenly it was as clear as the hot sky above. They had not come to welcome me. They had come for "dollar." I felt hurt and stupid. My heart dropped in me like an anchor. I needed one thing; they wanted another. Their welcome meant more to me than the money they needed, but I did not want to relate to them on that basis. They persisted and persisted. Once or twice I almost gave in, but my hands would not respond to my brain, for I was thinking about Donald in California. Finally it was over. Convinced that I was not a Big Man, they left in disgust to unload the ship.

Then I saw Jean Paul standing a short distance away. He had seen everything. Knowing Jean and the way his mind functioned, I knew he would never rescue a friend from a situation if he thought that his friend should experience it.

I had met Jean at the University of California at Berkeley when I was in law school. He was studying medicine, but had left America rather mysteriously. He had a kind and gentle spirit and a tall, beautiful black body to project it. Also, he was clever—brilliant. He spoke twenty-two languages, twelve European and ten African languages, including Swahili and Arabic. And when he learned a language, it was his. He spoke French with a perfect accent, and of course his English was Oxford. In his spare time he had become an authority on Islam, and had read every book a black man had ever written. He shared many of my political convictions, but he turned many people away from him because of his "aristocratic" manner. Once he had explained to me in California, "I'm glad I'm that way. My own life is a constant reminder that we need a revolution."

"Well, ole chap, I see you made it. You're looking fit. How are you getting on, Leslie? It's damn good to see you." He put his arms around me affectionately, and then pushed me away with his strong hands to get a good look at me. He smiled with pleasure.

I was glad to see him too. "I'm glad to be home." My words came slowly because I did not want to cry.

"Just cry. Let all that sickness out. In a week or so you'll be as good as you were four hundred years ago. No. I must be accurate; it was three hundred and sixty years ago."

We laughed. Jean could always be pleasantly cynical when it counted. The laugh was good. I dried my eyes, cleared my choked-up throat, and got myself together.

"What's the political scene like in the States?" Jean was serious again.

"So-so. Very little difference since you left."

"What's happening with the Afro-American Association?"

"It's moving ahead."

"Has Donald worked out an alliance with Rockefeller yet?" We laughed, because the few socialists in the Association were critical of Donald's explicitly black capitalistic orientation.

"I think Donald will have to become more radical." I was not trying to defend Donald, but I felt that he would see the weakness of his position.

"Maybe. I hope so anyway. How is your family?" Jean asked with concern.

"Fine."

"Did your brother go to medical school?"

"No," I said, embarrassed. "He became a minister."

"What!" Jean was a little surprised, but he was never really shocked about anything. He had a lot of ideas, a life-to-death commitment to a black world revolution, but very little faith in the present generation to achieve it. "What faith? I hope it's Baptist; at least he'll have some cultural rewards."

"No, it's not Baptist. It's probably Methodist."

"Same difference. Say"—Jean was laughing—"what ever happened to the white fellow student who used to predict that the revolution would be coming in two years?"

"You mean Phillip?"

"Yeah, I think he was the one."

"He went to jail for a draft conviction."

"Good. Those people are absolutely mad. Tell me, Les, what's happening with you and Judy?"

I hesitated to answer, but not for long, because Jean and Ken were the only two friends that I could really talk with now. "It's about over now. We broke up . . . got together again, then broke up again. When I left for New York the break was rather final."

"Politics?"

"Yeah, I guess you can say that." I paused. "But it was a lot of other things too."

"Like what?"

"Well . . . I don't know. I think we had just reached that point. We couldn't talk any more. The black-white issue constantly came up. Every day, we had an argument. It was just too much. It became too complicated. . . . Look, Jean, maybe we ought to change the subject. I'm in Africa now, let's not talk about America . . . it's too unpleasant."

"Whatever you say. You're the boss." He smiled.

"Wait! Before we change the subject, I've got something to show you." Hurriedly I opened my briefcase and removed an envelope. "Look, Jean, I've got a surprise for you."

Jean opened the envelope in his usual meticulous way. "Wow! Whose picture is this?"

"Eve Garden."

"And *who* is Eve Garden?"

"Well, I guess you can say that she's my new girl. In fact I think I'm beginning to love her. I met her shortly before I left Berkeley. She is from New York City, and while I was in the city I saw her almost every day. She is very nice, isn't she?"

"Leslie, you still don't know how to describe a black woman. She's more than nice. She is absolutely ravishing. And rather elegant. Is she clever?"

"Very."

"Wonderful, ole chap. And she's black too. We'll have you yet. . . . Is she a student or what?"

"She graduated with a degree in French. She wants to study African history."

"What about her politics?" He hadn't taken his eyes from the photograph.

"She is radical, but tends to be practical."

"That's good enough. Can't have them too radical. How are her other qualifications?" he asked, smiling.

I smiled too, because I knew that he was talking about sex. "Well that's working itself out."

"What you mean is that you haven't slept with her."

"Not yet."

Jean shook his head in disgust while looking at Eve. Then he put his arm on my shoulder, like a father getting ready to advise a son. "Damn, Leslie, you must stop this waiting nonsense. You take your training too seriously. Look at your life: The girls that you grew up with were *too nice* to fuck, and the other black women were *beneath your station* in life, so you didn't fuck them. So much for that stupidity. Now you go to Boston and don't have any of the white middle-class ass there, and then go to California, and after two years, *finally* a white Jewish surrealist Marxist has to almost drag you into the bedroom. At last you have a black woman, the movement of the earth, and you're still acting stupid. Leslie Lacy, you are absolutely rare. *Amazing. You have lost your African heritage.*" He laughed and then sarcastically added, "Are you sure your dick is still black? Look, my dear brother, let me tell you a story. There is an African Catholic priest here. Can you relate to that: an African priest in a Muslim country. Poor chap. He gets about one convert every ten years. But anyway, back to the story. This chap replaced a French priest who had served predominantly Europeans. One of the older European women had an 'illegal fuck' with an African and went to the new priest for absolution. As the story goes, when she arrived he was giving 'absolution' to another woman in his bedroom, and had to dress quickly to perform his religious duties. The sinful woman was very depressed and cried incessantly as she told him her story. His first question was, 'Was it good?' The moral there for you is never take yourself seriously. . . . By the way, where is Eve now?"

"Europe."

"Europe? Why don't you have her with you?"

"She's coming. I'm supposed to meet her in Guinea."

"Well, I'll straighten you out before you meet her." While he talked he put his arms around my shoulders and we walked toward his car. "You'll be in fine shape; don't worry about it. Tonight you will have your first black woman. Just think of it, you can lay between the legs of Mother Africa—no talking, no politics, no repression, no poetry—just natural fission."

Dakar! Dakar, Africa? My God, it's Paris! French culture hung over the city like the smog. Independent since 1960, and I saw General de Gaulle's official picture everywhere, including the new government building. French soldiers walked proudly and dignifiedly through the streets, and their overfed officers, with other French and European "Big Men," sat happily in sidewalk cafés, eating, drinking, and ordering the frightened waiters around.

Where were the Africans? They lived outside the Paris mainstream. Those inside, except the ruling African elite (who resided in the European section), lived in the "inner city," surrounded by modernization, which according to Jean, kept them from seeing out while allowing the Europeans the illusion that they were really home.

Now, after three weeks of seeing and hearing, I had land sickness. What Africa was this? But then, what did I really know about Senegal? I knew it was independent; that it occupied 76,000 square miles and had a population of about 3,490,000, mostly Muslims. The French had established this colony long before others on the Atlantic coast. Somewhere I had read that France had not considered Senegal or any of her possessions colonies in the general sense of the term, but in her imperialistic arrogance had considered them an extension of herself; that as soon as the "natives" could be civilized in the French language and culture, they could become Frenchmen. Its president, Léopold Senghor, was a distinguished scholar, and as a poet, he had helped to promote a black renaissance in Paris. He was Catholic and married to a French-woman. I knew that Dakar was the capital, with a rapidly growing population, and that many of these people were un-employed. In Berkeley, radicals, both black and white, said Senghor was conservative in comparison to Kwame Nkrumah and that he was very interested in a stronger relationship with France. Indeed, he was usually described as a "tool of de Gaulle." Beyond that, I tended to believe the opposite of what was said in the Western press, without knowing whether or not what I opposed was real.

It was a very strange sensation. I saw something which I only vaguely expected and for which I was only partially pre-pared: I could accept neocolonialism in theory, but not in practice.

But isn't this universal? Does not the sensitive man who knows that others are poor know something different once he sees the poverty? Probably. But that man has not been pre-pared in advance to identify with what he sees, and that is true even if he takes on their misery immediately. It was my problem. I was not looking at a frightened waiter, but at myself. My revulsion had nothing to do with Senegal; it was with *my Senegal*, the one I had created back home. I began to realize it when I noticed that the Senegalese who were disturbed by the same reality were never as mad as I was. Several times I thought my reactions were out of proportion. Later on, after I got to Ghana, the concept became much clearer.

I could feel that Jean Paul sensed my outrage, but—and I was confused by this—he never related to it. He was essentially a guide. As much as possible he avoided the French sights. We traveled outside of Dakar and observed how the *real* half was living, but I got no real feeling for the culture because my mind was always possessed by the *occupied city*. And although the majority of the Africans were still on the land, a land full of culture, known and unknown, Dakar was where the action was—where all major decisions affecting the republic were made, where power resided, and where the plans for nation building were being formulated.

Jean's family was very good to me, and in every sense, I was treated like the returned son. It was a fascinating household, and although Jean was not the head of the male-dominated family, he had a strange status. I think we would call him the translator. His father, the head man, was a professor of German at the University of Dakar. Sometimes his father had difficulty understanding the language he was born to. His sister, on vacation from Europe, spoke French *exclusively*. His mother always spoke Wolof. Jean did all the *unnecessary* translation, including giving instructions to the servants, who spoke Arabic. He could relate to everyone and tried in vain to keep the traditional values alive in a rapidly changing urban Senegalese family structure.

The night before I left, Jean and I had our first *real* discussion. It was perhaps rather a lecture, because I had seen very little in three weeks.

"How do you like our *glorious revolution?*" He was quite serious.

"It's interesting." I answered that way because I felt that he would continue to act like the guide.

"Rubbish. It's awful." He got up and walked around the floor. "Our real leader is in jail. Our president is Professor Senghor: poet, lover, philosopher, man of the people. In fact, ole chap, the president is a socialist. You may see, my brothers, the French are here (all praises due to de Gaulle) to help us carry forth our rapid industrialization. Your trouble is that you are a frustrated American socialist who always overreacts. We happy citizens of the republic are democratic socialists. And what is democratic socialism? I'll tell you: a system of government which gives a Big Man the opportunity to take money from the state without a receipt. It's not stealing, you see, because he gives it to his family, friends, enemies, and keeps half of it for old age. The ideology upon which the ingenious order works is fifty per cent Gaulist, ten per cent American, thirty per cent Catholic, five per cent symbolic logic, and five per cent Negritude. The Africans—very backward people—are excluded because they must first learn how to identify with power. Our exports go to France because Africans are basically humanistic and traditional and have no real need for a modern decadent society.

"The University of Dakar seems consistent with the Professor's plans for development. Ninety per cent of the staff and students are French. That's our revolution. . . . Wait, I almost forgot the French troops. They are necessary to keep the traitors from becoming subversive." Jean Paul smiled slightly, and said softly, "Now you'd better go to bed. Your plane is at an early hour."

Leaving was hard, but my three-week visa had expired. We had tried to get it extended, but could never find the "right" official to do it. Before I boarded the plane I received a present from Jean. He had gone to considerable trouble to get me an English translation of Frantz Fanon's magnum opus, *Les Damnés de la Terre*. With it, he gave me a letter, which I opened on the plane:

Dearest Leslie,
Promise me that you will be well. Head high. Your history is my history, and we must tell ourselves that it will not continue. My heart is heavy with my country, but it loves and I share it with you. Take care of Eve. Don't be too hard on her. Have children . . . do not let your heart die.
Don't become a Big Man in Ghana (smiles).
Fanon is good. We cannot use him now. Maybe some day, *oui?*
Jean Paul

Guinea

Like the average man in Senegal, the everyday citizen of the Republic of Guinea was poor. But for a different reason. Conakry, the capital, was not a French treasure chest. The 3,500,000 people of the country faced a difficult task of nation building. Their president, Sékou Touré—the grandson of Samory Touré, the nineteenth-century Islamic nationalist who delayed the spread of French imperialism—had been a stubborn man. In 1958 his country was the only French territory which rejected Charles de Gaulle's proposed *communauté* (community). Now, Charles didn't like that—who did that African think he was anyway? Mr. de Gaulle had visions of being very generous: besides giving Mr. Touré his own country, he was allowing him to have self-rule in all matters except *defense* and *foreign policy*. After all, African nations don't need an army. There's always South Africa to protect them. So, provoked by the politics in this 98,865 square miles, Mr. Charles quickly withdrew all colonial officials and economic aid. The grandson had one reply: "We prefer poverty in freedom to riches in colonial servitude."

Unlike Senghor, Touré was not a product of a French *lycée*. His roots were in the working class, and he had come to power through the militant trade unions. And with the help of Kwame Nkrumah's $30-million loan, the man who had defied a general was still in power.

After spending the first day in a Guinean jail, I must confess that I was less impressed with this militant history. I had committed a crime: I had entered the country without a visa. I had hoped to get one at the airport, but was arrested instead. My American passport was a liability. I thought about calling the American Embassy, but the thought of being *saved* by white Americans from Guinea was too ironical to be seriously considered. Sékou Touré had a lot of enemies, and his *very* efficient security police were taking no chances. In fact, the attack was not on me but on my passport, and I was glad to see black men challenge it.

Eve came to my defense. She had been in the country for two weeks and had met some of the influentials. With their help, her good looks and charm, she had gone right to the top, and I was free on one condition: twenty-four hours to leave.

I spent half of that time with Eve, putting into action my newly acquired African values.

The other half I spent seeing the city of Conakry. There was a bustling seaport, but hardly any industry. We were told that there were large amounts of iron ore, bauxite (perhaps the richest deposits in the world), and diamonds, but their economic potential was far from realized.

I was happy to see that the steps between politician and citizen were not that large: the governing officials had not forgotten about the common man. The highly disciplined party had brought its boot down on corruption and was walking quickly with the people toward full re-Africanization of the country.

I found out what had happened to the "Black Jacobins." They are all in Guinea. Thousands of skilled and progressive Haitians (many who have taken up Guinean citizenship) have settled there because they could not function in Duvalier's government. They are very critical of political conditions at home and see very little hope of ever returning. So they fight the poverty and the unbearable mosquitoes, trying to give some meaning to their lives. Funny, we had come from white power; they had come from black power.

We left the next afternoon. Farewell, Guinea; good luck, Sékou; courage to the Haitians, my countryless brothers.

Sierra Leone

Freetown—the capital settled as a refuge for freed slaves sent out by the Society for the Abolition of the Slave Trade in 1787—reminded me of Franklin without the added annoyance of Town One. And Prime Minister Albert Margai, who had led his people from a British protectorate to independence in 1961, reminded me of my Uncle Samuel, who owned a night club in Port Arthur, Texas. I told this to John Akar, the Minister of Broadcasting, and he assured me in his Oxford English, "Ole chap, I am sure that the physical similiarities of our dearly beloved head of state can be found on any peasant in the world. He is truly a man of the people."

Tongue-in-cheek Akar was an extraordinary man. Naturally he was the only qualified person in the country to lead the 2,290,000 people to glory, but the legislators did not share his opinions of himself, so they had passed a special law to restrict his political ambitions. John Akar, or as he called himself, "Mr. World," was kept out of his "rightful seat" because the law said that only a "pure" Sierra Leonean could be president. It was said that Mr. World was of mixed ancestry.

John (probably the most arrogant man on earth) and his

lovely Afro-American wife were very kind to us. We met all the important government officials except the president. I spoke on the national radio, and strongly criticized America's racial and economic policies both at home and abroad.

For two wonderful months we did nothing but relax. We had the best of everything. Some Africans we met were very Westernized, and of course, we were reminded to beware of the "natives." I did not like this look-down-on-them attitude; it reminded me too much of the Negro history I had left. Also we were warned about the "dictator Nkrumah"; in fact, advised not to go to Ghana.

In the first week of the third month we said goodbye to our friends. I kept thinking how much like Franklin it was.

Liberia

On the short plane ride from Freetown to Monrovia, the capital of Liberia, I was thinking about the young students I had met at the universities in Senegal and Sierra Leone. Without exception, they had all been very critical of their governments. And because they were afraid to express their discontent openly, most of them had become professionally cynical and hopelessly pessimistic. For Eve and me this was extremely demoralizing. In America black students were beginning to look at Africa with new eyes, with a new vision which was not dilated with notions of "primitive peoples"; and although they had read about the inroads of neocolonialism, most of them tended to be positive and surely optimistic. I had tended to be critical of Dakar and some of the negative foreign influences I had seen, but the fact of independence was sustaining enough: a great leap forward—a necessary precondition to real nation building.

Liberia, like Sierra Leone, tends to have a special significance for black Americans, because it was settled in 1822 by the American Colonization Society as a "home" for slaves from America, and in 1847 it became the first black republic in West Africa. This is true even though politically thinking Blacks are critical of William V. S. Tubman (president since 1943), his dependency on Firestone and Goodyear rubber plantations, and his inability to move toward a more pan-African direction. It is potentially a rich country, ranking sixth in the world in output of gem diamonds, ranking eighth in rubber production, and also having high-grade iron deposits. But the wealth in the country is divided between the exploitative American industries and descendants of the slaves. A very little gets down to the other two million inhabitants.

For me, Liberia had a special significance. Most of the African students who had come to Palmer were from Liberia, and a fellow called Edward Greenfield, a Liberian who had graduated in my Palmer class, was coming to Roberts Field (Liberia's only airport) to meet us.

Edward took us directly to his mansion. Then the last thing in the world I expected happened. While we were waiting in the spacious living room, which looked more like a museum, Dr. Edward Greenfield—a twenty-four-year-old physician—changed into his Palmer Memorial Institute jacket. He ran into the living room and insisted on doing some Palmer football cheers. Reluctantly, after ten minutes of his enthusiastic persuasion, I got up to join his ritual. But I just stood there and watched. I had neither the will nor the memory to participate. Eve was pretending to be fascinated, and annoyed me with her encouragement. He was absolutely amazing. Not only did he remember each song, saying, and yell, but also who wrote them, who said what, when, why, and so on, and so on, including esoteric details which I had never known. Edward was not satisfied with silent participation; I thought in his euphoria he had not seen. He was convinced—absolutely serious—that what I needed was the proper context, and excused himself and enthusiastically ran upstairs.

Down again, with record-breaking speed, he handed me a Palmer jacket. My God! Was he selling them?

For two weeks, in order not to hurt him, I had to wear a wool Palmer jacket. All of his friends had one, so I was right at home. Eve was luckier; she got a Palmer cap. What a two weeks!

Exhausted and hoarse, we left the third week, with fair Palmer—its sons and its daughters—giving cheer.

Ivory Coast

Their ivory and manganese are for the French; their diamonds are for the South Africans; and their cocoa belongs to America and Britain. Independent since 1960. Another French playground.

The capital, Abidjan, reminded me of Atlanta, Georgia, in 1950. Horrible place! I have talked about Dakar, so there's no need to repeat, except to say Abidjan's worse.

We were going to stay a month. But we stayed two days. How would you like to be discriminated against in a "free" black society? I wished the *people* well.

VIII

The Political Kingdom

GHANA. We had finally arrived. Nervously I followed the crowd—Eve next to me, holding my hand—down the landing stairs. I wanted to scream, "Ghana, Nkrumah, I'm here!" But not yet, I thought. The afternoon warm air felt good in my lungs; conscious of every breath, sucking it in, letting it out, gently—like a kiss. I took off my coat, pulled down my tie, and looked straight up at the sun until I could not see; looked down again, and walked slowly, counting each step into the terminal.

Police, security men, and soldiers occupied most of the space in the small airport waiting room. We had heard in Freetown that another attempt had been made on President Nkrumah's life. Everyone moved quickly and quietly, opened all bags, and waited to be inspected. No exceptions, no exemptions; everybody obeyed, especially the trembling Europeans, who knew this was not Dakar. I received in my head a fresh flow of blood from seeing white men wait, uncomfortable, not knowing what to expect from Blacks who did not move when they spoke. Give them hell, brothers; give them hell.

I moved to the inspection table. A captain my own age smiled, said good afternoon, and requested my passport. At the same time two other, older soldiers went painstakingly through my small bag, turning over and over all the new shirts and underwear I had happily gotten on my new, unpaid charge account at Sterns department store in New York.

"Afro-American?" the young captain asked rhetorically.

I shook my head in approval, for I was too twisted inside to say, "Yes, sir." I was free to go. So I stood next to the wall, waiting for Eve.

"Captain," shouted one of the older security guards, looking through Eve's baggage. The guard thought that Eve's Tampax were explosives. He was from a small village and the women there did not use tampons. Eve's were the first he had ever seen.

The captain graciously apologized to us and quietly explained to the old soldier, in his own language, what was happening. The old man's laugh was very long. We all laughed. A Ghanaian woman next to us explained essentially what was said: "Old man, this is not a bomb. . . . It is a blood catcher not blood producer. . . . It will be all right."

We were free to go, but I could not move my body. I was paralyzed by the sight in front of my eyes. I was looking at the captain—a black policeman. He was so proud, so efficient, stronger in one sense, an important sense, than I could ever be. He could never imagine the intense joy that his presence as a black policeman established for me. No man or woman born could ever know what that sight means to a black man who has never seen it. Nor could Eve, my woman, understand. It is a restricted type of social and psychological alienation. I claim that only a black male American can understand and appreciate the meaning of a black policeman. Because in America the police are white, evil. They stop you, search you, intimidate and beat you, and if there is any manhood left to stand up for more, they will kill it. A special relationship exists between you and the policeman: you can function, even argue with him, up to the point when he gets mad; to go beyond that point, which in essence is to change the nature of the relationship, is to invite death. He must always be dominant. He represents American white male chauvinism and racism over and against your erection. He is law and history, and you can never identify with it.

Once when I was in a friend's apartment in Oklahoma, the

police forced their way in. An Algerian student, fresh from fighting, whose frail body was held together by wire, jumped up *immediately* and ordered the police to leave. Our inability to be that spontaneous was a loss of manhood. We stood up minutes afterwards, but then it was too late. And each time it happens you lose a bit more, until something other than what you should be exists. The relationship did not exist between the Algerian and the rednecks. The latter were not dominant, because the Algerian had learned from his own war how to be spontaneous without being stupid.

"Leslie, let's go," Eve said impatiently.

"Sure, sweetheart, whatever you say." I was fine now. We moved out of the building.

My first days in Ghana were wild and beautiful; nights filled with tenderness and my growing love for Eve. I walked the streets of Accra, kissed and put my arms around strangers, calling them brother and sister, sometimes mother, many times father; they looked at me in bewilderment, but always smiled. I ate strange food, too much, too hot, got sick, threw up and ate more, ignored my ulcer, forgot about the pain. Eve watched with her cool self, each day getting more beautiful as the sun fought her cosmetics to make her more natural.

One day, alone, I took a bus to the Elmina Castle. I wanted to see the slave castle. I sat next to a market woman. She spoke to me in Fanti (a language of western Ghana); I shook my head, pretending to understand. I was passing, and I felt no need to be recognized.

I tried to relax, but that's a middle-class luxury, a wishful thought on a Ghanaian bus, or as the people call it, "transport." I had been on a crowded subway, but this was a totally new adventure in traveling. Once you take your seat, if you are fast enough to get one—it's like the New York subway at 5:30—it is impossible to move, as every inch is occupied with objects ranging from live chickens to small pieces of lumber; and you are constantly amazed because at every stop more people with more goods can be accommodated. No one seems inconvenienced or annoyed by the miniature market place or the gigantic heat this situation creates. I tried to suppress my headache and raging thirst and looked quite pleased with the box of cackling chickens in my lap. Also, I had little faith in the driver: passing other cars on hills I could not see over was not my idea of proper driving. Thousands of unrelated images, mostly about America, popped up in my mind, but like little bubbles which fly up and burst, they quickly vanished, except for my persistent impression: the city of Accra.

It was really an African city. Unlike Senghor in Dakar, the president of the ex-British colony was not keeping his peasants on the land. Their presence gave to this capital the touch of a confused boom town, crowded and noisy, everybody and his mama trying to sell you things from their sidewalk showrooms —very similar I guess, to a California gold rush town at the turn of the century, or maybe like Mencken's Baltimore, Maryland, in the eighteen-eighties. Things seemed pleasantly unorganized, but behind the confusion there seemed to be a logic and sense of direction. No, it was not a California boom town. It was a Southern black town without the lorries, with an African food-trading market, and beautiful African dresses and robes. The people of "Negro" Birmingham and every other black community which I had passed through in the South (and perhaps part of the East) had forgotten about the things I was seeing and hearing. They no longer spoke this language or carried this culture from generation to generation. But the spirit or character—something about the black people on these Accra streets—gave me, and also Eve, a feeling of belonging which I had only gotten in America from the dusky people who could still remember loud laughter, lack of European "refinement," festival nights and days, the bend of a black woman's buttocks; what Léopard Sédar Senghor had seen in Harlem, "humming with noise, with stately colours and flamboyant smells," saying to New York, "Let black blood flow in your blood that it may rub the rust from your still joints, like an oil of life." The historians who had said that there were no African survivals in the New World had not understood this, or if they did, had not appreciated its significance in the life of the New World Negro's culture.

But in an ever-changing city like Accra, tradition and modernization walk hand in hand, sometimes with a stride which inevitably leads them into confrontations. A mammy wagon (an old truck with wooden benches crammed inside to haul passengers) would cause a traffic jam because the driver had gotten out to talk to a distant cousin or because he had forgotten to fill up the gas tank. A political minister on his way to an important state meeting is understandably perturbed when there is no room for his new Mercedes-Benz to pass. The truck driver is not consciously indifferent to state affairs, but he has not seen his cousin in three months. So the minister and the other mammy lorries, trucks, cars, and taxis have to wait until the cousins have finished updating their extended family affairs or until a policeman comes from his shaded hiding place to get things moving. In the midst of this confusion are the market men and women, students, and Europeans, going about their business as usual.

A sudden stop brought me back to the reality of the bus. I sat up, adjusting the sleeping chickens in my lap, and looked around the bus. Like the chickens, everyone was asleep—except the reckless driver, who was happily entertaining himself by singing a Ghanaian song.

The countryside was beautiful. If only my brother, Nathaniel, could see this landscape; he would love the thick green trees, perpetually green in an everlasting summer. Some looked old, timeless, like the first in the world; others were young and defiantly erect, like the young men who had planted them; and together they stood spread out as far as I could see, a perfect loveliness between the ocean and me.

The bush and the trees are natural allies—a primeval condominium—like lovers perpetually in heat who constantly make war on the road. Everything grows fast in the tropics; procreation is part of the air. If you cut the growth, beat it back, the next week—sometimes the next day—you'll have to fight it all over again.

"Elmina. Everybody out for Elmina," said the driver indifferently, in English.

I returned the chickens to the market woman who had asked me to hold them, and when she reached for them I saw her mother's breast and refreshing smile; my heart swelled. She thanked me in Fanti. Still passing, I smiled back acknowledging her words, and stumbled over people and goods to get out of the door.

The lorry driver was annoyed because I had delayed him, but smiled when I smiled before he closed the door. He drove away singing, almost hitting a parked car. And I hoped that I would have another driver when I decided to return. Moments later, as the bus passed out of view, I was standing on the beach with my shoes in my hand.

Now it was afternoon, and cool; the sun was hot like always, but the ocean was stirring in her eternal movement and the breeze from her face gave me relief. It was Sunday too. I had heard the bells from the bus. Half of Elmina was asleep; the Christian half was in church. I was alone in an unbelievable silence—a stillness so intense, so complete, that I did not hear the waves. "O water, voice of my heart, crying in the sand," splashing upon and forever changing the prehistoric biology. I felt strangely detached and I tried to push my consciousness to the point where I would not remember my whole life. "O water, crying for rest, is it I, is it I?" Lines from "Of Our Spiritual Strivings" did not help. Arthur Symons could not write for me. I was a rare kind of nigger. Not a Bigger Thomas, nor a manchild in a promised land. Maybe I had experienced too much of the nausea of life to have an identity. And what I had internalized ached within me. Maybe Du Bois would help when I saw him soon. An old man helping a young man to answer a question about the soul of a black man. "How does it feel to be a problem?" A question he had not answered all his life long. Now he was dying, while I was living like "unresting water . . . crying without avail."

Where is my father? Where is my mother? San Francisco, I know that I am not supposed to miss you, but I do . . . I do. Eve, Eve, my black woman. And nobody understands you. Crying from a history of rejection which shapes your expectations. . . . I tried not to think of Judy. Outside, I was in a drunken frenzy and felt something like liberation. The beauty around excited me—the hell with alienation! I flexed my toes in the sand and threw smooth stones back into the great ocean. Then I ran. Fast at first, then slower, and when I got really tired, too nervous to stop, I walked and talked to myself and waited for the tropical breeze to fill up my lungs again so that I could scream and run back to my youth, a new youth. Oh, to be a child again—a little boy, twelve and romantic, looking on a seashore for smoother rocks, innocent and full because he has fallen in love. Was I being false? Maybe. Sorry. It didn't matter, nothing matters when you are trying real hard to be happy. . . .

When I opened my eyes I was in the fifteenth century, or so it seemed, standing before a castle next to the sea: Elmina Castle. A slave castle; the first European civilization in Ghana. The architects were Portuguese (had probably gotten lost on their way to Angola). They called themselves missionaries but had neglected to tell the natives that they had lost faith in their own civilization.

The gates of the castle were open and protected, but the guard was asleep. Why not? He's hot and tired, and besides, now there was no one inside to escape. Vacillating between contempt and anger, I gave myself a guided tour. Once inside the stone walls, I was outside of Africa. The sizes and shapes of the granite rock, a great temple defying the sky, did not express the African's conception of space and density. African chiefs and kings could not have ruled here. These structures did not express their way of life; the context was too restricted, un-African, emphasizing only brute muscles and power and not concerned with expressing feeling and modesty or with giving beauty and solemnity to faces and figures which paid homage to the gods they worshiped. Each tribe would no longer have had a separate universe and would have been forced to worship the granite instead of sacred art and natural gods. Elmina Castle was a place without beauty in comparison to the world outside. The cattle, color, humanity, and religion would have suffered, because in this place of European order, there was no room for the innumerable stools, masks, dolls, figures, pots, drums, rings, bangles, and decorative art—that endless treasury of Africana through which an immense love of life is expressed.

The castle was a place of business, a human stock exchange; a place of rest, waiting for the sun to rise, for the gates to open, and ears to close to the suffering sounds of naked feet. Elmina Castle was ancient, cold, regimented, a great host for shining people—like a wax museum, filled with dead things; built by rugged men with horrible smells, who did not trust the ocean, who did not like the sun—a naked sun, a yellow sun which made their white turn red.

Elmina Castle—a prison. Large rooms reserved for the officers; smaller ones for the men; holes for those who could not run fast enough. I saw each room, each rock, and was not surprised that the hole in which they had kept the female captives was next to the officers' quarters. My journey finally brought me back to the main courtroom. I stood there trying to figure it all out, where the granite men had sat waiting to pass judgment on the womb of Africa: these men of another mankind, strong, with big guns (too big to bring on one ship), men from the north who found the pathway back to where all life had come from; men with blue in their eyes, profit beating in their veins—these men, in this courtroom, had created me.

A distant Lacy, a poor farmer perhaps, named . . . well, any name but Lacy, had stood here—or on some spot like it in one of the many castles on the West African Guinea Coast— chained and pained, wondering why he and others who looked like him were leaving their perpetual summer to go beyond the land they loved. God was in heaven; he saw it all: the branding, the identification, the separation of this life from its womb. But his wrath of justice could not pierce the granite hell which he had built and blessed. He was committed in his eternal goodness to save these soul-stuffed natives once they had been whipped into shape, converted, and rehabilitated. So, after these pagans were organized, they moved from where I stood—the spot in the courtroom, the spot in African history, the beginning of Negro history—to be sold into a slavery which made their slavery look like small boys playing with sacred mythology.

We were tired and hungry—miserable, like orphans with nobody to care for us, but like God, who moves in mysterious ways—they moved us into the auction room. Each man, in single file, cut from his group, entered the room alone.

There was something sinister about this room. Someone was hiding behind the makeshift partition. . . . They could see us, but we could not see them. Bad for our psyches: our people, our kith and kin, were selling us to these strangers. "Five George Washington beads fer da nigra. . . . Do I hear six? . . . Nigra going once, going twice—sold!" To Mr. Lincoln.

Yes, the white men *sold* what the Africans *brought* to them, sometimes for beads and trinkets; the Ashanti held out for gold and guns. . . . "That's it fer today." The blue eyes had enough for today—more nigras tomorrow.

Then we were dropped into a hole. Fifty feet. Damp, dark. We tried to escape. Some found death. Tomorrow we would leave, leave the land we knew, our mothers' breasts, our rivers and fields; sweet mangoes, fu fu, thousands of years of being ourselves; giving up "beating . . . blood of the tom-tom, tom-tom blood and tom-tom," giving up our lives to sleep the long sleep of the nigger. But my distant gene, a summer's man, did not become a nigger. The Louisiana winter killed him and the granite God on his high white throne rejuvenated his witchcraft and made him over into a Negro, a proper one. So instead of dying, he gained energy and became younger. Funny—what a cycle. From Africa to Louisiana and back.

I pulled myself from my thoughts and ran back to the sea. I slept on the beach, a deathlike sleep over the blood-soaked sand, and I dreamed of black birds carrying me away. And when it was evening I awoke to the touch of the high tide and walked slowly back to the town—the remote cause of Town Two, the beginning of Essie Maes, Miss No Names, and others, throughout the world—believing in my heart that soon, probably not tomorrow, not even the next day or month, but one day soon, I would again be a summer's man . . .

> like
> the
> face
> of
> a
> god
> in
> a
> shrine.

Four Sundays later I left my state of euphoria, and on the same bus, with the same driver, I returned to Accra. That Friday, after spending five days seeing more of the capital, arguing constantly with Eve, and finally moving to the University of Ghana at Legon, some eight miles north of Accra, I met Wendell Jean Pierre, an Afro-American lecturer teaching French literature of African expression at Legon. Eve had met Wendell on her trip to Paris, for Wendell, like other Blacks from both America and the Caribbean, had lived in Europe for many years. And like the others who had come out to help President Kwame Nkrumah achieve his socialist revolution, he had become increasingly embittered by the rising current of French racism since the end of the Algerian revolution—a racism which had flowed into every level of French life.

I liked him immediately. He was warm, radical, a home boy, and although he was nearly fifteen years my senior, we had traveled much of the same ground. The major difference, and constantly a problem for Eve, was that Wendell was very much married to and in love with a Frenchwoman who had given them two wonderful sons. He extended himself beyond the usual niceties to make us comfortable at the university, a pleasant but adjusting change for most people who are accustomed to the technological efficiency of American life. Although the university was as modern as, and perhaps more beautiful than, most in its class in the States, it was connected to the wider world of Ghanaian life that was characterized by periodic breakdowns in social services which most people in a "developed" society take for granted. Sensibly, you prepared yourself for inevitable breakdowns. Weeks, sometimes months, you were without hot water, even if you were fortunate enough in the first place to be living in accommodations which had a hot-water heater. Even if you adjusted to cold showers, as I did very quickly—and liked them once I got used to them— there was still no guarantee that you would finish your shower. So you had a bucket of water near you, just in case the water was suddenly turned off in the middle of your soaping. And if there was no running water at all, one bucket of water per person was all you got. You were also wise to buy candles, and keep soft pieces of paper around, just in case of a blackout or a toilet-tissue shortage. Added to these minor irritants were the heat, rust, mold; malaria mosquitoes; harmless foot-long lizards everywhere; snakes; dishonest taxi drivers (who didn't bother me that much, because I could at least get a taxi); and the general inefficiency. Yet we were fortunate, because life in this nonindustrial society was far better at Legon than most other places in the nation.

Eve, like most women from the West, was constantly disturbed by the order of this existence. But unlike the white women, who despite the mechanics of this situation, generally lived at a higher standard than they had in Europe, she (like most of the other black women from America and the West Indies—many of whom I did not meet until after Eve finally returned to her middle-class comforts of hot baths plus racism) did not complain openly. For the Ghanaians, although they complained themselves, viewed criticisms as an expression of your disapproval of them as people, coupled with a general contempt of Ghanaian culture as a whole. Nevertheless, Eve was incessantly annoyed, and little personal differences between us were usually exaggerated; once or twice we almost exchanged blows.

This is not to say that I did not share many of Eve's adjustment neuroses and was not as guilty as she was in creating the tension in our personal lives. I was not an ascetic and had always been somewhat cynical of those individuals who claimed that they could practice without serious difficulty a life of asceticism. Rather, I was so profoundly elated to see black men with power and authority that I tried to ignore, suppress, and avoid inconveniences, complaints, and situations I felt that I could not deal with. That is, the psychological—and for a while, the political—benefits outweighed, overshadowed, if you will, made irrelevant the lack of effective social services, which intellectually I accepted as an inescapable consequence of nation building.

Beyond those neat rationalizations I had been cushioned by the romantic ruggedness of the American left. On a temporary basis extending, once, over a period of six months, I had lived in conditions in America which I can only call uncivil and ungracious, indeed harsh, but I had enjoyed it—again not *totally* liking them—because I was with people with whom I was deeply involved, individuals who had made a frontal assault on the very culture of efficiency which was missing in my present state of exile. Also, and perhaps more important, I felt that I needed to be in Africa, and I surely did not want to join either overtly or covertly the gang of European expatriates, who, as I discovered later, were complaining from a much more deep-seated level of grievances.

Wendell shared freely what he had to make us forget, including his two years of experience in the country. And Eve, although she adamantly opposed his "ugly white wife," found it increasingly easy to accept his wife's offers to let her use her bathtub and share whatever female articles she could not buy in the shops. In the meantime, Wendell was slowly—with tremendous patience—exposing Eve to the secular ethics of a coming-of-age revolutionary.

One day Wendell suggested that I, Eve, and he should drive to northern Ghana in order to get a feel of the whole country. I hesitated, because I wanted to see Dr. W. E. B. Du Bois, but Wendell, who was a prominent personage in the community of Afro-Americans in Ghana, a community I had not yet been exposed to, assured us that he could arrange an audience when we returned.

Traveling by car from the west coast up through the great Ashanti kingdom to the northern territories can be quite dangerous. Many people are killed each year in all kinds of unbelievable and freak accidents. One is forever, unless of course you have a death-wish, driving defensively on those new and very modern highways, trying to avoid stalled lorries or those parked by drivers who had gotten out to do their bush toileting; the half-naked peasant with his goods on his head, going to market; the occasional snake scooting across the road; and the important personality in government, whose underpaid chauffeur, like the bus drivers, *may* finally have learned to steer and shift (after his tenth kill) but still does not understand modern horsepower, safe speed, and why it is not nice to pass on a blind hill.

For Wendell Jean Pierre, Eve, and me, the trip to the north

included these hazards, plus others. I was driving a British car, with an American learner's permit I had never used. I was not used to the British style of driving. An American driver instinctively wants to get on the right side of the road, which from his perspective, is the *coming* rather than the *going* side. Moreover, we were trying to make this trek during the season of the rains, when the roads are forced to submit to the lust of tropical storms. But we felt young, alive, and drunk on Ghana.

In order to reach the town of Tamale by nightfall, we detoured from the main highway to a dirt road (a bush road, as it is called) right outside of the modern city of Kumasi, the capital of Ashanti. Kumasi was a passing political headache for Kwame Nkrumah's notion of nation building, since the historical developments in that region had created political and social conditions which made the Ashanti leaders more disposed to a federal structure with wide-ranging regional autonomy rather than the strong federal unitary government which the Convention People's party under Nkrumah had proposed shortly before independence.

And what a big detour! One moment we were in one world, which we understood and accepted; the next moment, with a single turn of the wheel, we entered another reality, another history—a road back to the past. A quiet road, except for the noise made by an occasional bush which broke under the impact of our fast-moving car. You could see that the men who cleared the highway had not been there for months. Now that was nice in spite of the constant obstructions to the car, because the inner bush had stretched over, and in some places, completely covered, the outer bush, and the inner growth is even lovelier than the outer—a twilight of history reaching out to be touched, vulnerable to the naked knife in a farmer's hand. I saw shapes, forms, trees, and birds too multicolored to be described; flying too fast from their eternal green to be apprehensive of the stalk of the hunter. The colors came at you like the lights of a carnival: greens, blues, reds, yellows, and colors I did not think of often—they would have been heresy for the artist who could not accept the natural integration of the original canvas, the Garden of Adam, the birthplace of Eve.

My Eve was watching too. And now that Wendell was driving, I did not have to view her beauty from the rearview mirror. She was quiet, and she looked very pensive. Her beauty kept calling to my eyes, as it had never done before. I had hardly recognized her when I met her in Guinea. Her hair was natural, her clothes plain, and I had noticed for the first time her pretty little ears. Now she was tired, fatigued, like us, by the heat, but too aware to close her large window-like eyes. The heat was long and piercing and true to what we had heard: that northern Ghana was unbearably hot and always humid.

The red mud was dead dry in spite of the previous day's rain. I had never experienced such heat and physical discomfort, not even in the place I thought was the hottest of the universe: Route 66, on which I had traveled to see an Indian reservation, from Los Angeles through Arizona, New Mexico, and Texas in mid-July. And strangely enough, this little nameless road looked and felt like one of the narrow dirt roads my father had traveled (before he became an urban-based doctor) to see his country patients. There are many nameless roads in countries like Ghana, a connecting footpath between the two Africas: traditional and modern. Ghanaians from the modern half would call them "proper bush highways," paths of life, supply routes between two changing cultures, which depend on each other and are trying to merge.

On both sides of this living highway, through the high bush, were living people: village and tribal people, young and old, chiefs and ju ju men; people who could not read English or French but who could speak of man in their own tongue—a language without cold wars, from a culture free of our problems; adjusted and natural people, who got from their land a subsistence; a beautiful people, who did not yet know about the power of the "Omnipotent Administrator" but who loved life nevertheless; a people who believed in Adam but not his stepson Smith; nor did they worship Marilyn Monroe or need Malcolm X.

Indeed, the new route brought us closer to the Westernized version of Africa: it brought us face to face with bush Africa, naked Africa, the Africa which is *developed*, although social scientists tell us it is *developing*. An Africa which is more concerned with subsistent compassion than with sophistication.

Suddenly Wendell jammed on the brakes, and we were thrown in disarray, for the car had almost turned over.

"What's wrong *this* time?" Eve asked.

Before Wendell could reply, we saw the reason for his action. To the right of our car was a Ghanaian woman who had apparently seen the car coming and was waiting near the road's edge until it was safe to pass. Wendell had stopped suddenly because it was difficult to tell from her movements whether she was going to wait or take the chance.

The road woman was very black, like ebony after it is shined. Except for disfiguring tribal marks, she was beautiful; indeed, she was exquisite, a picture of self-containment, a perfect form of the environment which had produced her.

"Well, Wendell, what are we waiting for?" Eve said impatiently.

But Wendell couldn't answer. His eyes were fixed on the road. As another black man, I could tell by his face (eyes wide open, with just a slight smile) what was going around in his mind: Goddamn, just look at that. . . . My God, she sure is fine. . . . What in the hell is she doing out here?

That is a strange kind of thought; in fact, rather contradictory (perhaps even a little chauvinistic), because in effect you are thinking, she does not really belong here because the men couldn't be foolish enough to let her out of their sight. Also, and perhaps more important, Wendell was thinking, as I was, as any sane black man would be, If I only had a woman like that. . . . Her man can't possibly be treating her as she should be treated.

Knowing Wendell somewhat, I decided he was probably (I was trying to be fair, because he was a happily married man) figuring out how he was going to get back there.

I thought she was near forty, but Wendell assured us (very emphatically) that she was nearer to twenty. Hard work, little leisure, well-defined female roles, inadequate diet, endemic diseases, and recurring malaria had robbed her of some of her youth, but whatever the culture in the bush which had made her older while she was still young, it had not made her ugly and tired out, like some of the Indian women I had seen on their concentration camping grounds in America. And she was a proud woman. She did not look at us, although I could tell by her bit of outward anxiety that she knew of our eyes on her. She was unbelievably human. She was pregnant, at least six months, and tied to her back with a piece of cloth that matched her dress was a sleeping child who appeared to be about two years old. And on her head, with a little pad of matching cloth, she carried at least two hundred pounds of wood, with the grace of a traditional Japanese dancer: more wood than I could have carried in my arms. She did not smile, and she was not angry, but seemed a little impatient, as though she was trying to tell us that Sunday was not a day of rest for her. Finally she looked quickly in our direction, adjusted the cloth around her child, and with much effort, crossed the road and entered the world of the bush. As we drove off, I thought about Senghor's lines, "When shall I sit at the table of your dark breast . . .? Perhaps, beloved, I shall fall tomorrow, on a restless earth. . . . And you will weep in the twilight for the glowing voice that sang your black beauty."

Now it was miles from our sudden stop. We were passing through a dense forest and we saw a strange and unwelcome scene. There, in the middle of a clearing, in the middle of Ghana, in the middle of nowhere, in the middle of the twentieth century, next to a forest infested with mosquitoes, we saw a white South African family—Wallace, Beastina, and their two children—having a picnic.

They flagged us down, and Wendell, a civil man, stopped to see what they wanted. The insipid-looking white man was attired in white Bermuda shorts, white knee socks, and an Albert Schweitzer-type colonial hat. His wife was indescribably hideous, and it was quite obvious that her blotchy skin and blond hair were unsuited for this climate. She was also pregnant. (According to a Ghana gynecologist we had met, white women seem to be able to have more children in Africa; he had cynically added, "Probably the force of the sun.") When they discovered that we were Americans they seemed relieved.

"Americans. Fine; we love America," said the white man.

"We are Afro-Americans," Wendell replied quickly. "And believe me, that's quite a difference."

"We like all Americans. Thousands of Americans come to South Africa every year. We have very friendly relations with your country."

Wendell was impatient. What in the hell did they want anyway? Eve was looking around in disgust, and I was thinking about a devil who had come to another garden to pervert Adam and Eve.

"What do you want?" Wendell asked with tremendous hostility.

I felt no need to say anything to this devil, because I had already proven to Eve that I could not whip every white man I met. If Marcus Garvey, from whom she quoted so often, said that every black man could beat any ten white men, then I was still very much *colored*. For I had not been able to beat even one. The fight had occurred on a New York subway in the heat of the rush hour. Some white man pushed Eve and apologized five times, but was reprimanded by her nevertheless. Then I stepped in, not so much to tame the beast as to prove my manhood to Eve. And this white man, twice my size, with underground working experience, had a good time on my head, then threw me off the crowded subway, whereupon the police finished opening my skull.

"Might we use your automobile lift? We don't mean to trouble you, but we have a flat tubeless."

The man was afraid. Wendell hesitated for some time. The tension mounted. I thought Wendell might kill them all and bury them in the forest, but I guess he gave the man what he asked for because he did not wish to stain the African soil. With no conversation from us, and with amazing speed, this white man fixed his car, and we continued our drive north.

Frankly, I was rather shocked to discover that a South African White was working in Ghana. I had seen and knew about other European expatriates working in various capacities, but a South African was another cup of tea. I was even more outdone when Wendell explained that this flat-tire man was not alone. Other South Africans ran a big gold field near

Kumasi, and there were a few others, doctors and teachers, working in the country. The government had nationalized three of the five mines now operating in the country, but the biggest, richest, and most productive were in the hands of these people. And, in fact, H. M. Basner, a white communist from South Africa, had a daily column in the *Ghanaian Times* (privately owned but government controlled), and it was common knowledge that he wrote speeches for Nkrumah and sometimes acted as a special consultant.

It was difficult to ascertain whether Wendell disapproved of these arrangements. Anyone who talked to him for two minutes could vouch for his militant black nationalist views. He was vociferously critical of France, more critical of America, a champion of Nkrumah's dream of a United States of Africa, and had been constantly taken to task by his university students, who called him Mr. Negritude and the Black Racist. But in the car (and on other occasions) he was never critical of President Nkrumah, and by extension, very cleverly rationalized the presence of those South Africans in the country. Most of them, he said, were very progressive and had struggled for the Blacks in South Africa before they were forced into exile; they had done good work for the government, and from all appearances, seemed loyal. Nevertheless, I felt that he had some serious reservations. Eve confirmed my suspicion later and assured me that he disapproved completely but did not yet feel disposed to take us into his confidence. Besides, she felt that Wendell thought that the President basically knew what he was doing.

Unfortunately for this trip, we did not reach the northern territory. The rains had destroyed the main road, and it was virtually impossible to continue. I was naturally disappointed, but looked forward to meeting Dr. Du Bois.

IX

Dusk of Dawn

WILLIAM EDWARD BURGHARDT DU BOIS had been the intellectual and political model of many in my generation.

He had become still more significant for the Blacks in the early nineteen sixties, because he left for Ghana (after many years of trying to get his passport returned for having "defied" the State Department). To the surprise of many, he became a Ghanaian citizen; denounced America, saying that there was no hope for social justice without radical changes in the basic institutions and that socialist Africa was the future of mankind. The radicals among us, with much less understanding of the American political culture than our intellectual leader, were coming to the same conclusion, especially after Robert Williams, leader of the Monroe Movement, was framed by United States government officials and forced into exile. Yet one question about Dr. Du Bois during this period had remained: Why had he joined the Communist party? I intended to ask him that question when I spoke with him.

But seeing the Old Man was not as easy as Wendell had anticipated. A great deal of security clearance was involved, because Du Bois was in close, indeed intimate, contact with the President. Being an Afro-American around that time was not necessarily an asset. I did not understand until I tried to see the Old Man why there had been signs around Accra reading "BEWARE OF AFRO-AMERICANS." From a reliable source we learned that certain Ghanaian officials had reason to believe that several Afro-Americans—possibly working for the Central Intelligence Agency, possibly not—had been involved in a conspiracy to assassinate Kwame Nkrumah. I do not believe that any of these officials entertained the notion that the same fate was in the works for Dr. Du Bois, but the security hand had been extended, and everyone remotely concerned with the Ghanaian revolution was touched by it.

On another level, Du Bois was being protected from tourists whose only serious business was to take the historical picture for the scrapbook back home. The Old Man loved people, and if it was left solely to him, would have met everyone; but his health was failing, and he needed all of his remaining time to devote to one of the major projects which had brought him to the country. For, at the age of ninety-four, he had founded and become director of the Secretariat for an Encyclopedia Africana in Accra. From America we knew about this proposed and long overdue project. In March 1962, not long after the Old Man arrived, work was begun. It was sponsored by the Ghana Academy of Sciences, and the government of Ghana had underwritten the cost of starting the efforts. The objectives of the Secretariat were to plan, guide, and coordinate the work of assembling, organizing, and publishing research which was *authentically African in viewpoint* and (as their monthly publication, *For Cooperation Toward an Encyclopedia Africana*, had said) "at the same time a product of scientific scholarship. . . . The Secretariat, the Director wishes it understood, is not merely a dream or a project, it is a directorate."

Because of President Nkrumah's personal interest in the project and Du Bois' presence in Ghana, Accra was the logical site at which to prepare the encyclopedia, in which despite the fact that many detractors had called it "Nkrumah's political history," all Africa was to participate equally. Advice and counsel of eminent scholars in various African states had been sought. The editorial board included Africans from other states, and in due course, funds for research and publication would come from other independent African nations. At the same time, it was the intention of the Founder, the Proximate Cause of Pan-Africanism, that the African scholars would draw on the skills of non-African scholars who had already advanced *accurate interpretation of African civilizations and culture.*

Favorable reactions to these endeavors had come from all over the world, including some from many well-known scholars: Dr. E. Franklin Frazier of Howard University; Dr. Melville J. Herskovits of Northwestern University; George M. Johnson, president of the University of Nigeria; Basil Davidson, free-lance historian and journalist in England; Kuo-Mo-jo, Academy of Sciences, Peking; The Honorable Jamal Mohammed Ahmed, ambassador of the Republic of the Sudan, Addis Ababa, Ethiopia; and Dr. Horace Mann Bond of Atlanta University, whose nephew Max Bond became the personal architect of Nkrumah.

On December 18, 1962, the year before I arrived in the country, W. E. B. Du Bois, ninety-four and ailing, formally launched his project in a historic speech at the University of Ghana:

I wish to express my sincere thanks to those of you here who have accepted the invitation of our Secretariat to participate in this conference. . . .

Had there been any doubts in your mind of the importance of African studies, I am sure the papers and discussions of the past week have dispelled them. The wide attendance of the First International Congress of Africanists attests the almost feverish interest throughout the world in the hitherto "Dark" continent. Remains, therefore, for me *only to lay before you the importance of an encyclopedia Africana based in Africa and compiled by Africans.* . . .

Some of you ask if an encyclopedia Africana at this time is not premature . . . too ambitious an undertaking for African scholars to attempt . . . enough scientifically proven information ready for publication. . . . Our answer is that it is long overdue. Yet, it is logical that such a work had to wait for independent Africans to carry it out. We know that there does exist much scientific knowledge of Africa which has never been brought together. We have little-known works of African scholars of the past in North Africa, in the Sudan, in Egypt. Al Azhar University of Sankore made large collections; *Présence Africaine* has already brought to light much written material in the French language. We can, therefore, begin; remembering always that an encyclopedia is never a finished or complete body of information. Research and study must be long and continuous. We can collect, organize, and publish knowledge as it emerges. The encyclopedia must be seen as a living effort which grows and changes—which will expand through the years as more and more material is gathered from all parts of Africa. . . .

It is true that scientific written records do not exist in most parts of this vast continent, but the time is now for beginning. The encyclopedia hopes to eliminate the artificial boundaries created on the continent by colonial masters. Designations such as British Africa, French Africa, Black Africa, Islamic Africa too often serve to keep alive differences which in large part have been imposed on Africans by outsiders. The encyclopedia must have research units throughout West Africa, North Africa, East, Central, and South Africa, which will gather and record information for these geographical sections of the continent. The encyclopedia is concerned with Africa as a whole.

It is true that there are not now enough trained African scholars available for this gigantic task. In the early stages we have need of the technical skills in research which have been highly developed in other parts of the world. We have already asked for and to a most gratifying degree been granted the unstinted cooperation and assistance of the leading institute of African studies outside Africa. Many of you who have gathered here from distant lands can, and I believe will, make valuable contributions to this undertaking. And you can assist us in finding capable African men and women who can carry the responsibilities of this work in their own country and to their people. For it is African scholars themselves who will create the ultimate *Encyclopedia Africana*.

My interest in this enterprise goes back to 1909, when I first attempted to launch an encyclopedia Africana while still teaching history at Atlanta University in Georgia, U.S.A. Though a number of distinguished scholars in the United States and various European countries consented to serve as sponsors, the more practical need of securing financial backing for the projected encyclopedia was not solved, and the project had to be abandoned. Again, in 1931, a group of American scholars met at Howard University and agreed upon the necessity of preparing an encyclopedia of the Negro, using this term in its broadest sense. There was much organizational work and research done in the preparation, but once again, the undertaking could not be carried through because money could not be secured. Educational foundations had doubts about a work of this kind being accomplished under the editorship of Negroes. We are deeply grateful to the president of Ghana and to the government of this independent African state for inviting us to undertake this important task here, where the necessary funds for beginning this colossal work have been provided. After all, this is where the work should be done—in Africa, sponsored by Africans, for Africa. The encyclopedia will be carried through.

Much has happened in Africa in the last twenty years. Yet, something of what I wrote in the preparatory volume of the *Encyclopedia of the Negro*, which was published in 1945, will bear repeating now. I quote: "Present thought and action are all too often guided by old and discarded theories of race and heredity, by misleading emphasis and silence of former histories. These conceptions are passed on to younger generations of students by current textbooks, popular histories and even public discussion. . . . Our knowledge of Africa today is not, of course, entirely complete; there are many gaps where further information and more careful study is needed; but this is the case in almost every branch of knowledge. Knowledge is never complete, and in few subjects does a time arrive when an encyclopedia is demanded because no further information is expected. Indeed, the need for an encyclopedia is greatest when a stage is reached where there is a distinct opportunity to bring together and set down a clear and orderly statement of the facts already known and agreed upon, for the sake of establishing a base for further advance and further study."

For these reasons and under these circumstances it would seem that an encyclopedia Africana is of vital importance to Africa as a whole and to the world at large. I now have the pleasure of declaring opened this Conference for the Encyclopedia Africana.

Against this background it was easy to understand and accept why the Ghana government unofficially was shielding a great talent from unnecessary interruptions. I was more than honored to wait like everyone else.

Indeed, politics in Ghana was proving to be an interesting but confusing experience. Perhaps a brief glance at modern-day Ghanaian political history might help to further elucidate some of my observations. The Second World War was a great impetus to the cause of African liberation. In Ghana, as elsewhere in the colonial world, a predominately nonwhite world which had been under European rule (primarily British and French) since 1885, the colonial regime had been weakened. Britian and France tried to recoup their lost strength by introducing wide social and political reforms in their colonies. But it was too late. Colonial rule was at an end. The colonial culture itself had created a new African, and the results of the war had given this new class even more reason to believe that Africans could always govern themselves.

In Ghana, and again elsewhere in the new world arising, political groups emerged to give explicit expression to this intense anticolonial feeling and also to chart a course for the new day when African nationalists would govern and rule. The United Gold Coast Convention (UGCC) was Ghana's official nationalist group, organized by wealthy middle-class lawyers and traders. Lacking the organizational skills to create a nationalist party, Kwame Nkrumah, then a student radical in England, was invited to be organizing secretary. When Mr. Nkrumah arrived in Ghana in December of 1947, he was thirty-eight years old and had been out of the country twelve years. Almost immediately, the young, active secretary was at odds with the men who had hired him. In his autobiography, *Ghana: The Autobiography of Kwame Nkrumah*, he said that he regarded the UGCC as a movement "backed almost entirely by reactionaries, middle-class lawyers, and merchants."

Kwame Nkrumah had a different brand of political ethics. Influenced very much by George Padmore, C. L. R. James, Dr. W. E. B. Du Bois, men with radical, Marxist, and pan-Africanist orientation, this young man wanted to organize a party with a mass-base national character and socialist objectives. In a bitter controversy with his employers, he broke away from the UGCC and formed, with the help of certain sections of the labor movement and other groups, the Convention People's party (CPP). Carrying out brilliant and well-calculated moves, the CPP won the elections of 1950, 1954, and 1956, forcing the British in March 1957 to grant independence to the first African state in Africa south. Nkrumah emerged a popular nationalist and international hero, particularly for Blacks, inside and outside Africa, who were still resisting various forms of colonial oppression. By 1959 he had become a progressive force in the revolutionary world of colored people. And Ghana's plans for economic reconstruction had become a model for other African, and non-African, leaders who shared his views of socialism and rapid plans for industrialization. Ghana became the tongue of the oppressed elsewhere in Africa, and freedom fighters from all over Africa flocked there for leadership and assistance. Moreover, Ghana had evolved a militant left-leaning foreign policy, which became highly critical and condemnatory of America for her attempts to strengthen existing colonial regimes. Last, but surely most important to people of African descent in every white racist society, Nkrumah called for the elimination of racial discrimination and prejudice, a United States of Africa, the restoration of African history, black consciousness, and the creation of a modern African personality.

This had been his glory outside of his political kingdom, a name given to Ghana because Nkrumah had declared that he was "a Marxist-Leninist, a nondenominational Christian," and said, "seek ye first the political kingdom, and all other things will be added unto you." Now that I was inside, it was obvious that sections in the population did not share my image of this great leader. The middle class had never forgiven him for bringing all those "uncultured" men into power, and general complaints about corruption, one-party rule, detention camps for security prisoners were heard.

At this point I had no real opinions. I would wait and see. Then, too, I was more immediately concerned about the status of Afro-Americans in Ghana. (At the insistence of President Nkrumah, all Blacks from America were referred to as Afro-Americans.) Because if our guys were involved in an attempt to murder Nkrumah, all of us *in* or *coming into* the country were probably being watched. We had heard in Freetown that half of the population was working for the government as security agents, and we had been cautioned to be wary of individuals who became "too friendly too soon." But given the pro-British character of the Sierra Leonean political culture and the overtly conservative sources from which these rumors had come, I completely ignored them. For if half of the population was needed to eliminate subversion, then more power to them.

Now, however, I became exceedingly paranoid, even though I had nothing whatsoever to hide. I constantly looked over my shoulder, under the bed, remained in my room when the stewards were cleaning it, and was very careful about what I said. In fact, Wendell told us—and his words made a deep impression on me—that except for a selected few, the Ghanaians were more suspicious of the Afro-Americans *who were most critical of America*, on the theory that professional American agents might try to infiltrate by identifying with existing anti-American feeling in the country. Things became so confused in my mind that I even suspected Wendell of being an agent for Nkrumah. Maybe I shouldn't even try to see the Old Man; or tour the country; or write home; or ask questions.

Two or three times I thought maybe I shouldn't be there. For the psychology of a black American exiled in an African country, you dig, creates a strange mixture of irrational reactions if his legitimacy is in question. Put simply, you are there because you hated America; given this hatred—blind and complete—coupled with the knowledge that the CIA is constantly subverting, embarrassing, confusing, disrupting governments which carry out or are thought to be carrying out policies which *seriously* jeopardize American interests, either in that country or elsewhere, you want to do anything within your power to help the country you have temporarily adopted. But if you think that you are being watched (which you are), it becomes difficult to function honestly and creatively. And you find yourself making statements, doing things—sometimes exaggeratedly—all in the hope of proving that you are really loyal to the revolution.

In any case, these were my feelings, and probably Eve's. Actually we never discussed it, and one day I hated myself because I suspected her first of being an American agent and then of being an agent for the Ghana government. I should emphasize that the fact that you have a clean conscience is basically irrelevant. Your beingness is interpreted and judged by men and women who may not understand *you*, and if they do, they may want to make political capital out of your bankruptcy. But more important, you have come a long way, and more than anything on earth, want to belong; be liked; eventually loved.

Finally, but only momentarily, my sanity(?) was restored: we were given an audience with Dr. Du Bois.

The night we were scheduled to see the Old Man I became very nervous. Added to my other concerns was a thought which hadn't occurred to me before: that the man we were to see shortly was almost a hundred years old, and what can a twenty-four-year old ask of a century? I had a lot of questions, but somehow none of them seemed real or significant.

Dr. Du Bois lived in the Cantonment. By Ghanaian standards it was considered plush; by American standards it measured up to the homes lower-middle-class whites would own in a very small Northern community. But it was the Sugar Hill of Ghana, because members of the cabinet, high court, parliament, high-ranking civil servants, professors, and important European expatriates lived there. Also Cantonment was the area where most of the diplomats lived, except the Chinese, Russians, and Americans, who all lived closer to the president's office.

If you were Ghanaian or an expatriate working for the government, the rent was next to nothing. The low rent (plus a loan to purchase a car) was a part of your salary. The houses —put up for British personnel during the colonial period— were simply built, usually with inexpensive lumber, and surprisingly modest. Most had two bedrooms, bath, a large living-dining area; some had a study. At the end of a large yard was a small, very small house with two closetlike rooms for the four servants and their ever-increasing families. To protect the (smaller) families in the big houses from mosquitoes, moths, June bugs, snakes, and other insects, of formidable size, which buzzed or crawled around at night, there were porch screens, and just in case of emergency, mosquito canopies. For the poor servants, without even a bathroom, no such amenities were provided.

Since independence, very little had been done to change the

natures or relationships of these colonial domiciles. The house in which Dr. Du Bois and his charming wife Shirley lived was typical, or perhaps a bit more elegant than most because of the pretty green hedges surrounding it.

They were standing on the screened porch as we drove up. In most homes like this one, the servants would have greeted us, but Dr. Du Bois' servants did very little domestic work, spending most of their time studying courses he had prepared for them. In fact, the Old Man did not want servants, but like a *few* others in the country—both Ghanaians and ex-patriates—who felt that having them was at variance with their conception of a "people's revolution," he accepted them as part of the natural order of life, aware that, since the government hadn't yet expanded its industrial base, this source of employment gave landless peasants in an urban economy sub-sistence pocket money. To rationalize his conflicts, he democratized the relationship, taught the servants useful skills, and unlike most other "masters," paid them a living wage.

Dr. Du Bois did not look well. Nevertheless, he was a gracious host. He was very interested in all of his guests, and I reminded him that I had met him before, in San Francisco at a peace rally. That led him into a discussion of American political history, and for nearly an hour he held us in absolute silence. His mind was clear; his words were lucid; and with tremendous honesty and modesty, he re-examined many of his earlier political positions. He reviewed with amazing accuracy his relationships with leading men and women of yesterday's history, and said, nearing the end of his talk, "I think that maybe the greatest difference between Booker T. and myself was that he had felt the lash and I had not." Dr. Du Bois did not discuss his motives for belatedly joining the Communist party, and for a number of reasons, I was not compelled to ask why.

Two days later, August 27, 1963, when hundreds of other Americans were marching on Washington, D.C., demanding reform, William Edward Burghardt Du Bois died, believing that such reforms were impossible. The news of his death was brought to the marchers who had gathered before the American embassy in Accra—to protest there what others were protesting back home—by Julian Mayfield, who would now become the political head of the community of Afros. With tears in his eyes, he managed to say, " 'The problem of the twentieth century is the problem of the color line.' The Old Man is dead. It is an end of an era."

A century was over. The marchers stopped. They had known Du Bois, of his illness, but did not want to believe. Maya Maka, an Afro-American teaching music at the university, came forth and sang the Old Man's favorite spiritual, "Let Us Cheer the Weary Traveller." Then, as they thought Du Bois would want them to, the protestors continued their march.

The next day, from early in the morning, hundreds of people entered the Cantonment to view his remains. Du Bois was dressed in the kind of brown suit Chinese leaders wear and was surrounded by all the traditional symbols which are always present at the burial of an African chief. Everyone passed the open coffin, which had been placed in a makeshift African hut. All looked in; a few prayed; a Muslim leader chanted a prayer in Arabic; a market woman put a flower on his chest; a few cried; most were very quiet. Even the cold war was relaxed, as the Russians, Americans, and Chinese came to the same historic spot to pay their last respects and comfort his mourning wife, Shirley Graham Du Bois.

The American representative, a Southern cracker, was obscene. For the second time in my life, I entertained thoughts of murder. What in the hell was he doing here? As if I didn't know. Immoral. Motherfucker. Representing a government which could never accommodate the likes of Du Bois. An evil white hand, which hit him while living, now, for political reasons, extends the same bloody hand around a widow it has not earned the right to touch. The cracker's presence desecrated the meaning of the sacred service. The Chinese were making their own political show, but it was a different kind of performance. They were there all day. They helped. They were not artificial and frozen. They were relevant—they understood the hurt the Great One had suffered.

Then, almost from out of the sky, I saw the President— Osagyefo Dr. Kwame Nkrumah—standing in the hut over his dead mentor. Security was good that day. My first look at

Nkrumah and my last look at Du Bois came together in my
skull and hammered home with unmistakable clarity that the
black man did have a history. Here was a part of it happening
before my eyes. I wish every black soul in the universe could
have seen that sight. It was beautiful. Do you hear me? Beautiful. My feelings, which began to kill the white man in me,
were expressed by the Senegalese poet, David Diop: "In your
presence I rediscovered my name. . . . And that turns love
into a boundless river."

And then, with tears in his eyes, Kwame Nkrumah reached
into the living soul of black folk and kissed him. Closed the
casket and gave "the sign of brotherhood which comes to
nourish the dreams of men."

William Edward Burghardt Du Bois, born February 23,
1868, died August 27, 1963, was laid to final rest, with full
military honor, on the afternoon of August 29 at a spot some
fifty yards from the pounding ocean, in a special grave next
to his friend George Padmore, just outside the walls of another
slave castle at Osu, residence of the President of Ghana. The
state burial brought thousands and thousands of people. Some
understood, but for those who did not (the little boys and
girls standing by the road, watching the coffin go by) it was
not important; some day they would know that that dead man
had started a history which had made this very day and others
to come possible . . . "days sparkling with ever-new joy."

Directly following the interment, Du Bois' last words to the
world were read:

It is much more difficult in theory than actually to say the last
goodbye to one's loved ones and friends and to all the familiar
things of this life.

I am going to take a long, deep, and endless sleep. This is
not a punishment, but a privilege, to which I have looked forward
for years.

I have loved my work; I have loved people and my play; but
always I have been uplifted by the thought that what I have done
well will live long and justify my life, that what I have done
ill or never finished can now be handed on to others for endless
days to be finished, perhaps better than I could have done.

And that peace will be my applause.

One thing alone I charge you. As you live, believe in life! Always human beings will live and progress to a greater, broader, and fuller life.

The only possible death is to lose belief in this truth, simply because the great end comes slowly, because time is long.

Goodbye.

Messages of condolence from institutions, organizations, and individuals in all walks of life came to his widow by the thousands. Kenya's Honorable Mr. Jomo Kenyatta wrote, "News of the death of your husband and my old friend has brought great sorrow to me and the people of Kenya. The world will always remember his long life of dedication to the cause of complete freedom of Africa and his vision of pan-Africanism. Our loss in this great statesman can never be replaced."

And the evening following the burial, Kwame Nkrumah made a special broadcast to the nation:

We mourn the death of Dr. William Edward Burghardt Du Bois, a great son of Africa. . . . Dr. Du Bois in a long life span . . . achieved distinction as a poet, historian, and sociologist. He was an undaunted fighter for the emancipation of colonial and oppressed people and pursued this objective throughout his life.

The fields of literature and science were enriched by his profound and searching scholarship, a brilliant literary talent, and a keen and penetrating mind. The essential quality of Dr. Du Bois' life and achievement can be summed up in a single phrase, "intellectual honesty and integrity."

It was the late George Padmore who described Dr. Du Bois as the greatest scholar the Negro race has produced and one who always upheld the right of Africans to govern themselves.

I asked Dr. Du Bois to come to Ghana to pass the evening of his life with us and also to spend his remaining years in compiling an encyclopedia Africana, a project which is part of his whole intellectual life.

We mourn his death. May he live in our memory not only as a distinguished scholar, but a great African patriot. Dr. Du Bois is a phenomenon. May he rest in peace.

X

Black Bodies in Exile

PEACE FOR DU BOIS. . . . But no peace for me. First, Eve returned to America. Her decision to leave was not sudden but was the culmination of our growing inability to decide on what we wanted from each other, and ultimately, I imagine, what we intended to do with our lives. Eve stood closer to the level of decision making. What was missing in the relationship was a basic sense of direction, which we agreed should come from me. I loved her. And like most women who can share in this wonderful emotion, she wanted to get married. But every ingredient of marriage I had grown up with had been thrown in disarray.

Rightly, Eve defined this confusion as irresponsibility, insecurity, and a lack of motivation to take what we mutually had and create something positive. I agreed. But my apprehensions went much further. My only conception of marriage had come out of the wilderness of my American experiences. I had seen the right and the left, the Negro, black and the white. From there, not only was I beginning to question the effectiveness of such a relationship but also to reject most of the values which went into making such a situation possible. I had seen beautiful individuals enter the sacred togetherness, only to end up hating each other. I rejected such statements as "Well, he [or she] was not the *right* person," "What they needed was a little more understanding," "Well, they just didn't love each other enough."

Certainly there was some truth in these characterizations, but at the bottom of them all, I saw what I thought was a far more fundamental dilemma, which challenged the very nature of the institution itself. How was it possible to have a reasonable, healthy, and creative marriage in a society which programed you into neurosis? How could I function in a world of competitive and inhuman values and then function sanely at home with a set of compassionate ones? And given the awareness and acceptance of this objective reality, what secret power could I muster in my private strength to fight off the inevitable bitterness and hostility which hung over the threshold of American households? Add to these problems my black skin, and the level of human alienation must rise. How was I as a black male to give credence to my manhood in a white male racist chauvinistic society?

What I could not explain was that the crisis of the Western marriage, especially for Blacks, was not substantially a result of personal inadequacies, but the inability of its members to create new norms which were consistent with their political and social experiences. Our society had trained us to have *dates* but had not prepared us to form meaningful relationships. What should be the definition of "love" for people who have been oppressed? Is black manhood an American myth? What is the role of the black female in such a situation? Education of the children? And more important, since none of these questions can be answered in one generation, what kind of marriage can we have in the interim?

Eve accused me of rationalization and an inability to surmount the personal hostilities I had internalized as a result of my mother and father, and alternatively offered me the black guide to the human heart. I agreed but attempted to show her that the failure of our family and most of the other families I knew was in part a manifestation of these very problems. As far as her black guide was concerned, I was only beginning to find my way. But then, how can you convince a woman in love? In any case we could not come to terms, and Eve arrogantly left, saying that when I was ready to deal with her, she would return.

In those days it took me a while to recoup from such setbacks. The little peace I found was suddenly interrupted. Eve hadn't been gone a week before I was visited by two agents from the CIA. Naturally they didn't call themselves that; as I remember, they represented themselves as having some vague connection with the United States Information Service. And as I was an American national, they were "concerned with my safety and protection." I must admit that at first I tended to accept their obvious credentials. My status in the country was rather tenuous: no contacts, no immediate job prospects, no return ticket, and a temporary visa which was up for expiration. Later, after they questioned me exhaustively, I had every reason to suspect them of being with the CIA.

The talkative agent was black (better call him colored) and the note-taking agent was white. (Political integration in the tropics.) They knew almost everything about me, even treasured trivia which had gone from my memory. They asked such questions as "Why are you here?" "Who sent you?"; questions about Du Bois and other people, whom I did not know; and a thousand other questions which made little sense to me. I answered only one question directly. "Why am I here? To get a nice sun tan."

At the end of the inquisition they cautioned me to "stay clear of the dissident expatriate element in Ghana" and *strongly recommended* that I leave before I got myself in real trouble. Finally they left.

Now I was puzzled and a little anxious. Why had they really come? Suppose they had been seen visiting me by the Ghanaian Central Intelligence? I walked around in my university room for almost four hours, trying to figure everything out. What would I do? . . . Wendell was out of town. . . . If only Eve were here. . . . Eventually, without coming out for dinner, I worried myself to sleep.

The next morning, bright and early, I went to visit an Afro-American who was subletting a professor's bungalow until school started in October. I wanted to share my experience and get some general advice. I had met a few members of the Afro-American community, but except for Wendell and a man called Preston King, most of them had said very little about politics.

"Hello. Anyone home? It's Leslie Lacy," I said as I knocked on the screen door.

"We're here. Come in," the woman replied rather indifferently.

In the room with the Afro woman were two South African friends. I had not met, except in the States, any black South African. I had heard from summer students at the university, and also from Wendell, that Ghana was a political sanctuary for South African freedom fighters. Nkrumah, consistent with his belief in African unity, had restored their dignity by giving these landless revolutionaries jobs, free social services, and a lively political environment in order to continue, from Accra, their efforts to overthrow the white fascist government in South Africa. Also, it was common knowledge that the South African refugees and the American Afros had a very close relationship both politically and socially. In fact, one of the prominent Afro women was married to one of the political intellectuals in the Pan-Africanist Congress, an all-African freedom movement which had successfully cut itself from the African National Congress, a group comparable to the American Communist party, at least ideologically.

I was quickly introduced to the South African brothers, who did not smile when I smiled, and the sister asked me to sit down.

"Well, Mr. Lacy, what brings you here at this hour?" Her words were very businesslike, and her eyes looked into mine.

"Let me say first of all that it is a pleasure to meet genuine freedom fighters. As you probably know, we have a lot of brothers in the States who preach revolution but very few men like yourselves, who are willing to make the personal sacrifices you undoubtedly have to make."

"Get to the point, Mr. Lacy. The reason for your visit?" Her voice was sweet, but I had the feeling that she was very impatient.

"Sure." I quickly responded and lit up a cigarette. "Well,

yesterday two white men—one black, the other white, and both American—came to see me. They asked me a lot of questions, mostly about the political situation here, and I have reason to believe that they were working for the Central Intelligence Agency."

"How do you know that?" asked the sister. "Has your experience endowed you with the vision to spot the CIA?"

"No, not really."

"So how could you tell?" She was now just a bit cynical.

"Well." I paused. "I just thought they might be."

"Okay. So two asses from the CIA came to see you. What does that have to do with your visit here?"

"I just thought I should tell somebody."

"Why us?" She sounded like the Negro fellow I had tried to introduce myself to in the lunchroom my first days in Boston.

"Well, because you are in the Afro-American community, and I was a little anxiety ridden and had no one else to talk with."

"What Afro-American community are you talking about?"

"The one here in Ghana."

"Have you ever seen it?"

"Not exactly."

"Does it have officers and a constitution?"

"I don't know."

"Then, Mr. Lacy, how can you speak about an Afro-American community?"

"Well, because it's common knowledge that there is one." I was somewhat uneasy at this point.

"Did the CIA tell you that?" Her voice was deadly serious. They all stared at me intently.

"Now, wait a minute. Why are you playing games with me? Two men came to my room and questioned me, and I felt that you could give me some advice."

"Mr. Lacy. That is your name, is it not?"

"Yes, it is." Now I was just a little annoyed, but underneath, I was a bit frightened.

"No one is playing games," she continued. "I just find it rather strange, quite strange, that you would come here to tell us about the CIA."

"Maybe this is the season for recruiting agents," the South African called Joe said sarcastically. The others laughed.

"Then why would they come to me?"

"Now, you can answer that better than we can."

"I resent that tone in your voice."

"First of all, Negro, you don't come into my house and resent anything. If there is any resentment here, it will come from me." She was firm and combative.

"But—"

"We have," the sister interrupted, "to go now. I suggest you take your problem to the local authorities, or better still, to the American embassy. Good day, Mr. Lacy." She got up and showed me out the door.

Nervously I returned to my room, to nurse a now worse case of paranoia. That evening a group of men from the Afro-American community came calling. I happily greeted them and instantly repeated—this time without interruption—my encounter with the CIA. They believed only one thing: that I got excited when I talked. They listened like indifferent men who are convinced of your crime and pretend to be concerned, hoping that you will confess. That was enough for me. I showed them out.

Months passed, and before long, a lively and healthy bunch of students returned from their between-term holiday. I enrolled as a graduate student in the Institute of African Studies and got a job as an instructor in the Department of Political Science. I assumed that my political loyalties had been confirmed, and from time to time I had seen and had had friendly informal conversations with different members of the community of black bodies exiled in Ghana.

Black bodies in Ghana? A Ghanaian friend of mine called us that because he said we were weird. "Weird" may not have described us, but we were probably strange to some, disjointed to others. On the whole I think we were a rather fascinating group, joined together in an amorphous community to express from different points of experience and knowledge our dislike and outrage for American racialism. Out of that madness we had come to this West African state, pressed by the words of Countee Cullen—"What is Africa to me?"—hoping to find for an incurable American sickness a drug of identity, a feeling of kinship with Africa and its "strong bronzed men . . . women from whose loins I sprang."

Consciously and unconsciously our presence was not just a second to that motion which had indicted America. More significantly, we were a confirmation, of immense importance, of those black voices—some loud, like Marcus Garvey, some adventurous, like Paul Cuffee, clever, like Martin Robinson Delany, some speaking about the pyramids as our dear Langston did, crying "among the skyscrapers"—which (however romantic, forgotten, or denied) have always, since the first day, damned the New World and cried out for the Old. And in rejecting America, for whatever reason, we had carried forth this glorious history. No, we did not speak Hausa, Twi, Akan, or Ga; our language and values had come from the States, from reservations of America, which had never become *America* because we were of African descent; and that fact—and that alone—established our historical legitimacy. Without arrogance, our presence in the country forged the link between the New World and the Old and made Ghanaian political independence complete. That occurred to me when I saw Du Bois. One of us had made all this possible. Because he had started it. True, there had been slave revolts, other men, other causes, and other forces, past and present, traditional and modern, which produced the complex pattern of independence. But as *Ghana* was the autobiography of Kwame Nkrumah, *African Freedom* was the autobiography of W. E. B. Du Bois. And we were a part of him. Strange, isn't it? I had more history there than I had in America, and by extension, more involvement in the revolution than the average Ghanaian.

It was beautiful—a day-to-day history, a living history. If you entered the country, you probably would see a group of Afros drinking beer at the airport hotel. If you stayed in that hotel or another and watched a television program you liked, you'd have to thank Shirley Du Bois because she was the director. If you wanted a book or speech written or to talk to the editor of the country's leading magazine, the *African Review*, the man to see was Julian Mayfield. Need Julian's magazine in the French edition? See Richard Wright's daughter

Julia—absolutely beautiful—but don't touch, because she's got an Algerian husband. Trouble with language? Don't worry, because there's an Afro to teach you at the Institute of Languages. Need an artist? Got three: Tom Feelings, Ted Pontiflet, Herman Bailey. And if you don't like artists, what about a sculptor? Just ask for Ray. Designer? Architect? Max Bond (M.A., Harvard School of Design), Jerry Bard (M.A., University of Paris). Advisor for a president? Go to Legon and ask for Preston King. Want to have fun, real fun—need a dancer, singer, poetry? See Maya Maka at the Institute of African Studies. Need someone to build what Max designs? See Frank Robertson and the other brothers at All Afro; they deal in heavy industry. Need a good doctor who is developing new techniques in tropical medicine? See Julian's lovely wife, Dr. Ana Livia Corderia. Want a creative children's book? See Jean Bond. Historian? Dr. Lewis. Have bad teeth? See Bobby Lee, and if you don't like him, his pretty wife, Dr. Sarah Lee, is right next door. Business? What kind?—legitimate, illegitimate, honest, underground, some other kind? Well, ask me, and I'll whisper it to you. Need a man of honor and integrity? Got a lot of them, but you can start with Jim Lacy, my namesake. Want a scholar? Well now, there's Dr. St. Clair Drake, and if he's too radical, see Dr. Martin Kilson. Want some soul? Ask for Jerry Harper. Want a really pretty girl (Southern too) with a lot of talent? Ask for Miss Lucretia Collins. If you want to go back to the States, go see Curtis Morrow; every hurt in our history is in his face. Want to see a happy Afro family? Go to Legon and ask to see the McCleans. Want charm, beauty, and intelligence? See Sylvia Boone; we all love her. Need a French master? See Wendell, he's a good friend of mine and a fine scholar. Want to start a revolution? See Vicky Garvin and Alice Windom. And for the women, how about a lover, a sixty-minute man replete with an authoritarian discussion about the history of China? Go to Tema and just ask for Max; he'll fix you up. Need a quick course in journalism? See the director at the Ghana School of Journalism; he is a brother too. Need a photographer who talks a lot? Well, go to Job 600 and get Earl Grant. Want to laugh, have fun, and see black people who have gotten the white man off their backs? Go to the YWCA in Accra any day at noon; you'll find them, sitting at their same table with their Ghanaian friends, having a ball, and you'll probably find me there too.

These people, and many others I have not named, were our tribe in Ghana. Like most tribes, clans, ethnic groups, or whatever, we had leaders and followers, assorted interest-class differentiation and political attitudes. Although each of us had the final say over his individual fate, there tended to be three distinct sectors in the community: the Politicals, the Nonpoliticals, and the Opportunists.

For lack of a better description, the Politicals can be called professional protesters. Many of them had been influenced by the same revolutionary ideology, and most had had similar activist experiences, in France, America, or England. The Politicals had had, as I did before coming to Ghana, connections— ties or membership involvement—with the white left in the countries they had come from. But they had dissolved or modified these connections for a more pan-Africanist perspective. Most of the men were married to European women, and the black women, except two, were single or divorced and faced the usual problem of chauvinism in a male-dominated society. The majority of the political exiles were near or over thirty, well educated or highly talented in literary and artistic ways. All were religiously loyal to Nkrumah, zealously rationalizing his political moves, and generally, if not always ostensibly, following the ruling party's line.

From the point of view of the government and from the vantage point of their various jobs, this minority in the community had a considerable amount of power. What they said or didn't say carried weight. When the government or party (a procedural distinction, since in substance they were synonymous) wanted an official statement, they were the ones who were consulted. Moreover, since, as a West Indian writer said, "They walked in the corridors of power," they had direct access to the mass media and could be as critical of any political position as they wished—just as long as their stand was not at variance with the prevailing party ideology. Like only a very few others in the country, they had a direct line to the President, as well as intimate associations with some of his key advisors.

The President used their skills, including their literary talents, for speech writing; took their advice rather seriously. In every sense, they identified with and were a part of the Ghanaian ruling elite.

Such benefits of power usually carry correlative burdens; and so it was with this Afro elite. They were watchdogs in the community and generally responsible for the activity within it. Negroes believed to be working for the CIA or carrying out subversive activities against the state always sent waves of fear and anxiety through the group. Its position of trust and power was always vulnerable. From inside and outside the party, Nkrumah's enemies were always trying to discredit the Politicals, either to weaken their position as an expatriate force or to embarrass the government. They were also attacked from the inner circle, by Ghanaian and European friends of the president who resented or hated them for their ideology, privileges, or more often than not, simply because they were Afro-Americans. Beyond all this, their power rested upon the overall stability of the CPP. Any day, hour, second, power can shift right or left, depending upon the exigencies of the moment, the strength of the opposition, or unrest in the army. A move to the right would have decreased their power, and a move to the left could have had the reverse effect. Either way, your position would change, and you would inevitably take on more friends or more enemies, probably both.

Being on guard against both external and internal forces coming at your heart produces a strange kind of head. You *must* suspect everyone, since you can never be sure. Everyone, Afro-Americans, even ones you rallied with in Harlem, are potential CIA agents or potential enemies. Every change in government or army and every presidential trip abroad is another headache to consider. In time, therefore, as an exile, you develop what I call a "refugee" mentality. The moves you make appear to reflect political acumen, but in reality they are based on acute anxiety, blind acceptance of an ideology you vaguely comprehend, a confused fusion of the political rhetoric you learned back home (which of course has nothing to do with the present political culture), and equally irrelevant, what you read in the daily newspaper. Naturally, you call all this nonsense "revolutionary," and are so smothered by this cloak that if real agents like the CIA . . . if CIA agents came to the country (as I'm sure they did), they could probably move around freely, because nothing in your political training would have prepared you to detect them.

I should say here that this group had a close alliance with the group of South African freedom fighters, which suffered from the same disposition. Small wonder that fascism still rides herd in their country. By default, Julian Mayfield was the unofficial leader of this neurotic contingent. He was very much aware of the psychology of his flock. But little could he do, since he spent most of his hours watching out for the knife against his own neck, trying to convince his immediate supervisor that a monthly magazine should come out each month, and doing his own writing. He worked on the average of fourteen hours a day just to keep ahead.

In the Politicals' behalf—one of their many virtues—they were honest, individuals of integrity, and in spite of their lack of revolutionary sophistication, devoted to their work. They could be trusted and did only what they believed. Also, they believed that Nkrumah was honest and committed and that some of the problems of political change—inevitable in these countries, given the world situation in which independence occurred—would be solved. If more of the Ghanaians had possessed their sense of history and honesty, at the very least there would have been much less corruption.

The Nonpoliticals would have faced the same problems, but fortunately they were not interested in "what was happening." I found that rather amazing, since what was happening would nevertheless affect their lives. Younger, they were the "hippies" of Ghana, and unlike the white hippies in America, had seen the worst in America, the side which had twisted and broken much of their spirit. Psychologically, Africa was good for them. It allowed them moments to think, relax, and feel a sense of development in a changing culture. Unlike the Politicals, with very few exceptions, they lived among the people and learned considerably more about the "real culture" than their radical brothers. Neither were they dogmatic believers. Conditioned by the hard steel of American racism, they were also hard, tough, and cynical; they had patience, a wait-see, or as the Ghanaians say "wait-small," philosophy which gave them a comfortable home among the urban masses. Most were artists and unpublished writers, a few students, and one, maybe two, did nothing. They were for Nkrumah, too, but expressed their support by loving the people they met. They taught the Ghanaian high school youngsters (who always flocked to them because they were "cool") black American music, especially jazz.

Tom Feelings, a talented artist from Brooklyn, led the Nonpoliticals, although neither he nor they wanted, needed, or would have approved had they thought of themselves in that way. But he stood out like a happy little boy, always joyful, always smiling, and drawing the happy children who smiled back. You could see the change in his work. His Brooklyn children looked angry, as our children feel as they grow up. Africa allowed Tom to live his youth all over, and this time he would be black, strong, and free. Tom did not know about their insides, their hurtings, their lack of nourishment—black bodies deformed by malaria, bodies which would not get old. Tom saw what he wanted and needed to see, and that was beautiful, because he created something, made them happy when they saw themselves; and that made him part of their lives.

And Ted Pontiflet, a fine artist too, became the model for many Ghanaian children. When he talked to them about music, I pretended to read, but listened too. The thought of coming to appreciate Charlie Parker, Miles Davis, John Coltrane, and Horace Silver in Africa blew my mind, because I was learning from men, brother men, beautiful men whom I probably would not have met back home. I had come from a mansion; Tom, Ted, Ray, Curtis from tenements, but they were giving and I was taking, because they, collectively and individually, were always closer to what we all were.

Naturally and understandably this group resented the power of the Politicals. Not out of envy, but because the existence of power creates pressures, conformity, obedience, and all our hippies wanted was a new sun, an undiscovered humanity, and as Ray said, "a little time to be me."

The Opportunists were many, always coming, always leaving, always stealing, never feeling—just going along with the tide. When business was right, Nkrumah was right; when business was bad, Nkrumah was bad. Men like these are always around. They are seen in American communities, and they look and smell the same out here.

Leslie Lacy was shaped by the Toms and the Julians. (And once or twice I sold some dollars on the Lebanese black market.) Whatever failings they had, I had. I was of both sectors. Sometimes, through me the community could express a wholeness. Both groups were honest, naïve—each in its own way trying to find itself. When Smith of Southern Rhodesia declared "his country" (isn't that a laugh?) unilaterally independent from Britain, Nkrumah called for the mobilization of a people's army. The Political males stayed up all night convincing me that I should join up with them, even if it meant the loss of citizenship. Finally I felt that it was the logical extension of what I said I believed in, so I—and all the Politicals—signed up. Heading the list were the brothers from the world of music and art, the first volunteers in the country. The Politicals were surprised. I was not.

Most Ghanaians viewed us, the Afros, as a community, and as far as they were concerned, we were the same breed. The more politically conscious Ghanaians, including some students and intellectuals, were aware of our political differences and levels of involvement and related to us accordingly. But overall, given their own ethnic orientations, they tended to view us as a group, because like any other tribe in the country, we spoke the same language: a language which was critical of America, a language which defended Nkrumah, a tongue which constantly spoke of brotherhood, which never complained about inefficiency or the corruption we knew about. We wanted so much to ask for love that we sometimes lied in order not to hurt someone's feelings; and sometimes we did a little Uncle Tomming (seems strange, doesn't it?) to convince the Ghanaians that, in spite of everything, we were glad to be Home.

And sometimes we didn't want to be around any Ghanaians. Blacks passing through or newly arrived invariably accused us of segregating ourselves from the people. We just said, "Okay, man," or, "Whatever you say, sister," and kept on doing our thing.

XI

The Case of
Wendell Jean Pierre

NEARING THE TURN of my first year at the university, a year full of new discoveries, there developed a bitter and protracted struggle between the university and the government. The character of this particular confrontation was new, but the cause was the result of years of government-university controversy about the objectives of education in a developing society. For almost two weeks the university had been under constant attack from the government press. Not a new occurrence, but now it was coupled with irate threats to specific staff and students. The *masses* (CPP activists, screaming market women, trade unionists, and idle streetwalkers that they had picked up on their way) had stormed Ghana's highest institution of learning, breaking windows, carrying out acts of physical violence, making political speeches about socialism, and screaming and shouting, "Deport the expatriates; discipline the Ghanaians."

In the middle of this scary confusion, Wendell Jean Pierre paid me a sudden visit. He had a strange look about him, like a man looks when he brings you tragic news, news which has affected him, news which he does not understand but is forced to tell you nevertheless.

"Have you heard the news?" Wendell asked, smiling just a bit to cover his real look.

"I guess everybody has," I said indifferently. "From the looks of things, Nkrumah's people will take over the university."

Wendell walked around the room, and as he always did, looked at me in a questioning manner. "That's not what I mean. I'm talking about me."

"What about you?"—again indifferently. I fumbled through my notes on the thesis I had just started.

"I'm being deported."

"Yeah, and so is Nkrumah," I said jokingly.

"It's true, Leslie. The Ghana government is deporting me. I have twenty-four hours to leave the country." He then handed me the deportation order, which read:

Dear Dr. Pierre,
Your presence in the country is injurious to the health and welfare of the Ghanaian revolution. You are no longer welcome in our People's Republic. You have 24 hours to leave the country.
By order of the President,
Osagyefo Dr. Kwame Nkrumah

"They have to be kidding. Look, Wendell, somebody's playing a joke on you." I handed him back the deportation order and continued looking through my index cards.

Wendell came up behind me, gripped my shoulders, and in a voice I had never heard from his lungs, said, "Les, this is not a joke. Police have surrounded my house, abused my family. It's dead serious."

I was shocked, confused, but because I knew Wendell, my belief still was not complete. "There must be some mistake," I said with authority. "Look, have you told Julian about this? What about Preston? Have you told him?" But Wendell did not hear my questions. His eyes were fixed on the wall in my little room in Mensah Sabbah Hall. His crying was disturbing, irritatingly disturbing. But what can you tell a man who is being put out of the country he has come to love? Who would do something like this to him?

"Les, my whole life will be ruined."

I put my arms around him and tried to assure him that

the Afro-American community would do all that was in its power to make things right. After a few minutes he got himself together and went home to see after his family.

That was the beginning of an ugly experience. I could not for a moment believe that Wendell Jean Pierre, the Wendell that Eve had met in Paris, the Wendell of Legon, whom I had heard over and over in his university classes trying desperately and painstakingly to get his students to understand the revolutionary thoughts of black men in the Third World—this Wendell, a man I knew, respected, and loved—could be working for the Central Intelligence Agency. There had been a gross error, a tragic mistake that a man—a man like Father— would make if he had lost his mind and developed in his insanity the unmitigated gall to accuse Malcolm X of being a CIA. The accusation would be absurd and heretical, and if you had a gun, you would probably kill the man. Certainly Wendell (or for that matter, any of us) was not Brother Malcolm, but I was unequivocally certain that Malcolm would have trusted him as I did. Fortunately, and shortly after Wendell left my room, I received a telephone call from Preston King informing me that the twenty-four hour deadline had been extended. Now we had time to work on a defense for Wendell, which we hoped would go through our channels directly to the president. The first thing was to rally support in the Afro-American community. Wendell had been an effective and serious voice at every level of life in our tribe. In French, he and Preston could discuss their letters to Fanon's wife, and with the "hippies" he was equally as responsive and involved. But the Afros, individually or collectively, did not come to his defense. We knocked on door after door, phoned until our ears were full of clicks and rings, and the response was always negative: "He's gone for the weekend." "Never did like that nigger." "Should'na got mixed up with that devil." "Told you so." "My name is Hess and I ain't in this mess." "I knew that nigger couldn't have believed all that shit he was saying." "Well, Pierre is all right, and I'd like to help, but . . ." And so it was, on and on.

I could understand, although I had to condemn it, the self-interested attitudes of the few, very few (brothers and sisters) who were afraid to get involved. Preston and I were both being watched, and the white cloud of guilt by association was beginning to form. But the overwhelming majority of our tribe members refused to form a defense committee because they were convinced of Wendell's guilt. Now, that was odd. Yesterday, the day before, all the days of their lives with Wendell, such a thought would have offended them, and if anyone of them accused him, the accuser would have found his neck on the block. With the exception of Julian Mayfield, who wrote a letter to the President in Wendell's defense, every other soul was on ice.

Because the Ghana government had accused him, he was guilty. Who were we to question the sovereign and progressive black government? We had never worked for the CIA, and did not, therefore, know its member agents. Maybe Wendell had infiltrated? But these doubts—questions however true, probing—did not enter my head. All I know was that the day before Wendell was cut down, he was my friend, our friend, a militant and understanding giant in the Afro-American hierarchy. Now the Ghana government had said that its judgment was clearer than ours and we had given him up.

Fear can cause people to do strange things; it is the timeless excuse for having acted irrationally. But our tribe was affected by a deeper illness, a sickness which went far beyond our inability to stand up for a principle, and in a very real sense, defined the twisted meaning of our black bodies in exile and the overall existential content of our human alienation. We had come from America because we hated it too much. Feeling ourselves sinking in a world of all-absorbing nations, worlds, parties, creeds and spirits, we, like others all over the damned earth, desperately needed something to hold on to. Nkrumah's kingdom was our promised land, a cubistic panacea for our lost souls. And in it, we lived honestly, did our jobs and whatever was our thing. It didn't matter if it was leaking, standing, falling, growing, or stopping; it was here, and we were in it.

Black, yes. But like most Americans, we were bent over by pragmatism, mixed up by poppycock. Because we saw the pragmatism and rejected the poppycock and ran into the kingdom's door, we thought we were free at last. And we were. But rather than do something un-American—like think—we simply got a robe from the kingdom keepers and covered over our self-hatred. We had power, prestige, and other things America could never give us; in addition, we had new norms, which we happily believed in. But we never used any of these things to create an effective ideology which our presence would have made useful to those of us still in America. We never understood power politics, least of all the Ghanaian kind. We could not be critical, as all creative revolutionaries must be, from a point of commitment. (We confused that with disloyalty.)

So when the government said, "Put Wendell out," we retreated, not so much in fear, but because we had not developed the tool to view Wendell in the changing complexities of an African political culture. We did not know about political deals; right and left movements; you take this and I'll take that; political envies and jealousies, suspicions, disputes; international economy, American pressures—all the dirty work politicians all over the world do every day. For the first time in our lives, we had power, black power, real power—not screams from the road. Nkrumah needed us, as we needed him. For we were a radical extension of thirty million other people in a country he constantly attacked. If the widow of Dr. Du Bois, Shirley Graham Du Bois, had said no, deals would have been made, and Wendell might have remained. Like a chief in Ghana said later, "They sold you once and they'll sell you again."

Preston King, his devoted wife Hazel, Julian, and I put Wendell and his family on the plane. It was evening, the air filled with mosquitoes and suspicion. Waiting to hide from the sun.

The black bodies in exile. . . . We were the believers, the affirmers of Nkrumah's justice. And from that perspective, Wendell Jean Pierre was a guilty nigger who had come to Africa to help the white man. We had not ascertained his guilt. We knew nothing about it. And if Nkrumah or any of his irretrievably corrupt ministers called for Julian Mayfield's blood the next morning, Shirley Graham Du Bois' the next day, and the beautiful person called Jim Lacy the day afterward —until we all had been asked for—we would have all left, blaming the white man as usual, never questioning, never knowing. Always believing.

XII

The Ghanaian Revolution

AND THE REVOLUTION went on. Wendell was one of four university teachers who were deported; finally, after many years of the party-university dispute, the CPP had achieved a victory. The Irish vice-chancellor, Conor Cruise O'Brien—who had defied the United Nations in the Congo crisis and had exposed Western imperialism operating there in his book *To Katanga and Back*—put up a protracted fight, but he and the university staff which supported him were no match for a government bent on creating a university which paralleled its political objectives.

To the extent that the government wanted to make the University of Ghana at Legon an African university, or as Kwame Nkrumah said, a "socialist university," it was indeed supportable. In Ghana, as elsewhere in Africa, the university had been established as part of the British plan to extend social and political reforms at the end of the Second Great War. Up until that time, Ghanaians who went on for higher education traveled to Europe, especially England and France, or went, as the President had, to America. The training the Africans received, both abroad and at home after the war, was essentially European in content, character, and orientation, and created the usual problems of cultural and intellectual alienation when the skills were finally applied. That is to say, university training, although useful in that it produced needed skills—in medicine, for example—was producing English gentlemen (crudely called black Englishmen) whose manners and orientations often set them apart from the people their training had prepared them to serve. Naturally then, since African independence implies a return to, or revitalization of, African art, culture, and values (which colonial universities had dealt with superficially if at all, since from their racist perspectives, Africans had no history), a new African political culture demanded a complementary intellectual culture, which would serve the new order.

Even before the government-university crisis of 1964, Kwame Nkrumah had moved in this general direction. In 1961, the University College of the Gold Coast had become independent of its mother body, the University of London, and had become the University of Ghana. To strengthen its intellectual autonomy and stabilize its new character, the government had reorganized and established the Institute of African Studies. Yet serious problems remained. The university was still staffed with colonial intellectuals, who still controlled the professorships in most of the departments and ultimately had power—which if not procedural, was indeed substantial—to decide the nature of the courses that were offered. Even in departments like those of economics and African studies (which was still in the hands of "radical and progressive Europeans") there was, given the all-embracing conservative bureaucracy, little anyone could do.

Ghanaian intellectuals formed an interesting elite. There were two main groups and some odd individuals who would no doubt have called themselves "independent thinkers." The pro-government "scholars" were a fascinating lot. Their hearts were in the right place, but their minds were products of schools like New York University, which, even in America, had little functional value. Through their minds, the party was able to see the inner dynamics of the institution, which of course meant that they were seeing nothing. More often than not, the educators of Ghana's youth simply repeated, but at a higher level, illusions which the party's political intellectuals already had.

To the right of this group stood those who opposed. These gentlemen intellectuals, for the most part well trained in Oxford habits and letters, had never (since they were the heirs apparent to British rule, and of the class Nkrumah had defeated at the national polls) been committed to the politics of Nkrumah's one-party government. In fact, most of them hated him not only for his "improper" American education but also because they considered his all-embracing power abusive and described his political norms and behavior as "medieval and rather Machiavellian." One professor once said to me, "You know, ole chap, *that* man down in Flagstaff is really unsuited to rule us. He doesn't really have a university education. At Oxford we surely wouldn't take his *training* seriously. . . . The situation, ole boy, is rather frightful. . . . Unlike Gandhi— you remember him, the man in India—Nkrumah with his bushlike tendencies really thinks he is an *Osagyefo*."

These gentlemen of English culture wanted Nkrumah out of the way(he was an embarrassment to "sane and responsible civil government") so that they could have a *proper society:* peopleless politics, acceptable standards of government. *Probably* most wanted British passports, and more than one political party, somewhat along British lines. What was amazing, sometimes a bit tragic, was that in spite of the intense tropical heat, they looked unperturbably comfortable in imported British gray flannel suits. I was constantly amused and never thrown off, because it was Palmer, but on a much higher level.

The best feature in the intellectual desert of cultural exchange was the students. Coming from all parts of the country, proudly bringing their culture with them, they were highly motivated, clever, and strong. Yet they had little faith in the future. Symbolically they were being trained in England, from Oxford high table. (This simply meant that in the dining room of each hall—the halls were designed by a Brazilian architect, after those of Cambridge University—one long King-Arthur-type table, with complementary shields decorating the wall behind it, was reserved for the *fellows* of the hall, who looked down from the little stage it was placed on, onto the future of Ghana, who ate Ghanaian food at low table.) Their *education* was further confused by the presence of the omnipresent Convention People's party, and student informers to complement the pro-government staff. The students did not generally accept the practice, or what they understood of the ideology, of mass party rule, and considered the practitioners corrupt opportunistic men and women completely lacking a sense of history.

Most of the students were afraid to express their grievances openly, for fear of arrest or the loss of government stipends, on which most depended. They registered their contempt for the party, which many of them, and their families, had supported while they were in secondary schools, by using party newspapers as supplementary toilet tissue. And at every opportunity they embarrassed the inept government officials who dared speak at open forums. Lacking better models, they tended to express the anti-government sentiments of the Oxonians in their classrooms. To that extent they were practically opportunistic, for they accepted the maids, dining-room stewards, loans, and other privileges which only their government could provide. And they looked forward to a big job, car, and house when they completed their course.

The government, as I have already explained, considered the university a "hotbed of reaction," and by extension, it considered the students "reactionaries." Now, a reactionary person in a socialist context is one who opposes that program, presumably to return to the former or another order, which in the Ghanaian context, could only mean colonial or neocolonial politics. Hence the party was intending to get these "hotbedders" over to its side.

Some clarification is necessary here. First, the Convention People's party was not a socialist party. It was anticolonial and nationalistic, with certain socialistic and Marxist features, never clearly defined. Outwardly it was similar to parties in Eastern Europe. It represented all the levels—classes if you will—in Ghanaian life, and to that extent, its major appeal, preindependence, was democratically based. But since 1961, when it started losing its support, not only from the intellectuals but also from the populace at large, it had been plagued by serious structural contradictions. Roles, functions, and party objectives had not been clearly defined, and there was no overall institutional control to get things moving again.

Much of this, one suspects, was inevitable. Nationalist parties struggling for independence, given the general activist nature of their struggle against colonialism, must securely tie down sound ideological and political programs for change. Depending primarily, sometimes exclusively, on political slogans and the general discontent in the society, a nationalist party can—if it is able to deal with other parties and work out some agreement with the colonials—come into power without a great deal of difficulty. Once there, the problems become more numerous. The party has to stabilize its power, and sometimes that means, as it did in Ghana, and elsewhere in west Africa, suppressing the parties that oppose its program; then the first enemies are created. Also, the party (now government) must now deal with the world, a big world of economics, power politics, and supergovernments, in which you have no *real* say (in spite of your shiny new seat in the U.N.), and a world generally not interested in your new flag, new power, or in you personally. Everything you need or want (or think you need or want) comes from cities you, in your colonial status, helped build, but which you do not control. The money you need to buy these *things* is called dollars, gold, or pounds, none of which you have. Since you are not Cuban or Chinese, the only way to get "dol-lah" is to see what you have and hope the white man will give you a meaningful price. Which, of course, he won't because, again, he is not interested in your development.

Somewhat simplified, but nonetheless true. The best, most skilled, most devoted nationalist leader faces at independence an imperialist and hostile world. If you criticize the order of things, as Nkrumah did, and turn to the communist camp (which in some cases is not an alternative), the imperialists make things that much harder.

Externally and internally the CPP faced the problems I have described. Alone, it could do little against the external problems, and given its structure, little was done with the internal ones. To appreciate what was happening in Ghana, add to these problems two others: corruption and anti-intellectualism. I am not in a position to say that Nkrumah was corrupt, but certainly his ministers and party chiefs were. And since he did very little about the situation—a situation which ultimately cost him his throne—his personal morality became irrelevant. Now, if that was the case, the student reaction was not to socialism, because it did not exist—except possibly in the mind of Nkrumah, who was described by a sympathetic student as being a "father who heads and loves his family but never figures out how to care for them." Beyond that, even if the party had been honestly socialist, it still would have encountered opposition from the students. Unquestionably the students were politically conservative. Being good products of their education, how could they be otherwise? But an honest socialist party with a meaningful program could have involved the students, who were, in spite of their political persuasion, culturally and spiritually very much African. They were young, dynamic, and ready for change, having come to awareness since the Second Global War. They did not want to look back to Britain and had serious reservations about America.

But they had no leadership. In Ghana, and elsewhere, nationalist parties are understandably (given their experiences under colonialism) anti-intellectual, anti-students, and so on. Many in the rank and file are insecure, because they were deprived of education during the colonial period, and also because education in the West, and by extension, in its colonies abroad, is elitist in nature and breeds contempt and snobbery for those below. If the CPP leaders had understood this and worked out a forum in which these conflicts could have been resolved, its brand of nation building (assuming its honesty) would have had more prospects.

Against this background Harold Duggan (an undergraduate student in economics from the Virgin Islands, and the first West Indian, like I was the first black American, to get a degree from the University of Ghana), Lebrette Hesse (a Ga from Accra and a third-year student of law), and I organized, three weeks after the deportation, the Marxist Study Forum. Presumptuously and optimistically we resolved that if we could develop a program in which radical and socialist ideas could be expressed openly, we would be helping the government and at the same time motivating the students to join the party in an effort to reform it. We had a lot of gall and were insanely young enough to think that we could get away with it. By then we had a rather firm knowledge of politics in the country, and what we didn't know was researched. When we had worked out our program, we took it over to Dr. Preston King, the only person we felt we could trust at this point, for advice. In a very real sense he was the intellectual and moral force behind us, without which we would not have been able to achieve that success which we did.

We knew that such an organization as we had in mind would eventually create controversy, so we had to plan very carefully. Understandably, Hesse was a little anxious during the planning phase: at the worst, Harold Duggan and I would be deported, but poor Hesse would be spending the rest of his years in a security prison. On the positive side, I had considerable experience in organizing. I remember telling two associates about the two communists who had infiltrated a Booker T. Washington club McDaniel had organized in Boston. (Their strategy amused Duggan, who, being young and impressionable, made it his official strategy, which he egotistically called Dugganism.) These two white boys, also students in the Boston area, wanted to join our club. Over the opposition of Mac, they were allowed membership. One day the one who did all the talking suggested that we type up and duplicate the minutes so that they could be distributed at each meeting in order to save time. Being lazy Negroes, naturally we protested, until they happily agreed to do it themselves. After several months Mac brought me some interesting information. Comparing the written minutes to the duplicated ones, we noticed slight and subtle differences. Where we had the word "Negro," the typed copy read "human"; where we had "civil rights," "human freedom"; where we had "deprived," they had "alienated"; where we had "advance," they had "struggle"; and on and on. With this and other tactics, they took over the club in six months.

We chose the name "Marxist" for tactical reasons. We couldn't have called it the Nkrumahist Forum because no one except the CPP students and staff would have come; while that would have been all right, we wanted a much broader base. Also, it would have been assumed that we were working for the party. The party would probably have preferred the other name, but we assumed that it would leave us alone if we seemed to be going in its general direction. And the university officials, while not totally approving of our "improper grouping," would probably allow us to function, given their vague rhetoric about academic freedom.

Even so, people assumed all kinds of weird things: some of the students, predictably, thought we were with the party; others thought we were crazy; the university officials were confused; the government thought we had been put there by Moscow; the American Embassy thought we were Chinese agents; the Afros thought we were CIA agents; and someone from the Chinese embassy came out every Monday at 8:00 to find out in person. Possibly there were a thousand other assumptions, but they created the necessary protection, and we were allowed to survive.

Our first order of business was to make the club *leftist* and *respectable*. Given the political and intellectual climate at Legon, we became respectable first. Our first speaker was an Englishman. A distinguished scholar from Oxford, teaching economic history at the university, Dr. Kay (whom I moved in with for a short time to update my own political personality) spoke on "Dr. Erich Fromm's Concept of Freedom." What resulted? Well, all of his two hundred students came and took notes (thinking that these might answer exam questions). All of his colleagues were present; fifty other students; members of the diplomatic corps; conservative professors, both Ghanaian and foreign; Chinese; Americans; Afros; CPP officials; and God knows who else. Everything was quiet and academic, and it allowed for different opinions to be expressed. Very Oxford, we served tea and cake after the question period. Everyone left looking forward to the next week, when a distinguished Indian mystic (Oxford, of course) would speak on "Freud,

Gandhi, Marx." Everyone was pleased. And who got all the credit? The Marxist Study Forum. The next week we had ten new members: all Dr. Kay's students.

We moved slowly and cautiously. All the members prepared assiduously for each meeting although the Big Three (and Preston) selected the topic, speakers, and made all the arrangements. We advertised in the school and local papers three days before the talk, and the evening before each speech all the fifteen hundred students who sat down to eat in the dining rooms of Legon's five halls read the *Marxist Forum Newsletter* before the steward poured their soup. Each newsletter gave four things: our aims and objectives (ha, ha!); what occurred the past week; the topic for that week; and activities planned for the future. We paid for this out of our pockets and quickly got it back when we started collecting dues. Our private lives had to be just right: (1) talk to *everybody*; (2) be civil; (3) never mention the CPP; (4) go to all the school's socials, church occasionally; (5) do well in school; (6) stay clear of scandals; and (7) be all-around nice guys. And it helped that Duggan was good in soccer and cricket.

In time we virtually controlled three of the newsletters each hall published weekly, and the two we didn't control were obliged to publish articles which we wrote each week. Moreover, we became an effective force in student politics. By the end of the first year we were five hundred strong.

But let me not exaggerate our good fortunes. We still had an uphill battle. Out of the five hundred, nearly a hundred accepted some variation of socialism as the most rational approach to solving political, cultural, and social problems in new states and tended to look to Cuba as a model without the Soviet strings. The others were more diversified. Some were sympathetic but uncertain; many liked the intellectual freedom the forum achieved; and some joined because it was the most "enjoyable" group on a campus which had very few social and cultural activities. I should also mention that it was hard to know how many students (and also staff) were actually converted by our efforts. I am certain that we converted some, but I am equally certain that many had previously accepted our point of view but had been unable to express it without fear of being identified with the unpopular party.

General observers at the university who may have come to one or more meetings tended to express either of two points of view. Most found the meeting interesting and were somewhat convinced that we were not working for Nkrumah. More specifically, about 30 per cent of the Ghanaian staff approved of our efforts because they had not been government inspired, motivated, or controlled. In fact, many of them liked the forum precisely for that reason. As one professor put it, "At least you chaps have something which is free."

Another 50 per cent were actively opposed for ideological reasons, and half of this group never gave up the idea that Nkrumah was behind us. The others were indifferent, for any number of reasons—like other people, elsewhere in the world, who look askance at political activities. European staff (in a sixty-forty majority at the university) generally did not participate unless invited to speak. Only a few speakers returned to hear other guests. My guess is that Europeans at Legon became a little apprehensive about political activities after the deportations. Nonetheless, about 5 per cent were actively involved.

We had many European speakers for several reasons: they taught the students, and the students respected them; and most Ghanaians approached to speak were apprehensive. As the forum became more secure and consistent with our original plans, we depended primarily on other Africans and West Indian scholars in the country. We had three speakers from the Afro-American community: Julian Mayfield, who spoke on "Robert Williams and the Monroe Movement"; his wife, Dr. Corderia, who spoke on the "Revolution in Puerto Rico"; and Preston King, who gave a lecture on "Pan-Africanism and Marxism."

XIII

The Coming of Malcolm X

"Malcolm who?"

Julian was shocked by my question and looked at me in disgust and disappointment. A second before, he was in a different mood. He had just jumped out of his yellow convertible Sprite, intensely elated, very un-Julian for that time of the morning. I could only think that he was coming to tell me that for once his monthly magazine was coming out on schedule. Before I could work up a complementary state of mind (a necessary adjustment if Julian Mayfield is to converse with you when excited), he had shouted, "Malcolm X is coming! We've got to get ourselves together!"

Now, emphatically enunciating each syllable, Julian said, "Malcolm X. Remember him? He's our leader from Harlem. Now, Harlem, in case you've forgotten, is in that sick society we just left. . . . But, that's right, you probably never went to Harlem. . . . You've been in universities all your life."

"Okay, brother," I interrupted. "I guess I deserved that. Is Malcolm really coming to Ghana?"

"That's what I hear."

"Who told you?"

"That's not important right now."

"When is he coming?"

"I don't know exactly, but he's definitely making it, and we've got to be ready."

"Maybe the Marxist Forum can present him," I said enthusiastically.

"Maybe."

"Why do you say 'maybe' like that?"

"Because we have to be very careful. . . . Must consider Malcolm's image."

"Right. I get it. His followers back home might not understand why a nationalist was presented by a Marxist forum."

"Les, you meet with your group and tentatively work out a program. But please, de-emphasize the socialistic rhetoric and concentrate on nationalistic themes. . . . Remember, Malcolm has his own stuff to run down. All we have to do is provide him with a platform."

"Wait a second." I hesitated. "Maybe the Marxist Forum shouldn't present him at all." For the first time in a long time I was thinking about my own experiences in America.

"In a sense you're right," Julian said as he paced the floor, thinking. "But you have the biggest and best organization on the campus, and you're closer to the problems which Malcolm will probably speak about. Handled very carefully, I think we can pull it off."

For the next two hours, over some early morning gin, we planned our strategy. By midday, half of the Afro-American community, representatives from all the sectors, were at Julian's house—twenty short feet from the house where Du Bois had lived. (Or as Julian used to say, "Twenty short feet from my own history.") Getting a group of the Afros there was not easy. Some were married to white women, and we wanted them without their wives, not so much out of respect for Malcolm, but primarily because of the sisters. So, painstakingly and discreetly, we visited these brothers, greeted their wives, took them outside, and ran down the program. They all understood and promised to come alone.

What a meeting! The sense of Malcolm brought a consensus which was rarely apparent in our exiled community, and out of this unanimity came the Malcolm X Committee, with Julian as the chairman, Maya Maka as vice-chairman, Vicky Garvin and Alice Windon as secretaries; naturally, given my success at the university, there was no doubt about who was to be the organizer. We arranged a busy speaking schedule and contacted our friends in the communications media. They promised us their "finest" hours. We worked twenty-four hours a day calling Afro-Americans throughout the country, telling them that the "tall, red man from Harlem" was on his way. Nothing was left to the innocence of spontaneity. Watching CPP activities, we had learned something about organizing a public meeting, so in the spirit of Nkrumah's political myth making, we were prepared to pack the halls with party activists, trade unionists, political opportunists, screaming market women (replete with their baskets and chickens) and Ghana's non-English-speaking street citizens if an overflowing crowd was not apparent for any of Malcolm's scheduled appearances. Our leader had to have the broadest possible exposure; even an audience with the president was not beyond our reach.

We waited. The first day, then the second, but Malcolm did not arrive; in fact, fifty of us slept in at Julian's place, hoping to greet him. Predictably, someone suggested that he had been kidnaped by the CIA. Naturally, that comment caused some concern, but most of us did not fret, because a thousand other explanations were equally as tenable.

The sight of all those black faces idly talking, waiting, was probably one of the most hilarious in history. An outsider would never have thought that among the serious watchers-for-Malcolm were some of the heaviest drinkers, night-lifers, and women chasers that had ever assembled in one country. Notwithstanding our political involvements, our private lives stood in open contrast to the life that Malcolm X had been leading since he joined the Nation of Islam. Ironically, we looked like the proper Palmer graduate, without the commensurate Palmer training. Out of respect for our disciplined leader, we had temporarily made truces with our inner drives and promised each other that we would abandon our habits until Malcolm left. Giving up a lifelong vice is never easy, especially if the abandonment is abrupt. But we endured, as I imagine a drug addict does, sweating and shaking away his first night in a Muslim mosque.

We all knew that the new-found austerity was temporary however. The red-eyed drinkers who grudgingly poured quarts of lemonade into their systems would return to the cause of their red eyes. The night-lifers, who kept us up all night talking and laughing, would again return to one of the many Ghanaian open-air clubs; and the women chasers (called "womanizers" by the inhabitants) seemed content with their present celibacy and past memories, undoubtedly dreaming of glorious conquests ahead. (I should add that the Ghanaian women were so beautiful that even bona fide celibates and married men constantly found their vows being tested.)

On a typically hot afternoon of the third day, our waiting came to an unexpected end: He had arrived. Like an army marching toward a review stand, we hustled ourselves into shape, cramped our bodies into the available cars and hurried over to the Ambassador Hotel to meet him.

Acting as if the Lord himself had come, we stormed into the government-owned hotel not only like we owned it but also like we were going to take it over. As usual, it was filled with European businessmen and expatriates, a few Ghanaians doing "business" with them; although undisclosed, the regular security men were undoubtedly present too. All eyes turned to us. Contemptuous glances. We responded accordingly. The whites in the hotel, and also more significantly, the Blacks, represented many in Ghana who hated us because we constantly reminded them that their country had, in spite of itself, radically changed since the "good ole days of British rule." By an ingenious extension, they held us responsible for what was going on in it. A few of us were hopelessly mystified; the rest had no illusions about our status: we were tolerated out of sufferance of Nkrumah, and if they could kill him at eight o'clock, our fate would be his at eight-thirty. A Ghanaian whom I saw that day, and every day, in this or some other hotel had once summarized the prevailing attitude: "You Afro-Americans are too arrogant. You think you are better than we are because you are more civilized. You may fool the common illiterate on the street, but we who know better are not so easily fooled. A few of your people are okay, fine chaps, but most of you and those so-called freedom fighters from South Africa are wasting our precious pounds, and taking jobs that are not rightly yours.

If that crazy man who calls himself Osagyefo could be put out, we would put all of you out too. . . . We like the West Indians because they are more like us."

Seeing his face today brought to mind the conversation that had followed.

"Why do you think we are too arrogant?" I had asked.

"Because you think you are. You act like you own this country. You think you are better than we are," the man replied quickly and angrily.

"But that just isn't true. We don't feel arrogant. Most of us came out here to get away from America, to get the white man off our backs, so to speak. . . . The U.S. is a racist society—"

"It may be racist," he interrupted, "but at least you're better off than you are here."

"It depends on what your values are. If you mean that black people have a higher material standard of living, then perhaps I could agree. But that's only a part of what makes a life meaningful. The other parts—peace of mind, sense of dignity, freedom from discrimination—are even more important, because they will determine the *real* value of the few material comforts Blacks receive."

"Rubbish. Tell that to a man in the street, and if he understands your nonsense, I can assure you that he will laugh at you. For in this society money is the difference between living and dying. You say that America is a white country, and being black, you have little freedom. Now take me. I'm black and everything around me is black. Yet even if I had the money to go abroad, I would need both a passport and an exit visa. They are hard to get if you are not rich or powerful; it is a waste of valuable time to try. How long did it take you to get your passport?"

"Two weeks."

"Two weeks! Did you say two weeks?"

"Yes."

"Well, I know Ghanaians who have been waiting two year. Why? Politics. Look, old chap, there is no freedom here either."

"Why is it so important to travel abroad?"

"If your government had told you that, you would have

picketed the passport office. If I did that here, I would be in jail the same day, and then you would have no one to educate you to the real Ghana. Look, Lacy, traveling is a basic freedom. I should have the right to travel, if I can afford it. Why should I let some corrupt official whose wife spends her holidays in the United Kingdom and whose children are too good to go to the local schools, but not to go to the English schools, tell me that I do not have the same right?"

"Much of what you say is probably true. But sometimes in new states such precautions are necessary for the good of the country. Don't you feel that things will be better in the future?"

"Hell, no. What future? Half of my family is in jail. They are called 'security prisoners.' Some politicians didn't like them, so they were locked up. Look Lacy, before you start talking about the virtues of Ghanaian politics, just talk to some of the ordinary people . . . just talk to them—they'll straighten out some of this nonsense."

Pushing that history to the back of my mind, I smiled when that same Ghanaian's eyes met mine, because on this afternoon, I did feel arrogant. Malcolm's presence (peace be upon him) excited our souls, and those among us who were violent wanted to throw all the Europeans out in the streets.

When Malcolm saw us walking over to him, although we looked like any other group of Ghanaians, he instinctively knew who we were and shook the hand and heard the name of each of us before he took his seat.

"So this is the famous Afro-American community of Accra. Brothers and sisters, I'm very glad to see you and I wish every black man in America could be sitting where I am. I bring you greetings from all those who cannot be here." Malcolm's words comforted all of us and we sat quietly, like children, as he talked about his trip, the political situation in America, then happily showed us pictures of his wife Betty and their beautiful daughters.

Malcolm was dressed like most tourists: he wore a white sport shirt and tropical gray pants, and he carried an inexpensive camera around his neck. He looked relaxed and refreshed, unlike the Malcolm X I had seen in photographs and on television. His long hair and neatly trimmed goatee made him look older; and the effects of the sun on his skin gave his face power, added masculinity and distinction. As he shared his experiences with us, I realized that I was seeing and hearing another Malcolm X. Or maybe he had always been sensitive and compassionate in his private moments. I knew the public Malcolm—argumentative, fiery, analytical—now, on the patio of this European-infested hostel, he sounded like a poet describing the Africa he had seen; his imagery was brilliant, his verse elegant, and I was touched deeply by his honesty and perception. Perhaps this Malcolm should not have surprised me, for I was sure other intimates had seen it, and much more. Failing to have imagined that a political leader passionately involved with the common man could be sensitive, elegant, and profound was another blow to the proper Negro still playing havoc with my intellectual development. Julian's cynicism was partially right. I knew where Harlem was, felt a part of its tragedy and genius, but I had never been there. My political liberation had come from universities and student protest movements, which had given me some historical indication of the importance of the Harlems of the world; and now I knew that a further liberation was yet to come.

"How many of us are out here, Julian?" Malcolm's question made us all sit up.

"About three hundred."

"Beautiful. That's beautiful. . . . What are we doing?"

Julian smiled, and some of us laughed. "All of us are trying to help the President from different levels of involvement. We are represented in most institutions in the country."

"That's what I call making a real revolution."

We laughed with relief at Malcolm's reply, and believe me, fifty Harlem voices are not easily accommodated in a British-African hotel at tea time!

"Malcolm," Julian said, "let's leave this place and go over to my house. Ana Livia has prepared lunch for us. Besides, this is not the best place to discuss issues!" Julian did not like the Ambassador, and in his five years in Ghana, had been there very few times.

As we walked out of the hotel, Malcolm turned, looked at the patio we had just left, and remarked, "When I get home,

I'm going to tell all those Negroes who still want to integrate that they should come to the Ambassador Hotel—'cause that's where the action is!"

Finally we were back at Julian's house. Most of the group had to return to their jobs; only ten of us, including the Malcolm X Committee, had lunch. Without exaggeration, it was the best meal of my life.

We laughed, slapped hands, listened to Bessie Smith, talked some more, ate Ana Livia's curried goat, looked at Malcolm and *felt good*, looked at each other and *felt good*, listened to Miles and *felt good*, and talked about Harlem, West Oakland, Chicago, ate some more; and finally, after all that Soul, we sat down to talk to our leader.

"Well, Malcolm, what do you have in mind?" asked Preston King.

Malcolm thought for a few moments, took out his notebook, and began to talk. "I would like to talk to my black brothers in Ghana. I want to explain to those who may not know the evils of American racism and its implications for black people everywhere. I am going to be here for four days and I'll do whatever I can during that period. . . . I look to you to give me some ideas about the political situation here and some of the things which I should expect and prepare for."

All of us shared our knowledge and experience with him, and ironically enough, Malcolm taught us much about Ghanaian life, just from the questions he asked.

Eventually, Julian said, "Malcolm, we thought maybe your first major speech should be at the university. Les here has helped to organize a Marxist study forum, and his group has tentatively arranged plans for your address tomorrow night. Do you have any objections to speaking to a Marxist study forum?"

"In Europe or America I would have some reservations, but out here I think I can deal with it. I assume that the forum is run by black people?"

"Yes, it is," I said emphatically.

Malcolm looked at me strangely and remarked, "Your name is Les Lacy?"

"Yes, I'm Les Lacy."

"Wait a minute." Malcolm looked through his pockets and brought out a crumpled sheet of white paper. "I met a brother called Larry Jackson in Lagos. He told me to tell you and Guy Johnson hello. I like Larry. He seems to be a good brother."

"He is. How's he doing?" I asked.

"He's doing fine. Trying to stay out of the way of white Americans. Otherwise he's in good shape."

After another two hours Malcolm's exhaustive schedule was ready. We left so he could rest for a few hours. Much later in the evening Malcolm held a press conference at the Ghana Press Club. A few American reporters asked the usual ridiculous questions, and Malcolm used this occasion to expose their subtle racism while at the same time bringing his message to the black people he had come to address. The next morning the *Daily Graphic* (privately owned but government influenced) carried the following story.

Help U.S. Negroes—Malcolm X

Mr. Malcolm X, the great Afro-American Moslem leader, declared in Accra yesterday that the struggle by Negroes for civil rights in the United States should be switched for a struggle for human rights, to enable Africans to raise the matter at the United Nations. Addressing pressmen at the Press Club, the Moslem leader said that the 22 million people of African descent in the United States were living in prison.

He described the U.S. as the "master of imperialism" without whose support France, South Africa, Britain and Portugal could not exist.

Mr. Malcolm X appealed for support from all Africans for their brothers and sisters in the United States. He praised Osagyefo the President and said as a result of his able, sincere and dedicated leadership, America feared Ghana. The Moslem leader pointed out that whenever a mature African leader, like Osagyefo, tries to unite the people of the continent they always label him as a dictator in order to discredit him.

Meanwhile, the Marxist Forum prepared for Malcolm's address at the university. As expected, a few university officials tried to sabotage our efforts, but we outmaneuvered them without too much difficulty. These officials had made peace with the forum but did not consider Malcolm's politics within the scope of the forum's objectives. Their prime concern was that the government and the press might use Malcolm X against them in the power struggle, and make it seem like the prominent university officials were anti-Malcolm. This may have been true; however, the university's grievance was primarily against Kwame Nkrumah, not Malcolm X.

I had tried without success to meet Malcolm earlier in the evening so that I could explain in greater detail the government-university dispute. I knew that living at the Press Club and being constantly surrounded by party officials and supporters would surely give him a distorted picture of the actual situation. I was right. Malcolm came to Legon that evening with the government's conception of university politics.

Hesse, Duggan, King, and I met Malcolm at the entrance to the Great Hall and walked down the aisle with him to the podium as the audience stood and clapped politely. We took our seats. The atmosphere was tense. A massacred soul had come to speak to a demoralized youth. . . . What would Malcolm say? Had the party given him instructions? It was too quiet. Duggan's breath heaved like a wounded gland. If only someone would cough. The world was our audience; every aspect of international politics was represented. . . . Someone said fifty CIA agents were there. No one knew what to expect.

I wish Preston would get up and introduce him, I thought. But he can't. Even though the hall is packed, it's only seven-forty-five . . . got to wait until eight.

Finally, finally, the man from Georgia with an upper-class London accent did his thing.

Sit down, I kept thinking. You're talking too much. I give you . . .

Then came Malcolm. The audience was still again, waiting. Suddenly the television Malcolm spoke out. He praised the president of Ghana, the party, and struck out at their detractors. I hoped he would not go on that way. . . . He spoke of Nkrumah like he spoke of Elijah Muhammad; then he gave his address:

. . . No condition of any people on earth is more deplorable than the condition or plight of the twenty-two million black people in America. When we are born in a country that stands up and represents itself as the leader of the free world, and you still have to beg and crawl just to get a chance to drink a cup of coffee, then the condition is very deplorable indeed. . . .

I don't feel that I am a visitor in Ghana or in any part of Africa. I feel that I am at home. I've been away for four hundred years [Laughter], but not of my own volition, not of my own will. . . .

This is the most beautiful continent that I've ever seen, and strange as it may seem, I find many white Americans here smiling in the faces of our African brothers like they have been loving them all the time. [Laughter and applause.]

. . . But actually what it is, they want to integrate with the wealth that they know is here—the untapped natural resources which exceed the wealth of any continent on this earth today. . . .

The President of this nation has done something that no American wants to see done . . . and that is he's restoring the African image. There is probably no more enlightened leader on the African continent than President Nkrumah, because he lived in America. He knows what it is like there. You come there and take off your national dress and be mistaken for an American Negro, and you will find out you're not in the land of the free. [Loud applause.] America is a colonial power. There is a growing tendency among black Americans today . . . they are reaching the point where they are ready to tell the Man no matter what the odds are against them: it's liberty or death.

The students loved him. They cheered and they chanted. They shouted at the top of their voices songs of praise in different Ghanaian languages. Lebrette Hesse called that the Ghanaian "violent elation." I felt very good that night, because in a way I was responsible for those young voices shouting for Malcolm—voices the government called "reactionary." One student ran up and kissed his hand. A female student stood in front of him and cried, but said nothing. Only the CPP-ites seemed annoyed. A bloodless war with the university was over— they had lost the last round.

That night a crisis developed in the Afro-American community. Malcolm had returned to his place of rest. A few of the males in the community wanted to talk with him—needing, you might say, a soul session. The sisters who watched over him like mother hens would not hear of it. As one sister said,

"Malcolm is tired and has no time to be concerned with your foolishness." Malcolm was tired, completely knocked out. The brothers understood but were having problems, severe ones, and they wanted the master's advice. If Malcolm had known of their needs, he would have come, but the sisters were having none of this "foolishness." On the surface I supported the sisters. Underneath, the situation was far more complicated, because ultimately it had nothing to do with Malcolm.

The Afro-American women in our community, at least the unmarried ones, were going through a difficult period in Ghana. Aside from the normal adjustments, they had emotional ones to make too—to the benefits and burdens of a male-dominated black society. Since there were no rigid rules, male chauvinism prevailed. They were exceptional women, so they survived, but not without its costing them some of their emotional strength. Balance that off with the fact that some of the brothers were married to white women and that the others tended to prefer the local ones. They had Ghanaian men, but these invariably had other women. Again, they could deal with that, but only a very few liked it. Around this time I wrote, "Black woman, you, my sister, are a sadness. . . .

"You cry for men, strong men, and your voice grows stronger. . . . You hate and you blame, because your security has been threatened; a tragedy grips your consciousness—a history of rejection shapes your expectations. . . . We let them open you —your sexual outhouse . . .

> exposed,
> blamed.
> We gave the white woman
> your place, our
> name,
> and believed
> that our children from her
> would grow up
> black,
> beautiful,
> brave,
> big,
> American,
> and free,

". . . and would marry the children which we gave to you out of wedlock. But our children grew up absurd,

> hated you and
> your children
> 'cause they were
> black,
> and we were mixed with
> fear,
> dreams,
> a mood of freedom,
> blood
> from a devil's cup,
> where life is perverted,

". . . and with apologies to Hughes—deferred. Now you are here—here in Mother Africa. Home.

> Forced to hide your beauty,
> forced to hide your anger,
> forced to bed with small boys
> with big voices,
> commercial manhoods
> who dominate but
> do not love you.
> Who blame you but
> do not fight to free you.

> No love for you, black woman,
> No love for you,
> No love for you,

". . . until a new manhood is born out of violence and revolution which loves you, respects you, marries you and closes your sexual outhouse for ever and ever. Amen, black men, Amen."

Malcolm represented that new black man: strong, responsible, angry, compassionate, and committed. They knew that they could not have him though. He was "had" already. Betty was waiting. They were just watching. Why bother with men who are only enjoying the pleasures of exile, anyway?

The following day the brothers and sisters relaxed their

differences and turned their full attention back to Malcolm. We read with interest the reports of his Legon address. "Negroes Need Your Help" was the title of the article published the following day about the speech in the *Daily Graphic*. "Mr. Malcolm X, the militant Afro-American nationalist, has called for concerted efforts by African states on the governmental level to bring pressure to bear on the United States government to solve the racial problem of that country. Mr. X was speaking at the University of Ghana on the 'plight of the 22 million Afro-Americans in the United States.'. . ."

The article highlighted Malcolm's speech, but interestingly enough, did not mention the exceptional student reactions, which were anything but "reactionary."

Pushing through our hectic schedule, we next accompanied Malcolm to Parliament House, where he had been granted an audience with the members of Parliament. The *Ghanaian Times* was there to cover the story.

Malcolm X Addresses MPs

In keeping with the policy of getting to learn facts on every issue, Members of Parliament yesterday granted audience to Mr. Malcolm X, the visiting militant Afro-American Black Muslim leader, at the lounge of Parliament House, Accra.

Mr. X spoke on the degrading status of the Afro-American in the United States. A lively discussion followed his address, during which the MPs asked questions of topical interest.

His last engagement was at the Nkrumah Institute, a political indoctrination center where the students were stuffed with Nkrumahisms which were to prepare them for eventual political activity. Malcolm was tired—the Afros had encircled him during his few free moments—but he was as eager and excited as he had been on his first day among us.

He left for North Africa the next day.

XIV

The Return

HIS SECOND coming caught us by surprise. Why was he back? Hadn't he read the Ghanaian newspapers? He had been severly criticized for his Legon speech. Two days after Malcolm's first visit, Mr. Basner had written a highly critical article in the *Ghanaian Times*.

Mr. Basner, better known as H. M. Basner, was a professional Marxist from South Africa. He was white. He had practiced law in South Africa before coming to Ghana, and he had always been known to be on the right side of the freedom struggle in South Africa. There was a warrant for his arrest awaiting him in Cape Town. Like other South Africans, both white and black, Basner had obtained a job in Nkrumah's government. But unlike his South African compatriots, he held an extremely important job. He wrote a column, "Watching the World from Accra," for the *Ghanaian Times*, and he served as an advisor to President Nkrumah. Without a doubt he was one of the most, if not the most, important of the expatriates on Nkrumah's payroll. So what he wrote was relevant.

Basner had written that our leader was a nationalist, and therefore a racist. In new Marxist terminology, he attempted to expose the weaknesses of Malcolm's political philosophy, and of course, concluded that there was but one hope: Blacks and Whites working together. To use Basner's words, the only hope for the races was "the army of the oppressed."

Julian had written a brilliant reply to this Marxist nonsense and covered in a much briefer form what Harold Cruse later covered in his book *The Crisis of the Negro Intellectual*. In substance, Julian's point was that communist theories of class and race are not applicable as a solution for black America. Shirley Du Bois wrote a similar article in support of Julian's position, but Basner had the last word, for after his second article the debate was mysteriously stopped. It was rumored that Nkrumah had ordered the dispute discontinued.

We had all known Basner's private political sentiments, but they had appeared in a government-controlled newspaper. Had Nkrumah approved of his views? Did that mean that the Ghanaian government would support Basner's African Nationalist Congress, a predominately white communist freedom movement, in South Africa in preference to the black nationalist breakaway group called the Pan-African Congress? Did that mean that Nkrumah was leaning more toward the Russians than toward the nationalist Chinese? And, more important, what implications would this have for the black-nationalist-oriented black community in Accra?

Malcolm gave us only twenty-five minutes notice, a call from the airport. But we were ready. Most of us had not gone back to our old lives. Malcolm the man, the father, the person, the revolutionary, and all that we had seen and felt as a result of his visit, had had a converting effect upon our lives, and he had outlined specific plans for how we could aid our struggle for human rights in America.

Julian met him at the airport and brought him to my place at Legon. I greeted them outside and the three of us entered my living room. Brother Malcolm looked tired, very tired—like a black man who has looked for a new apartment and is tired and disgusted, first because he did not find a place, and second because he has walked for many hours. Or perhaps what I saw on Malcolm's sun-tanned face was fear. He had been preoccupied with thoughts of death and assassination on his first visit, and now, as he talked, sometimes incoherently, I felt a strange feeling of finality.

I tried to relax him. I offered him a glass of water. I was sorry that I did not have any Ghanaian food, because I knew how much he liked it. I had some oranges in the kitchen, so I made him some orange juice. He drank the first glass and I gave him another.

Malcolm sat down in one of the chairs. It was my best chair. He moved up and down and from side to side, trying to find the spot which would allow him to relax. The chair was a product of local industry, and the Ghanaian carpenters had not yet discovered how to make a seat comfortable. Huge and inviting pillows gave the chair the look of comfort; but as was often the case in Ghana, outward manifestations were misleading. Soon Malcolm gave up his search and settled for a chair that he could at least sit on. There was a mildly irritated look on his face, but he smiled and sat down.

"Is there much corruption here?" he asked innocently after he had picked up a copy of the *Ghanaian Times* and had seen the headline "Down with Corruption."

Malcolm continued to read the ten-page government-controlled newspaper, but after a few moments, looked at Julian for an answer to his question.

"There is some corruption."

"How much?"

"It's difficult to tell."

"How does Mr. Nkrumah deal with it?"

Julian smiled and searched his pockets for a cigarette. Apparently the question had made him a little uneasy. Corruption in office was a subject few people wanted to discuss, because no one knew to what extent it existed. The Afro-Americans tended to overlook minor forms of corruption in Ghana, and only the select political elite knew the workings of the inner kingdom. Julian was especially sensitive on the issue. We always knew that he *knew*, but he never spoke. I knew him well, but much of our relationship was nonpolitical.

The only thing he had ever said to me about the government was: "We don't need a lot of party loyalists. What we need are committed men and women who are willing to live on their own salaries."

Julian lit his cigarette and said, "The President has taken several steps to crack down. Three months ago he set up a commission to investigate corruption in public office. But if he were to shoot a few of his ministers, other crooks would soon get the point."

Julian then told us a long story about another Nkrumah watcher, who had gone to see the President about the "guilty men" in his government. According to Julian, this watcher had told the President: "Mr. President, there are men in your government who are stealing. They are stealing every day. We know they are stealing, and we think you know they are stealing; and since they are not arrested, some of us think that you are stealing too." The next week this party loyalist told Julian, "I have been reduced to the status of a caterer. I am no longer in politics. I am now in charge of the state bakery."

Malcolm seemed perplexed by the whole account. Like most of us before coming to Ghana, he admired Kwame Nkrumah for his militant policies and his strong advocacy of black solidarity.

"I guess Mr. Nkrumah knows how to best deal with his people," Malcolm said with a shrug.

Julian remained silent.

Suddenly there was a knock on the door, and Julian went to open it.

"Is Mr. Lacy here?" asked a soft voice from outside.

"Yeah, man," Julian said with disgust. He stood at the door in his stocking feet, with his hands belligerently thrust in his pockets and a scowl on his face, for several minutes, then let the young Ghanaian enter. He had little love for students.

"Mr. X!" the student said with surprise. "We thought you had gone." The student paused. He seemed overcome by elation. "Mr. X, I'm glad to see you."

Julian smiled cynically and went into the kitchen.

Malcolm seemed touched by the concern of the student who was genuinely happy to see our leader. His elation was so completely revealed even Julian could not deny it.

By now Malcolm was on his feet. He gave the student the brotherhood handshake, which other students had taught him on his first visit. "What is your name?" he asked.

"Kwame," the student replied in a manly voice. "I come from Kumasi. I am Ashanti."

"Very good. What are you studying?"

"I'm reading law."

Malcolm didn't understand "reading law." The student explained that it was the same as studying law, but that the English say "reading" rather than "studying."

"How is the struggle in America?" the student asked excitedly.

"There are always problems."

"What kind of problems?" Kwame asked with concern.

"Well, the white man has poisoned the minds of black people in America for so long that it will be hard to organize our people and teach them black nationalism."

"Well, if we can help, let us know," Kwame said authoritatively. "Mr. X, will you be able to speak to us again? I'm sure the Marxist Forum could arrange it."

"I don't know yet, but we'll see. I hope so, Kwame."

The student got up, gave Brother Malcolm the shake, and left, running to tell his friends that Malcolm had returned.

Malcolm was pleased. He loved students. Kwame and hundreds of other students who had heard his historic speech at the University of Ghana seemed to sense that. In my two years at the university, I had never before seen the students in such total agreement. They had talked about Malcolm for days after he left. One folk singer had created a song in his honor, called "Malcolm Man."

> Malcolm Man, Malcolm Man,
> You speak your tale of woe,
> The red in your face like the
> Blood on the land,
> You speak your tale of woe.
> Malcolm Man, Malcolm Man,

The anger that you feel
Will one day unite our people
And make us all so real.
Malcolm Man, Malcolm Man . . .

Malcolm Man had also inspired the students to political action. To the surprise of everyone, ten students at Legon had formed a Malcolm X Society. And, of course, the question which no one, especially party activists, could answer was, why had "reactionary" students cheered and applauded a revolutionary?

Then came another knock on the door. More students, I thought.

"Kwame, did you forget something?" I asked as I opened the door. I remembered that he had originally come to see me but had been distracted upon seeing Malcolm.

"No . . ." he said in a very soft voice.

We could tell that he had something on his mind, but he seemed afraid to speak. He paced the length of the living room twice, and then stood near Malcolm's seat.

"Speak, man, speak," Julian shouted impatiently. "Mr. X has other appointments."

"Is there something you have to tell me?" asked Malcolm sympathetically.

"Yes, Mr. X," the student replied as he looked into Malcolm's face. "I want to say that the students do not believe what Mr. Basner said about you in the *Ghanaian Times*. None of us here like him. We wish he would go back to South Africa."

"Who is Mr. Basner? What article do you mean?"

"Hasn't Mr. Mayfield told you about it? He wrote a reply to those vicious remarks." The room became silent, and after a few moments the student excused himself and left.

Malcolm looked at both of us. Who should tell him? I thought.

"Mayfield, what is this about?" Malcolm demanded.

Julian told Malcolm everything, and Malcolm sat perplexed until he had finished. Then Malcolm stood and stretched his arms. "I guess Mr. Nkrumah knows what he is doing. I've got twenty million other black people to think about right now, and I guess I should get back to them soon."

Malcolm looked around the room, letting his eyes linger on that invitingly stuffed chair he had earlier struggled with. He still looked tired. Thanking me for everything, he left with Julian for Accra. Two days later he left the country.

His second coming, unlike his first, was quiet and un-eventful. On his first coming, he had received a hero's welcome, speeches all over the country, addresses to Parliament, excellent press coverage; he had met the President. And of course, there had been Mr. Basner.

XV

Toward My Last Days

As HISTORY would have it, the "Mayfield-Basner Bride-Groom Squabbles" as they were called over and over again by the Ghanaian students (who were good at creating slogans), brought me closer to these young men who would one day inherit the political kingdom. It was an embarrassing development, because I had thought, after two years, I knew them; and it took several months for me to recover from this over-confidence and arrogance, by which time they had taken me a long way toward beginning to understand their real attitudes— and also, their families, friends, and the people of the villages, towns, and cities they had come from. In essence they exposed me to their cultures: diverse, complicated, strong, flexible, but "primitive" to those who could not understand them. By "culture" I do not simply mean language and traditions, but the way in which a man views the world, the power sources behind the values, the source which motivates an individual to live. I came to see that the strength of Ghana was still on the land. If only that power could be brought to the national level.

I learned a lot about Ghana that summer; spent my days working in various villages and nights fighting mosquitoes and thinking how we would express these discoveries in the forum. Nights were always the hardest. I could deal with the heat and the insects, but not with my thoughts. How could you express African ideas through a Marxist forum? The whole idea seemed absurd. Changing the name or even the direction of the forum was not sufficient either, for ultimately you faced the problems which none of us could fathom. How do you express a way of life through structures which that life has not created? How could Kumasi, Ho, Cape Coast, Tamale, Senghor, black glassmaker, Aburi, listen to their own rhythms like children on their mothers' back? How could Africans return to the ancient while still remaining modern . . . linking thought to act, "ear to heart, sign to sense"? How could Africa become modernized without being Westernized?

Perhaps these were the wrong questions, but even if they were the right ones, we had no answers, no direction. For the first time I did not envy the black men and women who had power. Outside and inside, they had powerful enemies. Outside, if they could *see*, and even if they couldn't, there was Mr. Western World: tall, white, powerful, arrogant. Walking, stalking. Waiting to judge—"I told you so"—and if necessary, getting down from his police horse to draw. And bang, bang—you're dead! Look out, black man, white power can get your mamma and my wife too.

And inside? The problems of a society which has not developed naturally. And socialism, mobilization theories, were only part of the answer.

One day I had a glimpse into the future. I was in a small village near Sekondi in western Ghana. Typical of those in other villages which I had seen, the people were poor, but proud, At the end of the second week, the headmaster of the village's only school came to see me and the student I was staying with. He knocked on the door and entered at the same moment that the student's father told him he could. Since *strangers* are not strangers in a Ghanaian household, he was made comfortable immediately, and he came right to his point.

For my benefit the old headmaster spoke in English. "*Tell me*," he began, "*what is going on in Accra? I am confused. . . .*

What is the CPP doing? I can make no sense these days of Accra. Not so long ago I was very active in the party. I knew Osagyefo, like everybody knew him. Then that man was very dynamic, a hard worker, and spoke well against the British. We followed him. We believed. Now, which is why I came to you, I do not know what has happened. You are students. You speak well of him; I have heard you talk to our people here. The returned son"—his eyes were on me—*"does not speak our language, but we hear him, and he, too, speaks well of the Old Man.*

"I want to know, what is this socialism? I can make no sense of it. Every month, a CPP man comes to speak to my people. He stands a safe distance away from the people"— the headmaster smiled—*"reads for fifteen minutes from a printed speech. He then gives to us many copies of the paper called* Spark, *then he goes and gets into his Mercedes-Benz and drives away.*

"Now. When he leaves, those of us who read English find this in the paper: the first page is a discussion of the African personality versus Negritude; the second page is a discussion of the Sino-Soviet dispute; the third page is a discussion of the World Federation of Trade Unions versus the International Federation of Free Trade Unions, and the last page is a discussion of Osagyefo's version of socialism, which he calls conscientism. Why?

"Now. We are very simple people here. We work hard and we get what we can for our lives. . . . Again, I ask because you are students, what is this socialism?"

The student whom I had come to stay with—and once the headmaster's student—answered him in the language of the village. Some words were English, but most were Fanti. I understood enough to get a general sense of what was being said. I was surprised that the student, who was not an admirer of Nkrumah's politics, was trying to explain (without being critical of Osagyefo) the concept of socialism. Into the early morning hours, the student tried to make his meanings clear to his former teacher and the other men who had joined us. But the Legonite was laboriously working against himself. The crowd possessed no idealism; Nkrumah had brought the word "socialism" to their village as he had brought it throughout the land, and from their perspective, the CPP and socialism were synonomous. If socialism was for the good of the Ghanaian people, why were the people powerless and poor and the leaders powerful and rich? The student had confidence but no answers for men who had brought Padmore's disciple to power. And it was also impossible, in Fanti, English, or any other tongue, to explain to these poor but intelligent men of the land how the Sino-Soviet dispute had any meaning for their crops.

Finally the headmaster said, "It is late. We must get up early tomorrow. We believe you, but we do not believe what you say. . . . We are simple men, and we believe what we see. May your sleep be good."

When they left, the student looked at me and said, "This is what you could not have learned in America. May your sleep be good also."

In early October I returned to Legon. In town after town I had heard the headmaster's feelings repeated. "What is this socialism?" And more than once I had wondered whether the president was aware of the growing popular alienation and disillusionment with his policies. Surely his advisors were conscious of this disaffection and discontent. Maybe they believed their own rhetoric? Or perhaps I had seen an unrepresentative sampling?

The university was still on vacation. I had lots of hours to think and study because school was not scheduled to open for another couple of weeks. Although the students were not at Legon, they would nevertheless be studying. In 1964 the government had ordered that every student at the university spend two weeks before each academic year at the Winneba Ideological Institute letting the Russians, eastern Europeans, and a few Ghanaians straighten out their political education.

Near the end of the first week, I had an unexpected visit from one of the party's students. I stood up, opened the door and sat down. I had a passionate aversion to him, not because of his practical politics, but because on very reliable authority he was known to be Legon's chief informer. Presumably informers are necessary, but I had by then (and still have now) an intense dislike for any of them: Black, white, right, left . . . whatever.

In a commanding voice he said, "Lacy, Mr. Addison wants to see you immediately. I am to inform you that it is very urgent."

I ignored him, as I always did, and that usually angered him, because in spite of his incredible innocence, he was very much aware of my hostility.

"Lacy! Lacy . . . you heard me. I said the party wants to see you."

Five second pause.

"Now, Lacy. Right now."

"Why, hello, Edward. How are you doing? Thought you'd be lecturing down at Winneba."

"That's where you need to be. You need to learn some real socialist theory."

I smiled contemptuously. "You're probably right, but you see, I didn't get my invitation. Did you bring it?"

"No. We don't send invitations. Unlike you, the other students go because they are interested in the development of the country."

"Then, why aren't you there?"

"Because I already have my political education."

"Okay, let me give you a test. What did Stalin have to eat at his twenty-fifth birthday party?"

"Look, fool, I am not here to be tested by the likes of you. I have already proven my loyalty to the people who matter."

"I'm sure you have. How many students did you inform on last academic year? Was it fifty or a hundred?"

"I am not an informer. If anything, you might call me a political watchdog."

"Yes, dog is probably an appropriate appellation. Back in Louisiana we had a watchdog, and he barked so loud that one day I poisoned him."

"Lacy, your capitalist jokes are not funny. I am not here to be amused, in any case. The party wants to see you and I would advise you to get dressed and go over to see Mr. Addison."

"Why should the Convention People's party want to see me? I am a small boy; you are the Big Man. Wait. I know. They need a new group of informers for 1965–6?"

"Lacy, one of these days I'm going to personally put you on a plane back to America."

"But that isn't fair. You are a just man. Why not take me to jail? I hear the security prisons are very romantic. They tell me that the rooms are air conditioned—"

The informer interrupted, "If you are trying to be witty, you need not. Security prisons are necessary in a developing country with so many British and American agents around."

"Splendid. Then go and arrest them and leave me alone. I don't have time for your machinations. Now leave my room before I forget that I am a gentleman."

"Is that a threat?"

I stood up and looked directly in his face. "Call it what you like. You are good for making up names. But get the hell out of my room."

He backed up to the door, opened it, and I sat down.

"Lacy, the trouble with you is that you are *hopelessly pompous*, and we have no use for people like you in our country. You should be grateful that we let you Afro-Americans stay here, for if I were running things, I'd put all of you out."

"Your country? Well, Mr. Informer, let me tell you that this is my country too. My ancestors did not ask to leave here. More than likely, your ancestors did the selling. Now I'm back and I have just as much right to be here as you have. *Now leave!*" I began to write at my desk.

"Lacy!" he shouted. "I am not joking. Mr. Addison wants to see you now. Today!"

I started from my seat, but before I could get my hands on him, he ran out of the building.

Not for a second had I assumed he was joking. With his mentality, he would never use the party name in vain. But what did they want from me?

Later that afternoon I went to see Mr. Addison. Comrade Addison was a Big Man: not only was he a high-ranking party member and director of the Ideological Institute, but more important, he was one of three men on the vice-presidential commission, a body which ruled the country when the President was away.

When I arrived at his modest home, a stone's throw from the President's office at Flagstaff House, one of his stewards showed me into his small living room. It was filled with student leaders from all over the country, and they smiled friendly as I entered while they continued listening to Mr. Addison. My smile was controlled, because I was completely in the dark.

Comrade Addison was a big man physically as well. His Chinese-like eyes and large nose made him look rather interesting, and most of the Ghanaian women I had talked with thought of him as attractive. Indeed he was.

From what I could gather, the party had held a high strategy meeting, and had decided, among other things, to reorganize *their* students throughout the country. Being late, I had missed all the details. For the rest of the afternoon Comrade Addison summarized with the standard CPP slogans: "Down with Reaction," "Up with Socialism," "Death to Colonialism," "Life to National Reconstruction," and so on. When he finished, the students clapped politely, and gradually departed, after they had asked all the right questions. Finally Mr. Addison and I were alone.

"Well, so you are the famous Mr. Lacy." He was very flattering and excited.

"I wouldn't call myself famous." I smiled somewhat more than I had when I entered.

"Well, to us you are famous. You have done a lot of interesting things since you come to this country two and a half years ago."

"Thank you."

"The party is pleased with some of your accomplishments, which is one of the reasons I sent for you."

"Thank you again."

"Fine. Would you like to have a drink?"

"Okay," I said indifferently. "It's kind of early for me, but I'll have something."

"Gin, whisky, or beer?"

"I guess I'll have beer."

He clapped his large hands and his steward ran into the room, almost stumbling over his own feet. Mr. Addison spoke to him in Twi and told him to bring me beer and to get him a glass of whisky.

"I understand you are doing a degree at the Institute of African Studies."

"I am."

"What do you think of our Institute?"

Naturally I said, "It's a fine Institute."

The steward who looked frightened returned with the drinks, quickly left the room and we drank a toast to the revolution.

"Now, Lacy"—Mr. Addison put his glass down—"as I said earlier, the party is pleased with the work of the forum. It was a great idea. Was it your idea?"

"Three of us organized it. It was a collective effort."

"Was there any outside help?" He took a sip of whisky and looked at me suspiciously over the glass.

"What do you mean by outside?" As if I didn't know.

"Well, you know. . . . I mean to say, were you independent of any other group?"

"Absolutely." I was very emphatic.

"Good. Now this is what you have to do. The party has decided that the Marxist Forum is good for the university. We liked the programs and your general political style. But one thing must change immediately." He was confident.

"And what thing is that?"

"You must change the name of the Marxist Study Forum to the Nkrumahist Forum. Starting the new school year, the new move is to go into effect. You are to work with the CPP students on the campus and you will get every assistance which you need from me."

"But why must we change our name?"

"Because the party has decided that in the interest of national issues, the name change is necessary." He was just a bit annoyed.

"Mr. Addison, with all due respect for the party and its wisdom, I think that might not be a wise move to make at this time."

"Why not?"

"Well . . . " I hesitated.

"Go ahead, be frank. The party likes frankness."

"Well, I think it would be unwise because if we change our name, it might have an overall negative effect on our program."

"Now, let me understand you. Changing the name to the Nkrumahist Forum would have a negative effect on your program? How so?" He was polite but not pleased.

"Well, maybe 'negative' is just a bit strong. Let me say it might make us less effective."

"Why?"

"Because the students would have every reason to believe that we are being controlled by you. Many of them had that impression when we first organized, but I can happily say that most of them no longer think so. Being frank, I don't have to tell you what the prevailing political attitudes are. You know much better than I ever will. All I can say is that a great part of our initial success lay in the fact that we were independent. If we change our name, work openly or secretly with your students, and depend on you for assistance, I think we will lose much of what we have been working for. You also know, Mr. Addison, that in order to change deep-seated prejudices it is sometimes necessary to move very slowly.

"Again, speaking frankly, I believe that the party failed at the university. You have made 'socialism' an ugly word and alienated many students. The Marxist Forum has not succeeded in recouping your losses, but it has gone a long way in enabling the students to re-examine radical political concepts without feeling that they were being forced to do so. If you must change the name, which is probably a good thing, since Marx was a European, call it the Legon Forum, call it anything but the Nkrumahist Forum. In time you will be able to call it the Nkrumahist Forum, but by then—perhaps three years from now—you will have re-established your dialogue with the students. What I'm saying is this: Let us do your job for you, and in time you can have the university on a silver platter."

"Rubbish." He was on his feet and very angry. "You are an American and you don't understand our ways. The party has decided, and that decision will be carried through. Inform your chaps immediately upon their return from Winneba, and get the changes through right away. That's an *order*."

"But, Mr. Addison—"

"The party," he interrupted, "has spoken, Mr. Lacy. There will be no further discussion. Good day."

Thus spoke the party. . . . A decision to change the name, and by extension the content, and immediately the direction of the forum had already been made. We had not been consulted, because they were wise Big Men, and their wisdom and bigness were impervious to the impressions of small boys, even if they had developed out of an overall commitment. Yet assuming, as I imagine one should, that the party was genuine and seriously interested in recapturing the university, you would think that before making a definite decision about such an important issue—especially at that time in Ghanaian history—it would have wanted some firsthand knowledge from individuals who had had greater success in their efforts than the party had had. It would have made good political sense, an excellent characteristic, which the party had displayed in its earlier evolution.

Addison and those he represented had power. From that vantage point, I was seen as simply an Afro-American Hamlet figure, distracted, pursuing a ghost. Because, surely, if they had thought we had domestic political ambitions, Harold Duggan and I would have been writing letters from America to Lebrette Hesse in a detention camp.

Also, and indeed more relevant, Addison's anger and impatience were out of proportion to the objections I had raised. Politics aside, he viewed my criticisms as an attack upon him. This psychological behavior was a constant problem. People who are or have been oppressed in modern times have interesting and contradictory reactions both to the oppressor and to each other. In this case, both Mr. Addison (representative of many others in Ghana and elsewhere in Africa) and I had experienced oppression, but from different points of time, history, and culture. Even before I met him, I had attitudes about him, as on his part, he did about me. I was prepared to accept him, follow, and believe in him as part of the evidence needed to convince myself that Blacks were not sub-humans. His background—colonization in Africa had often been oppressive in ways paralleling those of enslavement—

had created a slightly but significantly different psyche. Which had not prepared him to accept, follow, or believe in me. (Thank heaven, he didn't.)

In his country he felt both inferior and superior to me. The latter because he had power; the former because I was an Afro-American. Being oppressed, he thought himself inferior to the master, especially since he had confronted, assimilated, touched, or internalized all or part of the latter's culture. In this state, if only subconsciously, he would assume that black people who are closer to the white man are more civilized. Hence better. By his definition, then, an Afro-American would be better than a Ghanaian. And thinking that Afros are better, he would feel, as many Negroes do feel, that the "betters" feel better. (An interesting form of unconscious identification quite similar in substance to that which the rural Negro, who does not understand, has with the urban Negro, whom he resents for not being himself, or like he is, and whom he feels oppressed or intimidated by.)

Given this state of mind, the Addisons of the oppressed world must protect themselves from the real or apparent arrogance of the Lacys in that world. The Addisons are authoritative and in command when they deal with the Lacys, so that the "more civilized" ones will see that the "less civilized" ones are as big (usually bigger) than they are. The greater the inferiority felt, the greater the hostility. Even if a black person does not act or think like the Negro, he is still not free from the hostility, even if he "proves that he is not arrogant," since he might say something which is interpreted as such.

Ironically, and tragically, the perceptive and conscious New World Black is likely to find himself doing a little black Uncle Tomming in Africa in order not to be disliked, since that is why he came, and also because, in his own confused inferiority, he believes that criticism of Africans would support the racist notions Whites have about all black people. Any *serious exchange* is ultimately impossible, because it hurts too much to be honest.

So I followed Big Man Mr. Addison's orders.

When the students returned with their heads packed with communist humanisms, I added to their miseries by informing them of what we *had* to do. They listened but did not want to believe. Hurt too, because for the first time in their young lives, they had done something they assumed the party (however annoyed because it had not been the initiator) would have approved.

It was looking at them—some unable to speak, most quiet, one or two smiling painfully—that I understood, for the first time, demoralization. Later, however, I realized that I had seen it before, but never quite so vividly. The men and women I had seen and heard that summer in the villages and towns were also demoralized. I could not see it as I could see this, but it had been there—perhaps more so, because they had seen Nkrumah when he was younger. And now, because he had become Osagyefo Dr. Kwame Nkrumah, they did not recognize him.

For days the students tried to see the President, but always they received the same words: "Sorry, he's busy." Too busy to see his own future. The students returned to their studies. Hesse's words remain in my mind: "They just don't care. We will become old without becoming anything, because for the thousandth time in our history, we can become big men in our country, but small boys in the world."

Before I resigned from the new forum, we met with the CPP students, handed over our records, and shared freely with them our experiences. Later that week, the *Spark* made Mr. Addison's words flashingly clear: "Anyone to the right of the party is reactionary; anyone to the left of the party is an adventurer."

And as we thought, the Nkrumahist Forum lasted a few months; by the end of the year it was a forum in name only.

Meanwhile, in my new nonpolitical life, I enjoyed myself. My mother came. Emotionally I was much further along the road, and for the first time in a long while, I could love her and the Real One without much difficulty; and I understood and no longer blamed her or him for what had happened to our family.

She looked as young and beautiful in Africa as I remembered her when we lived in Franklin. The Ghanaian girls braided her hair as she had braided my sister's hair when Beatrice was a child. The sight pleased me immensely, and at the same time, reinforced my love for Ghana. Mother loved it too. She was saying incessantly, in her well-preserved Southern accent, "Leslie, this place reminds me of Franklin." Yes, it sure did, because she decided to stay. Not in Ghana, but in Sierra Leone with the man she met, loved, and married. Go ahead, Mother, and do your thing.

Then Julian's mother came. Herman's mother. Preston's mother. Tom's mother. Jim's mother. And when Herman's mother stayed so long, out come the grandmother. It was really wonderful. And these Southern women were right at home. . . . And Preston's father, when he heard what had happened to my mother, got on the next plane to Ghana, and told us when he got there that he didn't "want none of these colored fellows out here stealing my little peach."

Ron Matthew's mother (and she's got to be the prettiest woman in Brooklyn) came out because Ron was getting married to Ruth, a lovely little girl, a woman from Accra.

The night of the wedding I looked for and finally found seclusion and comfort in a local bar on the edge of Accra. Having been the best man—a thoroughly consuming and exhausting task at an African wedding, for I was required to meet, introduce, make comfortable, and remember the names of hundreds of members of an extended family, who had not met since the last important family function—I needed a year of uninterrupted rest. The lonely bar was a resting room half-way back to my bed at Legon, and a bottle of gin was an additional remedy for a heavy fatigue. I tried to think of nothing, but the bar radio's Congolese high-life music—much more dynamic and varied than the dull Ghanaian popular music—kept the day's activities looming in my mind.

It had been a beautiful day for a wedding. Ruth was a happy, handsome bride, the ebony black woman Ronald had been searching for since his arrival. To that extent, we judged it to be a perfect marriage. For Ron the marriage was a factual resolution of his social and psychological dilemmas; and for Ruth, who came from poverty and was moving toward an uncertain end, Ron represented security, freedom from the past, and the important passage to the lights and benefits of New York—the place of evil and insanity Ron had run from to find her. All day I saw their eyes and heard their words. Ron wanted those moments of joy to last forever, to fill and for a while also sustain his husbandless mother, who could not stay, because she had to return to her eight-to-four American factory and her three little rooms in a Bedford-Stuyvesant tenement. I crossed and recrossed his yard that day alternating between the reality that was his mother and the reality that was Ruth. She was poor like Ron had been poor, but the poverty was not comparable—and the commensurate alienation had produced different kinds of blackness. The former Ruth Hall was not haunted by headaches of racism and did not think her toiletless house was profound. And Ron's mother made more money in one week than she could make in six months. Ask Ruth about America: "When are we going? Tonight would not be fast enough!"

By about three o'clock in the morning the horde of laughing, jostling relatives and friends had begun to get to me. I was ready for my bed. I pushed through the screaming crowd still high-life-ing and finally got to the door. I felt just slightly dizzy, but my mind was clear. Then I hesitated. A pleasant thought entered my head and affected my body: should I take home the beautiful woman who had been smiling at and watching me for the last two hours? No, not tonight. Just me and my bed.

I stood under a street light, waiting for a taxi. I was glad that I was not in New York, because I knew I would get the first cab to come along here—no off-duty signs, no questions except, "Where are you going?" But my blackness could not assure me of a just rate. There were no metered taxis, and sometimes one had to bargain for fifteen minutes to get the price down to standardized rates. That done, it was often wise to help the driver watch the road. His cousin (distant or near) in the Department of Transport may have *given* him his license, or assuming he can drive, he might be new to the job. With four eyes looking, one's chances of getting home safely, without heart failure, are improved—unless the driver had filled his tank up in the morning, then forgotten that a constant gas supply is a necessity.

It's 1:00 A.M., you are his last passenger, and he's driving

on a bush-on-both-sides highway back to the university; you
help him watch for the first mile, or until such time that
you are convinced of your safety. Then you relax. You are
tired. Maybe drunk. Close your eyes. Might even sleep.
Suddenly you are aroused to the spurting and jerking sounds
of the car. That sound is familiar, but you refuse to accept it.
Finally the car stops. Now you know. But the driver, innocent
and embarrassed, tells you anyway. "Master, sorry." Pause.
"Petro finished."

The first time it happened to me I argued. "Didn't you
know that your car needed gas? Didn't you watch the gauge?
You are a businessman. . . . The first thing you should . . ."
and so on. The second time, I argued too. The third time, I
said nothing, knowing the drivers only smile while you rave.

That time, I got out to walk.

"Master. The snakes be big-o."

"Snakes?" I said slowly. He was not joking. It dawned on
me that during the night, snakes are around, and sometimes
stroll across the road. I remembered that a workman at the
University had been bitten and rushed to the hospital, where
he was told, "Serum finished." Immediately I ran—zigzaggedly
down the road, hopping, screaming, praying, making strange
sounds, but not stopping until I was safely in front of my door.

And the courteous taxi driver was right behind. Before I
could thank him, he *demanded* his money—not part, or half,
but all of his money.

Reason, logic, and "suppose I had been bitten" were useless.
I paid, for the same reason that I listened to Mr. Addison.

This night, I was going to make sure that the taxi had
enough "petro," because I was too exhausted to run.

"Mister, wanna buy some razor blades?" asked a soft voice
behind me.

Turning around, I saw a woman about nineteen. She was a
market woman, and it was not unusual to see such women
offering their wares around the clock. I was going to say
no, but she was already on her knees, showing me her blades.
What an assortment. She carried the United Nations on her
head. There were blades from Britain, France, Japan, America,
Brazil, India, Egypt, and China.

"China is not in yet." I laughed, and we laughed together, even though she did not understand. That's when I saw her face: surrendered, pressurized, naked, famished, futile—and still hoping for me to say yes.

I was seized by what I saw. In a thousand black faces I had seen her look, her flat nose, lips that kiss, eyes sad, looking inward to the earth. I had called all this beauty. "Black is beautiful, great, eternal," had come freely from my lips, but it had been a lie, a goddamn lie, a political whip to beat Marilyn Monroe.

But in this woman, this night, weary, waiting under a street light, I discovered that a black face is really beautiful. Its meaning screamed inside of my skull, healing my wounds, relaxing my anger. Kneeling down with her to touch her face— so she would smile—I discovered my own beauty, since the recognition of hers was the affirmation of mine.

I squeezed her. Exploded my tears in her face and laughed and screamed with joy into the sky because her innocence could not know of my suffering.

"Mister, wanna buy some razor blades?"

"Blades? Yeah, all of them. I'll buy all the blades in Africa. Africa! Africa! Africa! Africa! Africa! . . ."

XVI

The Resurrection

"Leslie! My God, Leslie. What's wrong with you?"

"Christina, you're back." I jumped up and sat on the edge of the bed while reaching for her hand so she could come and sit near me. "Christina, you are beautiful, beautiful, beautiful. Did you know that?"

"Leslie, are you sure you're okay? Haven't been smoking, have you?"

"No I'm fine! I'm fine, absolutely wonderful. Christina, from now on you've got to call me *The Blade*. That's my new name."

"Why *The Blade?*" She got up from the bed to open the windows.

"It's a long story. I'll tell you about it one day." Pause. "Christina! My God! I almost forgot. What's happening in Accra?"

"Well the coup was a success." Her voice was firm. "Now we have 'freedom,' " she added cynically.

"What happened to all the party officials and people connected to the President?"

"They are either dead, detained, in hiding, or under house arrest. The CPP has been disbanded and outlawed, and the constitution has been suspended."

"What about the Afros?"

"William Gardner Smith and a few others will be deported. I think you'll be all right for a while because you're here at Legon. Look, Leslie, I'm a little tired. I'll come over and see you later. Right now I want to rest."

"Sure, sweetheart. I'll go home. See you later."

Later that afternoon I made a journey into Accra. I was afraid that someone would shout, "There's one of those no-good Afro-Americans who supported Nkrumah and organized the Marxist Forum." But I was too anxious and curious to stay at home. The city was occupied by the army and the police (the two institutions which formed the new government), and they checked and inspected thoroughly each transport and person that passed through. They were looking primarily for contraband and ex-party-officials who had escaped the drag-net. The black men with guns were smart-looking and efficient, and most of the nonofficials were extremely young.

The capital was bursting with enthusiasm. Hundreds of civilians were roaming the streets screaming, "Down with the corrupt CPP; praises to the National Liberation Council." They broke into the party's headquarters, destroyed every piece of property in the building, and were refrained from burning down the structure itself by the few army men who guarded it. Symbols of Nkrumah—as statues, pictures, names on streets —were prime targets, and after the mob hit, there was little that could be recognized. Another main target was the Trade Union Congress building, where books, records, furniture, and other pieces of movable property were destroyed in a huge bonfire, with the mob cheering hysterically as each piece was hurled into the flames. Observers said the smoke could be seen for a hundred miles. The demonstrations seemed spontaneous, and all the actors in agreement. I had been aware of the government's growing unpopularity, but I had never dreamed that the hatred and resentment were so deep seated. Diverse elements of the population had joined together their violent disapproval of fourteen years of a one-party state. I thought about Dr. W. E. B. Du Bois' vivid description (in *Black Reconstruction*) of the Blacks in the American South after they had learned of the Emancipation Proclamation.

There was so much happening at once. And moving painfully, cautiously as I did, it was impossible to see everything.
The university had closed, declaring an official holiday, and
the students had marched eight miles to hail their new military
rulers. Market women—some who had cheered Nkrumah
off several days ago, before his trip to Hanoi—were this day
of unconstitutional change hanging Kwame Nkrumah and his
cabinet in effigy. The security prisons were opened, and each
political prisoner who spoke was cheered before, during, and
after his speech. The angry mob of Accra's best and worst
did not have to listen, since all of the prisoners would say the
same thing. In the middle of one of the speeches, one student
from the university came over to me and said quietly, "Leslie,
I'm sorry for you. Nkrumah was for you, but not for us. I'm
also sorry to say that the Du Bois Avenue sign on the campus
has been destroyed, and the street renamed." He then squeezed
my arm affectionately and said, "Long live the revolution." He
also told me that the two Chinese students at the university
had been severely beaten and chased from the campus. That
bothered me as much as the Du Bois episode. No American
or British students had been touched, though acts of violence
were constantly being hurled at Ghanaians studying in their
countries. But the Chinese students were communists, and
represented Nkrumah in his absence; hence they were the real
targets of the violence.

Chinese officials were being deported, and already there were
rumors that diplomatic relations with "socialist and communist countries" would be broken off. Tragically, and understandably, other Asians, who were afraid of being identified
with the leaving Chinese, put signs on their cars and houses
reading "We are Japanese [etc., etc.—depending on the
country], not Reds." One sign read, "We Nationalist Chinese—
we rather be dead than Red." The mob beat them anyway,
because, as one man said to me, "A Chinaman is a Chinaman."
The Europeans, except the "progressive" ones, who were
being beaten and deported, were twitteringly happy. Quiet
and well mannered for years, they were delighted that "the
reign of black terror" was over. They had a grand picnic at
the Ambassador Hotel, shouting at the stewards and laughing

and remembering the good old days. The West Germans, crude and profane as always, extended their obscenity by standing on the tables and singing Nazi songs in English.

By the end of the week there had been a decisive move to the right. The chairman of the National Liberation Council re-established diplomatic relations with England. (The Nkrumah government had broken relations with Britain because of Southern Rhodesia.) In a fantastic radio speech, doing what can only be described as political begging, he pleaded with the West to forgive Ghana for Nkrumah's abuses, and quoted from the 750-year-old Magna Charta to prove his sincerity.

It was heard from impeachable sources that the International Monetary Fund and the World Bank, both controlled by American dollars, would grant the loans they had refused the former government. The American ambassador, Franklin Williams, a charming and handsome Negro from San Francisco, was having a great time. He was always on hand to make congratulatory comments on the "virtues of the new freedom" and made the grand tour with other officials to close down the training camps Nkrumah had organized for various African freedom fighters. I wonder how he felt when this "new freedom" deported black South Africans to South Africa to be murdered. I know what the Ghanaians thought about him: after the coup they were saying, "Now maybe we can have a proper ambassador—white, Harvard trained."

The rest is history. I survived for six months. I left for Nigeria to get a job at the University of Lagos. They were having a coup there, and the civil war was easily predictable. It finally occurred to me, sitting in Lagos, that it was time to return to America. And so, after four years away—years crowded with discoveries—years of struggling and despairing to develop a new me, of completing school, of fashioning a new image of the world, of seeing Africa and participating in her revolution, of partial success and added recognition, I arrived at Kennedy Airport in late summer 1966, ending my exile in Mother Africa.

XVII

How My Heart Now Beats

FOR A YOUNG man this odyssey has created a heavy burden. Half of my life has been consumed, and in this period I have done more, seen more, cried and loved more—despaired, swallowed, taught, learned, damned, and wondered more— than most men who have lived much longer, men whose wise gray temples have already formed. Making the move from Franklin to the Political Kingdom and back—as well as under-standing the inevitable contradictions, deceptions, and dis-coveries that such an intense voyage produces—is by no means easy or conclusive, in such a short life, and is not recommended to those who are not at some point prepared to be ruthlessly honest with the world they come to perceive. Yet honesty can be a dangerous virtue in a dishonest world, and where it is not explicitly dangerous, it can be unpopular, irrelevant to those who believe that what works is honest and true, or alienating to others, especially the young, who believe that all history which preceded their quest for disalienation is meaning-less. Aware of all of this, I nevertheless want to present some idea of what now beats in my heart.

My early years, growing up in the company of my older brother and younger sister, were well guarded and sheltered by the authority of my parents. Reared with concern for loyalty and honesty, for achievement and integrity, with a love for God, I learned at Palmer the correct way in which this being had to live and to get meaning from life. Until then, approaching my manhood, my existence had been a spiritual struggle, unmoved and untouched by the *actual* world and without political consciousness, though I was always told to beware of evil. When I discovered another world and the contradictions and limitations of the universe in which I had served with honor, I hated and despised my parents and my training, and took other parents and other training, without understanding them either. Out of these rejections and reversals, I, like most sensitive people in search of clarity, created my psychology and philosophy of life. But I still could not find a truth or a continuity to live by. The more I rejected, the more I accepted, until I reached a point of diminishing utility, and finally left America because I lost faith in her and in her power to redeem and save our lives. Tormented racially as I was, in search of sanity, I went to Ghana. For four long, revealing years I was in what might be called therapeutic exile, looking for new insight, a new definition of emotional freedom which would allow me in my confusion the needed years to decide what I could be. By being an African, I thought, replete with a new psychology and sense of history, I could be saved—absorbed by the culture.

This aimless way of life came to an end after my first year in Ghana. One day I relaxed. Don't know when, or even how, but the spinning top in my system came to a halt. It was hard, but I endured. It was then that my exile took on significance. I made discoveries. The socio-political space in which I floated did not enable me to function at the level of my emotional and political expectations, and I was unable to be *black* in terms of my American-made Africa, since neither was needed or wanted in this political culture of decolonization. The Ghanaians were healthier psychologically and generally more conservative politically. I discovered that trying *to belong*, to be saved, was at best ritualistic and misleading, covering over my disintegration rather than bringing to myself some reasonable kind of order. I was a being of reaction, a confused black creature trying to stabilize a painful neurosis without knowing, except in general terms, what had made me sick; and having been trained in the best of American institutions, I could not think, and again and again had accepted general solutions as a cure for everything—including myself. I had never understood the problems of American racism, or the aspects of its interrelations to other problems, or the degree to which I had suffered —or the life style I needed to construct in order to deal with it.

Strange, and again extremely significant, these bits of reality came together more coherently when I returned to America and went to visit Ron and Ruth Matthews in their Bedford-Stuyvesant two-room apartment. Ruth was happy, as always. Ron was not. He called me into his kitchen; "I do not love Ruth any more," he said with conviction. He explained that Ruth did not seem like the same woman he married, that "things seem different in America," and that he had discovered to his embarrassment among a group of his radical black friends that his wife was never in support of Nkrumah's politics. A few of us could have told Ron about Ruth's political views in Ghana, but he would not have accepted them, because he wanted "a soft black woman," and Ruth, with her desire to get to the big city, would have been anything Ron could deal with. Ron had not married Ruth; in his way, like most of us in our ways, he had married Africa. Ruth did not exist as a person; in the same way, the Africa we needed did not exist as a continent. Our concept of Africa was formed in America, an Afro-American Africa based primarily on a reaction to the white man's Africa and what we thought Africa would be like. Now, the white man's Africa never existed. He went to the African land mass and carved up political subdivisions, named them and created beliefs about them. By extension, our concept of Africa never existed either.

Hence we were doomed to be disappointed, because what we saw and felt could not conform to the Africa in our skulls. Nevertheless, we immediately labeled the government and the people: Nkrumah was a revolutionary, and those who did not find his revolution pleasant were called reactionaries. This was in essence a projection of our own psychological and emotional need, since that was the Africa we needed. Some of us, as I did, soon discovered that our Africa was an illusion, and tried to relate to and love what they saw. The psychologically weak could not make this adjustment; even if he discovers the "real Africa," he is unable to embrace it, since it is not the Africa he wants. He would be criticizing himself. And given his understandable insecurities, he is unable and unwilling to do this. Therefore, in order to protect himself from what he sees, he must continue his tragic forms of mystification, because in his confusion he has the perverted notion that he would be affirming the white man's conception of Africa, and by extension affirming America. In short, he cannot dig Africa for what she is—changing, developing, confused, corrupt, beautiful, uncertain, flirting with revolution—but must see her as his mistress, beating to death the white man in his own skull. And he will surely leave blaming Africa for his inability to deal with objective reality.

Here in America black people are plagued by this same madness. So, pressed under by white racism, we are unable to create a revolutionary posture beyond reaction. Immediately upon my return I did not understand this. What I saw and heard at first excited me—new black faces, new music, new programs; and in Harlem once or twice I was reminded of Accra. Revolt, rebellion, protest came freely from black voices, and before hearing them, I had heard about Watts and Harlem, and they had burned in my imagination too. Essentially what I saw was what other black people were feeling, changing their relationship to America; not one, not two, but hundreds were saying "Hell, no!" to an America I had gone away from.

Now, that frightens me, because how can "Hell, no!" deal decisively with the America I left, the same America I returned to, the old America, too powerful to change by her own will and too ugly to turn her face from screams in the street? Listening to her, she sounds new; her face even smiles when you scream; and her ears are open to your programs of change. But it is a delusion. In our years of feverish strugglings to be a part of her, we are easily bedeviled, and only because we have never been in the command of circumstances, never reasoned out our fears—deciding that we would never be great . . . but only pleasantly mediocre.

No, America has not changed her relationship to us. She has not changed her nature, or subjugated her egotism, which has refused to be satisfied with anything but the ultimate, the greatest. She suffers from a national psychosis which everyone can now happily call racism. And that illness, my brothers and sisters, the outward form of her deeper life, cannot be cured by simply giving us more jobs, establishing Black Studies programs, and letting us do our thing. We would still suffer from the anxiety—become paralyzed and inert, if only subconsciously. And America, given her commitment to be "involved in the world" for the rest of her history cannot *now*, even if she wanted, deal therapeutically with her deeper illness. She is like a whore who has syphilis but hasn't the time to get the shots. Even if she found a physician of trust, she's too busy serving her other worlds to bend over for us. It would cause a national emotional breakdown.

So America, slowly but certainly moving toward fascism, must prepare for us. All the signs are here: an affluent and politically indifferent middle class; a losing war in Vietnam (and there are sure to be others); seriously alienated white students; breakdown in order; and of course, people like me— restless, angry—whom no one (not even ourselves) can figure out what to do with. Fascism is an ugly word, especially in this society, where there is a certain kind of freedom and a national character built on a democratic myth. Look closely, however, at the political and cultural history of America, and see that fascist tendencies have always been there, repressed and waiting for more Indians to put on their war paint.

Nothing on the present political scene is relevant to deal with this America. The rhetoric is meaningful, inspirational, and a force of togetherness. History will probably tell us that we needed it.

But dealing with American racism is serious business, requiring serious planning and commitment, the lack of which kept nationalist movements in Africa from achieving little else than independence. Ironically perhaps, the most unfortunate thing is that we have been using the word "revolution." Like the word "socialism" as Kwame Nkrumah used it, it covers over a multitude of social, political, cultural, economic, and psychological problems which are all in dire need of examination. And, like Nkrumah, our black leaders speak for the "people," but with only a vague notion of what they taste, touch, and want, and equally vague notions about the world which has closed the door to progress on them.

Black people are hopeless, downtrodden, the result of mass exploitation. They are alienated from themselves and their families, suspicious, materialistic, cynical, and like most other Americans, hopelessly practical. Also they are anti-intellectual, or to put it a better way, they are anti-people, against ideas and concepts they have vaguely heard about but which have had little substantive effect on their lot. When a leader, or one who wants to lead, comes to preach his brand of freedom, authentic or otherwise, he does not usually understand the faces of the men who stand before him. The black faces are poor, oppressed, angry, and their owners may have struck out at the oppressors from time to time. The brother who comes to speak assumes that they are as ready as he is to do their thing. He may tell them about the good life, a life that they could have, and they may applaud him because he told the truth or made them laugh. But they may not follow him, because they may not believe him. They say in their hearts, Why does he care about us? He says that we should arm ourselves, but Jesus will take care of us. Sure, the system is corrupt. But how do we eat tomorrow?

It is hard, maybe impossible, to be a black revolutionary in present-day America. Living in a black community, married to a black person, having literary, cultural, linguistic, and political support, plus a closetful of African clothes, it will still be difficult, because the objective conditions of our lives do not demand a full-time commitment to revolutionary action. Racism makes you self-conscious and angry, and it is necessary to become an "anti-racist racist" to deal with it. But this is not Cuba, Algeria, or North Vietnam. Our industrial society confuses us. It is possible to get involved in so much, and sometimes, especially when we are partying, we forget that we are supposed to be radically changing our lives.

Maybe the trouble is that we have created a model of revolutionary behavior which is at variance with our actual conditions. You are indeed a sellout if you work for the CIA as a spy. But you can pass if you are forced by economic necessity to be a mail clerk or secretary in one of its branch offices. Again, you are a sellout if you write "revolutionary" books and participate in related activities while married to a white woman. But you can pass, be black, if you have the right marriage, in the right community, saying or writing the same views, even if you wear $250 suits while the black people around, who do not read your books, wallow in the poverty to which they have been accustomed.

Once while I was in Ghana I met two men whom I would like to call revolutionaries. They had come from Vietnam to speak to Africans about the evils of American imperialism. I did not hear them speak publicly—no one did, since the political fathers did not want them to confuse the educated masses—but saw them privately at a reception and learned a great deal about men involved in radical social and political change. If they had not been pointed out to me, I would never have recognized them, for I was looking for men with long hair, political clothing, hysteria in their voices, and words of passion dripping from their mouths. These strangers from the East looked rather ordinary—suits, ties, clean shaven—and talked to everyone who had questions. I watched and listened to them half of the night. I, as everyone there, was impressed. They were calm, intelligent, civil, practical, violent, sensitive, secure, modest but certain, possessed by a sense of history, and they showed concern and love for their families, who stood near their sides. Now it was clear to me why men like these could beat a whole world of American marines.

We who have chosen to give our lives to changing the nature of American society from within have not reached this stage of development. Our militant reactions to racism constitute "a stand against this death" but not an alternative, never a solution. Essentially what we have failed to grasp is the full significance of a revolutionary experience. It is not a one-shot deal, a one-lifetime thing. To radically alter the nature of an unhealthy and corrupt order of two thousand years necessitates a continuing process. At one stage you have your LeRoi Joneses. At another stage your Nkrumahs and

Malcolms. Then your Fanons. So men like the brothers from the East can come forth. But we must know when to move, when to retreat, when to go beyond a present leadership because its purpose has been served.

Our great-grand-sons and -daughters of another history will look back upon these years and ask many questions: Why we repeated ourselves so often, why Malcolm's movement died with him; why Nkrumah did not stop corruption in Ghana. If we are honest with ourselves now, we can give them something to stand on, for they will make the revolution. They will have the benefits and burdens of the reform period afoot. They will want to relate to the real Africa. They will have organized a black culture which is disciplined enough to sustain a revolutionary struggle, and in this nation of nations, develop secular ethics, without gods, without heroes. Psychologically secure, they will know the difference between acts which are emotional and acts which change political relationships.

It seems to me that our task is to make their revolution easier. The issues must be clarified. And black people must always have the heart to be critical of each other, from a point of commitment and love.

To the black youth:

You are very beautiful;
Love each other.
Be honest.
Do not become negative, cynical or self-righteous because the black
    world does not move as fast as we would like it.
Do not be too hard on Mother and Father;
Look at them historically,
And you will understand and love them as I have come to love mine.
Be strong and positive.
History did not begin when you became conscious.
This can still be our century.
Oh, to be "young, gifted and black."

WESTMAR COLLEGE LIBRARY